Bringing Finance
to Pakistan's Poor

Bringing Finance to Pakistan's Poor

Access to Finance for Small Enterprises and the Underserved

Tatiana Nenova
Cecile Thioro Niang
with
Anjum Ahmad

THE WORLD BANK
Washington, D.C.

© 2009 The International Bank for Reconstruction and Development / The World Bank
1818 H Street NW
Washington DC 20433
Telephone: 202-473-1000
Internet: www.worldbank.org
E-mail: feedback@worldbank.org

1 2 3 4 12 11 10 09

This volume is a product of the staff of the International Bank for Reconstruction and Development / The World Bank. The findings, interpretations, and conclusions expressed in this volume do not necessarily reflect the views of the Executive Directors of The World Bank or the governments they represent.

The World Bank does not guarantee the accuracy of the data included in this work. The boundaries, colors, denominations, and other information shown on any map in this work do not imply any judgement on the part of The World Bank concerning the legal status of any territory or the endorsement or acceptance of such boundaries.

ISBN: 978-0-8213-8030-7
eISBN: 978-0-8213-8032-1
DOI: 10.1596/978-0-8213-8030-7

Cover photos: © World Bank/Curt Carnemark

Library of Congress Cataloging-in-Publication Data

Nenova, Tatiana
  Bringing finance to Pakistan's poor : access to finance for small
Enterprises and the underserved / Tatiana Nenova, Cecile Thioro Niang ; with
Anjum Ahmad.
      p. cm
Includes bibliographical references and index.
ISBN 978—0-8213-8030-7 - - ISBN 978-0-8213-8032-1 (electronic)
1. Microfinance—Pakistan. 2. Small business—Pakistan—Finance. I. Niang,
Cecile Thioro. II. Ahmad, Anjum. III. Title.
HG78.33.P18N46 2009
332.7095491—dc22
                                                                2009021680

Contents

Contents

Boxes

Figures

Tables

Annex Tables

Acknowledgments

This report owes much to our colleagues at the State Bank of Pakistan, especially Dr. Saeed Ahmed, Director of the Financial Inclusion Program. The data collection would have not been possible without the guidance, onsite assistance, advice, data provision, and expert statistical contribution of the Federal Bureau of Statistics. The cooperation, assistance, and joint work with the Department for International Development, FinMark Trust, Swiss Agency for Development and Cooperation, and the Pakistan Microfinance Network have been invaluable. The coordination and leadership of the survey work by Fatimah Afzal of PMN have bridged the boundaries of the impossible in pioneering this major new data-gathering exercise in the country. The ACNielsen (the survey house) staff, and especially Faiza Jamil, have put in long hours of dedicated effort and diligence. Finally, the team thanks all major Pakistani banks and other financial institutions, who took time to discuss and brainstorm on pertinent issues, as well as various stakeholder groups and especially the Pakistani men and women who patiently went along with our enumerators during the pilot launch of the survey.

The effort has benefited from able advisers, including Haroon Sharif (DFID), Zoi Andrew (DFID), Stuart Andrew (DFID), Sarah Hennell (DFID), Sarah Zaka, Gregory Chen (Shorebank), Lioba Solbach (Reconstruction Credit Institute), Michael Kortenbusch (Business and Finance Consulting), Khalid Siraj, Ijaz Nabi, Faisal Bari, Namoos Zaheer, Isfandyar Zaman Khan, Anjali Kumar, Asli Demirguc-Kunt, Consolate Rusagara, P. S. Shrinivas, Yoko Doi, Shabana Khawar, Kaspar Richter, Zahid Hasnain, Nobuo Yoshida, Tomoyuki Sho, Paul Wade, Bob Cull, Bilal Zia, Ann Rennie, and Mahesh Uttamchandani and Rachel (Raha) Shahid-Saless (who together contributed the expert annex on secured transactions). Eric Manes was instrumental with advice and data for chapter 4. Kiran Afzal provided outstanding research assistance. The team owes particular appreciation to Shamsuddin Ahmad and Simon Bell for overall guidance, review, and advice. The excellent support from Aza Rashid, Sakm Abdul Hye, Imtiaz Ahmad Sheikh, Rubina Geizla Quanber, Marjorie Espiritu, and Margaret Murray have above all made this work possible.

The chapter authors are Anjum Ahmad and Tatiana Nenova (chapter 1), Cecile Thioro Niang and Tatiana Nenova (chapter 2), Stephen Rasmussen and Tatiana Nenova (chapter 3), Aurora Ferrari and Mukta Joshi (chapter 4), and Martin Aslop and Cecile Thioro Niang (chapter 5). Shanthi Divakaran contributed to research for chapter 1. Cecile Thioro Niang further contributed the technology sections to all chapters. Cecile Thioro Niang, Mukta Joshi, and Anjum Ahmad tirelessly helped with the overall research, report drafting, and review. Tatiana Nenova coordinated, edited, and led the survey and report work.

Abbreviations

A2F	Access to Finance (survey)
ABL	Allied Bank Limited
ADB	Asian Development Bank
AJK	Azad Jammu and Kashmir[1]
AML	Anti-Money Laundering
ATM	Automated Teller Machine
BFC	Business and Finance Consulting
CIB	Credit Investment Bureau
DFI	Development Finance Institutions
DFID	Department for International Development, UK
EC	Exchange Company
FANA	Federally Administered Northern Area
FATA	Federally Administered Tribal Area
FBS	Federal Bureau of Statistics
FIP	Financial Inclusion Program
FY	Fiscal Year
GDP	Gross Domestic Product
GOP	Government of Pakistan
HBL	Habib Bank Limited
HIES	Household Income Integrated Survey
ICA	Investment Climate Assessment
KfW	Kreditanstalt für Wiederaufbau (German government–owned development bank)
MCB	Muslim Commercial Bank

[1]Azad Jammu and Kashmir (AJK) is the Pakistan-administered portion of an area which is in dispute between India and Pakistan. This report does not intend to make any judgement as to the legal or other status of any disputed territories or to prejudice the final determination of the parties' claims.

MFB	Microfinance Bank
MFI	Microfinance Institution
MTO	Money Transfer Organization
NBP	National Bank of Pakistan
NGO	Nongovernmental Organization
NIFT	National Interbank Financial Telecommunication
NRSP	National Rural Support Program
NSS	National Savings Scheme
NWFP	North West Frontier Province
OECD	Organisation for Economic Co-operation and Development
PAR	Portfolio at Risk
PLS Account	Profit and Loss Sharing Account
PMN	Pakistan Microfinance Network
POS	Point of Sale
PPAF	Pakistan Poverty Alleviation Fund
PPSB	Pakistan Post Savings Bank
PRISM	Pakistani Realtime Interbank Settlement Mechanism
PSLM	Pakistan Social and Living Standards Measurement Survey
PSU	Primary Sampling Unit
ROA	Returns on Assets
ROE	Returns on Equity
ROSCA	Rotating Credit and Savings Association
RSP	Rural Support Program
SBP	State Bank of Pakistan
SDC	Swiss Agency for Development and Cooperation
SECP	Securities and Exchange Commission of Pakistan
SME	Small and Medium Enterprises
SMS	Short Message Service
SSU	Secondary Sampling Unit
SWIFT	Society for Worldwide Interbank Financial Telecommunication
UAE	United Arab Emirates
UBL	United Bank Limited
USA	United States of America

Currency Conversion

Exchange rate at the time of the study (Dec. 2008) was Rs 1 = $0.012837.
All dollar amounts are in U.S. dollars.

Executive Summary

Access to financing is now widely acknowledged as a path to meaningful economic inclusion and reduction in poverty. Policy efforts to increase access to finance in Pakistan have taken time to bear fruit, but now access is indeed expanding quickly in certain financial sectors (microfinance, remittances)—albeit from a very low base. Nevertheless, policy measures cannot single-handedly increase financial access; financial institutions' willingness to expand access in Pakistan has been stinted by slow technologic advances, weak legal foundations, and unsuitable financial processes and products. Poor socioeconomic conditions, gender bias, and low levels of basic education and financial literacy remain barriers, but perhaps the single strongest driver of low demand for financial access has been income.

The average Pakistani household remains outside the formal financial system, saving at home and borrowing from family or friends in cases of dire need. Fourteen percent of Pakistanis are using a financial product or service of a formal financial institution (including savings, credit, insurance, payments, and remittance services). When

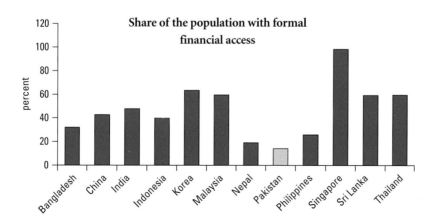

informal financial access is taken into account, 50.5 percent of Pakistanis have access to finance. Informal access can occur through the organized sector (though committees, shopkeepers, moneylenders, *hawala/hundi* money transfers, and so forth), or informally through friends and family. In comparison, 32 percent of the population has access to the formal financial system in Bangladesh, and this figure amounts to 48 percent in India and 59 percent in Sri Lanka (World Bank, 2008c). Of the nearly 50 percent of Pakistanis who do not engage in either the formal or informal financial system, we estimate about 19 percent have voluntarily excluded themselves through lack of understanding, awareness, or need, due to poverty, or for religious reasons. Financial exclusion precludes people from reducing risk, managing fluctuations in income, and investing in microenterprises or in health and education.

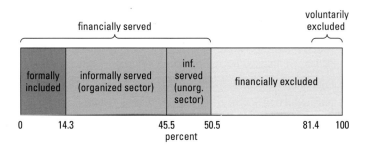

Major constraints to financial access, in spite of policy reforms, arise from the high levels of poverty, combined with low awareness of and information about available financial services, as well as gender bias. Currently, financial institutions limit expansion of services to individuals and enterprises with a high and predictable income. And yet there is nothing inherently unserviceable about low-income, informally employed, rural, or female clients. In fact, the considerable gender bias is completely eliminated among formally serviced individuals. Differences between urban and rural financial inclusion are completely eliminated once the effect of income and other individual characteristics is taken out. Technology can be harnessed to help expand geographical outreach, as well as overcome low literacy levels. Physical access can be stepped up using a two-pronged strategy, in view of limited financial infrastructure and penetration—via existing agencies with higher penetration, such as the Pakistan Post Office, as well as via new technology solutions, such as branchless banking and mobile banking. Simplified financial processes and procedures, client segmentation, and product diversification can help lower costs and manage risks better. New approaches suitable for smaller enterprises, such as bank downscaling, are workable tools to achieve sustainable small and medium enterprise (SME) lending products. Further integration of financial services for the underserved—microfinance, remittances, small enterprise finance—would strengthen financial provider sustainability, via improved competition, efficiency, and exposure of financial institutions to market discipline. A major obstacle that has rendered product and client expansion difficult and unnecessarily risky has been the limited information on markets, segments, and instruments. **This report and**

the attendant pioneering nationwide access to finance survey, part of a considerable donor-supported State Bank of Pakistan (SBP) financial inclusion program, is meant to fill in the gap.

Despite reforms, access to financial products remains limited. The SBP has embarked on an aggressive path of expanding financial market coverage via enabling, if strict, regulation, yet outreach has lagged behind the country's growth and development needs. Reforms in the past decade have resulted in strong banks

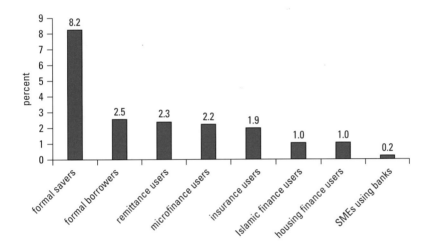

with a steady performance. As a result, Pakistan's financial system has grown significantly in the past few years, and access and penetration of financial products have been expanding, though again, from a very small base:

- More than half of the population saves, but only 8 percent entrust their money to formal financial institutions.

- One-third of the population borrows, but only 3 percent use formal financial institutions to do so.

- Microfinance has grown at 40 percent per year since 1999—*yet* microfinance access extends to only 1.7 million out of an adult population of about 80 million.

- International remittances have grown at 29 percent since 2001—*yet* only 2.3 percent of Pakistanis send or receive remittances, while half of remittances, including domestic flows, are transmitted informally.

- Agricultural disbursement grew by 44 percent in 2003–7—*yet* rural credit demand remains unmet—the financial system reaches only 15 percent of farmers.

- Life insurance is the most-used insurance product, and demand is high for crop insurance products—*yet* only 1.9 percent are insured.

Financial access is low among the poorer, women, and small and microenterprises and in rural areas, though market studies suggest they are viable customers. Formal

markets could learn from and cooperate with informal arrangements, to increase outreach. In testimony to the commercial viability of these client segments, informal finance seems to be capable of profitably serving such groups at a reasonably low premium to formal services. Most formal financial products remain high-end, limited to urban, rich educated males employed in the formal sector. The formal sector could learn a lot from and partner with informal providers—their services are perceived as being more geographically accessible, less complex, with fewer requirements, and easier to understand. For one, formal finance could differentiate its products more, attuning them to the specific needs of various population segments, such as women. Requirements could be less onerous, using technology and flexibility—strict documentary, guarantor, and collateral requirements for becoming a customer, and income and information/awareness constraints have obstructed more aggressive growth in formal financial access.

Disparate as formal access might be among rural and urban areas, men and women, income levels, as well as along education and employment sectors, interest in financial services is virtually identical. The challenge is to translate financial interest into formal access and usage. Poverty and lack of information on financial services predicate lack of interest—the perception of irrelevance of the financial system to the everyday lives of a considerable share of the Pakistani population. Low geographic outreach, complex procedures, and products poorly suited to client needs strengthen the perception of formal sector irrelevance for the vast majority of the population. An analysis of perceptions of financial services links the popularity of informal finance to its minimum access requirements—in direct contrast to formal finance documentation, creditworthiness requirements, and associated fees that overburden population groups such as women, low-income, or rural populations.

Microfinance

Microfinance in Pakistan represents a low 0.2 percent of total financial assets, though formal markets growth is second fastest in South Asia (after Afghanistan). The formal microfinance sector reaches less than 2 percent of the poor, as opposed to over a quarter in Bangladesh, India, and Sri Lanka. The informal sector can be competitive, and has good lessons to offer to its formal counterpart. There is still considerable room for growth of microfinance in Pakistan—the estimated potential market size is in the range of 10–20 million active borrowers, and some estimates place the number as high as 35 million. Women are a poorly explored clientele with tremendous potential. While microfinance policy and services have focused on credit, there is a considerable potential for other products, especially savings.

A key challenge to microfinance institutions (MFIs) in Pakistan is raising considerable funding to grow, attaining sustainability, and better integrating with financial markets. MFIs rely considerably on noncommercial funding—commercial liabilities to gross lending portfolio are barely 21 percent. Profitability and performance in the microfinance sector is low but improving. In 2000, microfinance was elevated to a core aspect of the government's poverty reduction program. In spite of SBP encouragement, commercial banks have shown little appetite to service microfinance clients. The SBP strategy of offering a bank license to stronger MFIs has proven more successful, though the hoped-for deposit mobilization has not materialized with the pace expected, and the outreach of microfinance banks (MFBs) remains limited. MFBs account for 31 percent of the microfinance lending portfolio, and 85 percent of its growth.

The Pakistan microfinance market has much potential for a rapid outreach expansion, and faces considerable unsatisfied demand, especially for savings products. Mobile technology can help expand access considerably, especially in the informal sector. The financial sector has not yet taken up SBP encouragement to that effect, and will unlikely change course given the recent financial crisis fallout. Yet, it is important to persevere in this agenda, which directly links into poverty reduction. Promising strategies include financial awareness campaigns, strengthening of MFI viability and commercial sustainability, inclusion of women and client segmentation, and development of savings products. Smaller-size products, and bulk service might better attract lower-income groups. The increasing use of technology will make this approach a viable business proposition for banks as well as affordable for clients. Two approaches have been used internationally to address high transaction costs due to low population density, small average loans, and low household savings—the Grameen and Brac low-tech, low-cost, high-volume models of microfinance, and the high-tech, low-cost, high-volume approaches developed in Kenya or the Philippines. With close to 90 percent coverage and 59 percent reach (and no gender divide), mobile banking holds much promise to increase access. A potentially major player in access to finance for the underserved is the Pakistan Post Office, with its more than 13,000 offices, and current efforts to upgrade technology. Under government policy encouragement, some microfinance banks (MFBs) have experimented with linking up with Pakistan Post in a bid to expand outreach (such as in Brazil and China).

Small Enterprise Finance

Small and microenterprises have seen access to finance worsen, while medium-size enterprises have seen it improve. SMEs are the growth engines of the economy due to their ability to create jobs, foster entrepreneurship, and provide depth to the industrial base of the economy. Yet SMEs get a disproportionately small share of credit relative to their economic importance. There are 3.2 million SMEs in Pakistan, which constitute more than 90 percent of all private enterprises in the industrial sector, employ nearly 78 percent of the nonagriculture labor force, and contribute more than 30 percent to gross domestic product (GDP). Yet SME lending accounts for 16 percent of total lending volume and only 4 percent of total customers. Similarly, 3.6 percent of firms use loans for investment (as compared with 12.7 percent for South Asia), and only 13.9 percent use them for expenses (34.5 percent in South Asia). Small and micro firms finance internally 90 percent of working capital and 81 percent of new investment. Studies estimate a small enterprise credit demand gap of Rs 277 billion (compared with total current SME credit at Rs 400 billion).

Enterprises do not seem to be excluded from financial markets due to poor performance. Instead, an incomplete legal and regulatory framework and non-SME-friendly products and procedures hamper increased SME lending. Indirect costs—legal fees, collateral registration, and documentation—make bank lending expensive for SMEs. A typical small business loan requires up to 27 steps for the bank and 9 meetings with the client. An enabling role has been played by the expansion of the Credit Investment Bureau's (CIB's) scope in 2006, the SME Policy 2007, which emphasized SME access to finance, and above all the new SBP Prudential Regulations for SMEs. However, banks continue to find it difficult to serve SMEs profitably for several reasons. First, the legal framework (namely, the secured transactions regime and, to a lesser extent, the credit information infrastructure) limits the pool of potential applicants. Further regulatory challenges include a slow court, the stalled "SME Act" of 2006, and a problematic tax system. Second, bank products are not tailored to SMEs, resembling instead corporate lending practices. Finally, banks do not have organizational structures and monitoring tools conducive to achieving high efficiency. SME demand-side factors further constrain the market, including limited SME accounting, budgeting, and planning capacity and poor entrepreneurial skills.

Continued promotion of an enabling environment for SME lending and large-scale downscaling efforts involving both the public and private sectors can forge rapid growth in SME lending. Increasing access to finance for SMEs also requires creating a secured transactions law that allows all SMEs to use movable collateral, attracting an institutional investor with a track record in SME lending, and assisting other banks to go down market. While progress has also been substantial on credit bureaus, more could be done to facilitate the creation of credit histories by SMEs.

Remittances

Remittances to Pakistan are estimated at around $16 billion and growing fast, but formal flows do not reach the poor, women, and rural areas, where service is mostly informal. International flows (through both formal and informal channels) total $9 billion, with domestic flows at approximately US$6.95 billion. These remittance flows can play a valuable role in providing foreign exchange, but more importantly also offer significant potential to support incomes of poor and vulnerable groups. In Pakistan, however, formal remittances have not been a major part of income for poorer households, mainly because of limited access. Transmission networks work well in urban areas, though outreach to rural and remote locations is difficult, and services are not sufficiently customized to client needs (such as women who might need doorstep delivery, and the poor who rarely have the requisite documentation and accounts). Pakistan Post has a large rural network and is the most common channel for domestic remittances, but services remain relatively inefficient. Home consumption constitutes the largest use of remittances.

SBP has taken various measures that have significantly increased remittances through formal channels, though a large share of domestic remittances remains

informally transferred. SBP has been encouraging the private sector toward providing mobile banking solutions. The mobile coverage (at about 90 percent of the population of Pakistan), and the success of mobile money transfer solutions in other countries, suggests that mobile phone banking offers significant potential to scale up access to financial services in Pakistan. To stimulate outreach to remote locations, SBP has been encouraging the private sector to provide mobile banking solutions. Other solutions from international experience include Indian innovations, such as the non-governmental organization (NGO) Adhikar, which developed an efficient domestic customized transfer service, and ICICI Bank, which extended its outreach to remote village centers via computer kiosks. New partnerships among remittance market players and other financial entities both within Pakistan and abroad hold much promise. Further advances in formalizing money transfer flows will bring new clientele and motivation for efficiency gains and customization of services to client needs.

The Way Ahead: Policy Options

A major drive to enhance financial inclusion would involve a joint effort of SBP, the national government, private sector, the community, and donor efforts. The best formula for a rapid scaling-up of access is to rely on technology, literacy gains, financial reengineering of processes and products, and an enabling legal and institutional framework.

Access to All Financial Services

The Role of the Private Sector

Diversifying the product range and segmenting clients to increase outreach, simplify procedures, lower costs, and manage risks, to better cater to client needs. Specific suggestions include:

- Use of alternative forms of collateral, such as social collateral, compulsory savings, personal guarantees, crops or machinery purchased, household assets;
- Use of traditional saving arrangements and Rotating Savings and Credit Associations;
- Smaller size of products, and bulk service, to better attract lower-income groups;
- Lower loan size and deposit size to better match women's needs, given their lower incomes;
- Frequent repayments so that installments are smaller and correspond to women's income cycles;
- Literacy should not be a requirement to access financial service;
- Innovative ways to reach customers, such as decentralized operations, use of mobile units, operating units located near women clients, transactions at clients' doorsteps, use of female staff. Focus on the promising market niche of financial access for heads of households, especially of interest in rural areas).

Reaching out to the female client: Women's abilities to better manage debt and their stronger savings patterns and client loyalty present an untapped profitable client base for the financial and microfinance sectors in Pakistan. Understanding women's needs more precisely, and reflecting those in the financial products and the provider's policies and procedures, would ensure an increase in women's access to finance in spite of cultural norms, gender segregation, low literacy, and incomes. Global experience suggests offering women credit that is untied to specific use, instead allowing the borrower to suggest the activity.

(Continued)

Learning from the informal financial sector's minimum requirements, flexibility, and cost/time efficiency: Developing linkages with the informal sector would help formalize the sector, increasing the formal sector's client base.

Reaching out to the rural client by leveraging technology: Technology can lower costs, enlarge geographical outreach, increase product quality, help enhance credit information, and provide innovative applications for service delivery. Despite some regulatory and operating challenges, technology solutions have enabled poor people to access financial services, for example:

- Innovative bank devices can enhance outreach/correspondent banking (such as India's ICICI Bank computer kiosks in remote village centers).

- Branchless banking via mobile phones and other devices has the potential to decrease operating costs by as much as 12 percent and can help shift some of the financial flows from informal to formal channels, in particular if combined with other correspondent banking channels. Challenges include regulatory, security, and supervision difficulties, and limits on the range of services (as in the Philippines G-Cash and Kenya M-Pesa models).

- The Grameen and Brac low-tech, low-cost, high-volume models present successful experience for microfinance.

- Partnerships among financial institutions (commercial banks and MFBs, linkages with Pakistan Post and NGOs) can unleash remittances and other financial services for the rural poor. A useful example is that of the Indian NGO Adhikar, which developed an efficient domestic customized transfer service.

- Basic banking has had some success (India, Mexico, South Africa), in particular when banks have voluntarily offered commercial basic banking.

- Home-grown solutions include United Bank Limited's services for bill payments and money transfers; Bank Al-Falah's mobile banking with Warid Telecom; and the remittance service of Etisalat's (UAE)-Smart (Philippines).

The Role of the Public Sector

Creating awareness of the benefits of access to financial services: Further gains in financial literacy are critical, though more critical is increasing awareness of financial services to promote trust in the sector, as well as information about services and products available. A national awareness campaign can support financial inclusion, especially for women, as well as encourage people to open bank and savings accounts. Awareness creation and trust building could be forged through social mobilization and mass media.

Strengthening institutions: Growth in access to finance will be accelerated by an integrated financial system and a strong regulatory framework.

- Stronger institutions (including Securities and Exchange Commission of Pakistan and CIB) are a major part of a rapid increase in financial inclusion.

- Upgrading the existing credit bureau managed by SBP and consolidating the achievements in increasing its coverage to the whole finance service sector, including NGO MFIs, can place many more potential borrowers within reach of some access to finance. SBP could also facilitate the creation of a credit history for SMEs by mandating the credit bureau to collect information from utility and telecom companies.

- To facilitate SME lending monitoring, SBP should amend SME portfolio reporting requirements to include volumes/number of loans in four sub-brackets (Rs <2M, Rs 2–6M, Rs 6–25M, and Rs 25–75M).

- A more efficient Pakistan Post is a must (following the successful examples of Brazil and China) to capitalize on its large network and outreach in rural areas. Government should explore ways to improve remittance and other services and speed up the automation of postal branches. Given the significant developmental potential of Pakistan Post to enhance financial access, it needs modernization in operations and regulations. Following most success cases in East Asia, as well as many other continents, PPSB should be placed under the supervision of SBP.

Creating an enabling environment for expanding access to the underserved: Regulations should keep up with the needs of the sector and technological developments, to enable expansion. Simultaneously, an enabling environment should go hand in hand with a carefully chosen government presence. Indiscriminate subsidies, especially focused on interest rates, can be detrimental to the expansion of the sector, as they not only distort prices but crowd out efficient institutions and products. The government should resist populist perceptions that low interest rate funding can serve a developmental purpose. Even more detrimental are state-owned institutions created to promote financial access. Evidence in the case of Pakistan that such institutions (for example, SME Bank) actually improve access is weak; rather, these efforts waste valuable public resources that could more usefully be deployed elsewhere, and eliminate the level playing field for market participants.

Access to Microfinance

The Role of the Private Sector

Improving MFI sustainability and ability to muster commercial funding/savings deposits, and their further integration into the financial system: MFIs need to improve efficiency, risk management, and profitability to increase reliance on commercial funding.

A further strategy is **refocusing on microsavings and deposits collection,** given the large untapped demand for such products, and is supported by international experience: savings methods that have worked for microfinance include doorstep collection schemes and periodic contribution or "commitment" programs.

The Role of the Public Sector

Encouraging positive public perceptions on accessibility and safety would help.

Refocusing on microsavings: International experience points to regulatory methods of promoting savings, such as matching schemes and tax-advantaged schemes.

Access to SME Lending

The Role of the Private Sector

Carrying out a thorough bank downscaling program and modernizing SME banking. Key features of the downscaling programs that have worked include:

- Long-term technical assistance to implement the necessary substantial changes;
- Careful selection of bank advisers and content of the technical assistance;
- Participation of a mix of committed banks to create competition;
- Adequate performance agreements for participating banks.

The Role of the Public Sector

Creating a complete and well-functioning secured transactions regime: Security interests over movable assets should be easy and allowed on most assets and by every entity (both physical and juridical persons). Priority rankings should also be clearly defined among those who might have claims on property offered as collateral. The new secured transactions regime should also include a place (such as a registry) for making priority interests publicly known, and enforcement of security interests for all assets should be fast and low-cost.

(Continued)

Promoting bank downscaling initiatives with the potential for a demonstration effect:

- Introducing an institutional investor with a track record in SME lending, ideally via selling the SME bank or giving controlling rights on its board to an institutional investor.

- Supporting long-term technical assistance programs for selected banks (a good example is the China SME lending program).

Access to Remittances

The Role of the Private Sector

Reducing informality: Informality will decrease upon the introduction of efficient, low-cost, easy-access remittance services without prohibitive identification requirements. Increasing bank accounts can also help increase remittances through formal channels.

New technologies can reduce costs and make it possible to service areas where traditional bank branch models are not viable.

Expanding Pakistani bank presence and remittance service provision abroad, particularly in the major remittance source countries. These include partnerships, or innovative ways to reach customers (for example, Habib Bank Limited's model for cultivating clients and fostering regular remittance habits in the Middle East). Paperwork should be kept to a minimum, recognizing low literacy levels, and technology interfaces should not be excessively complex. Doorstep delivery models would help remittance recipients, who are generally women or elder groups.

The Role of the Public Sector

Formalizing informal remittances, particularly domestic: Public policies aimed at supporting technical and financial literacy, combined with education on the benefits of formal systems would also help.

Supporting remittance services of Pakistani banks abroad, to boost international remittances and forge alliances with international banks. One strategy would be to set the reimbursement rate through partner banks higher than remittances through Pakistani bank networks. Pakistani missions abroad could disseminate information to immigrants on lowest-cost and best sources of money transfer (as is done by the Mexican mission to the United States).

Promoting the structuring of international flows into investments: International good practices include (1) packaging remittances with payment services (such as Bansefi in Mexico); and (2) organizing and targeting diaspora networks rather than actual remittances flows. At the macro level, diaspora bonds issues (for example, in Israel, India, Ghana) or securitization of future remittances flows (in Brazil, Salvador) have been used, although securitization is costly. At the micro level, governments have facilitated targeted diaspora funds.

The Role of Public-Private Partnerships

A concrete way to make progress in expanding access to the underserved is to form public-private working groups on microfinance, small enterprise finance, and remittances to start a dialogue to tackle key challenges in the sector. Priority themes should include legal and regulatory issues, market transparency, competition and cost, and research and data issues. Public-private discussions on branchless banking could focus on barriers to industry response to recent SBP regulatory incentives, as well as review the Payment and Electronic Fund Transfer Act, data privacy, or security regulation that could facilitate e- or m-payments, and the branchless banking regulations providing for bank-nonbank partnerships and use of agents in money transfer services (building on the UK Public-Private Working Group on Remittances and the Remittances Task Force, and the World Bank remittance initiative).

Chapter 1

Overview, Financial Market Structure, Regulations, and Policies

Expanding Access to Finance, Links to Growth, and Poverty Reduction

Financial access is now widely acknowledged as a path to meaningful inclusion and reduction in poverty. Increased access to financial services has a significant impact on poverty (Claessens and Tzioumis, 2006) (box 1.1). Access to finance in Pakistan has an important potential for significant improvements. Credit to the private sector amounts to 29 percent of gross domestic product (GDP), as individuals and small and medium enterprises (SMEs) prefer to rely on retained earnings to finance their working capital, investment, housing financing, and other financial needs. Of the total population, 14 percent have access to formal finance, and about 40 percent have no financial access to formal or informal financial systems altogether. In comparison, 32 percent of the population in Bangladesh has access to the formal financial system, as do 48 percent in India and 59 percent in Sri Lanka (World Bank, 2008c). Policy efforts to increase access to finance in Pakistan have taken time to bear fruit, but access now is expanding quickly in certain financial sectors, albeit from a very low base. To understand the difficulties in policy measures to single-handedly raise financial access, one has to recognize the importance of socioeconomic conditions, basic education, and financial literacy on access. Lack of information on available financial services, combined with high levels of poverty, low literacy rates, and gender bias, results in low levels of financial inclusion.

Access to a savings account, to credit, to insurance, to micro- and SME finance, and to remittances reduces risk and vulnerability by allowing households to better manage fluctuations in income, and it enables the poor to invest in microenterprises or in essential services like health and education. Lack of access to the formal financial sector perpetuates the poverty trap. Lack of well-functioning financial markets

> ### Box 1.1   Finance and Link to Growth
>
> The importance of broad financial services outreach can be justified in several ways. The first argument builds on the theoretical and empirical finance and growth literature, as surveyed by Levine (2005) and the importance of a well-developed financial system for economic development and poverty alleviation (Beck, Demirguc-Kunt, and Levine 2004 and Honohan 2004a). Financial market imperfections, such as informational asymmetries, transaction costs and contract enforcement costs, are particularly binding on poor or small entrepreneurs who lack collateral, credit histories, and connections. Without broad access, such credit constraints make it difficult for poor households or small entrepreneurs to finance high-return investment projects, reducing the efficiency of resource allocation and having adverse implications for growth and poverty alleviation (Galor and Zeira 1993). Second, one of the channels through which financial development fosters economic growth is the entry of new firms (Klapper, Laeven, and Rajan, 2004) and the Schumpeterian process of "creative destruction." This implies that talented newcomers have access to the necessary financial services, including external finance. Access to finance for large parts of the population is thus seen as important to expand opportunities and assure a thriving private sector with efficient distribution of resources (Rajan and Zingales 2003).
>
> *Source:* Beck, Demirguc Kunt, and Peria (2005).

has disproportionately adverse consequences for the poor, who have credit requirements but few assets that can serve as collateral. They are thus shut out of formal finance markets. Poorer households depend mainly on expensive informal or noninstitutional sources.

This report examines both the formal (regulated) financial sector, and the informal sector (moneylenders, credit from supplier of goods, *hawala/hundi* money transfers, savings, and lending via committees and friends/family). Informal finance is discussed in Chapters 2 and 3. In the Pakistani context, the final financial sector includes the banking sector regulated by the State Bank of Pakistan (SBP), the nonbanking financial institutions regulated by the Securities and Exchange Commission of Pakistan, Pakistan Post Office, Directorate of National Savings, microfinance institutions (MFIs), remittances through licensed exchange companies, and the insurance sector. The report suggests strategies for stronger cross-pollination between the two sectors, formalizing or adopting practices of the informal sector, and putting the sector on a more sustainable footing; it also points out lessons about client knowledge and orientation, and (sometimes) efficiency, in the informal sector, from which the formal sector could benefit or emulate.

Recent advances in access to finance technology make it possible to reach broader groups of people at lower cost and risk. An estimated 1 billion people are currently connected to payment systems in developing countries. Yet financial institutions in many countries have been reluctant to expand into that market, including in Pakistan, due to poor information, low public awareness, inappropriate technology, and unsuitable financial processes and products. Equally widely acknowledged are the data gaps that persist when attempting to understand barriers to access. Greater availability of data in Pakistan can provide precise measures on financial access to the poor, to rural areas, as well as information on the characteristics of the financially underserved and informal finance.

Objectives of the Report

The primary purpose of this study is to measure and describe the state of financial service provision to underserved segments of the market in Pakistan, particularly those with low incomes and small enterprises, and to identify ways to improve investment and create inclusive markets that meet the needs of underserved people and enterprises. The new data and study are of value to commercial providers who are able to design product strategies around the segmentation and trends highlighted by the data, to policy makers who may be considering new legislation aimed at improving the functioning of financial markets, and to donors who may be making investment and funding decisions to increase access to certain regions or population groups. Further, the data can be used to conduct cross-country comparisons and construct a baseline for future reference that will help guide policy development on financial inclusion. The survey has already been conducted in several countries, including Brazil, India, Mexico, and South Africa.

An in-depth picture of financial access was obtained by a national Access to Finance (A2F) household survey focusing on the demand side of financial markets. A specific effort was made to capture the elements of access to finance that lie outside of the formal financial systems—such as informal financing from shops, family-based business run out of the house, socially based rotating savings/lending schemes, and others that might not even be recognized as finance by survey respondents and therefore require specific techniques to elicit the data and facts. The national household survey also provides insights into regional issues, including access to finance concerns specific to urban and rural areas. The survey data on household access to finance is a first of its kind and is not currently available for the country. Combining demand and supply aspects, the findings can be of considerable benefit to those currently underserved by the financial sector.

The report focuses on the underserved population groups and enterprises, those with informal access to finance or with no such access altogether. It does not cover large corporate lending, consumer lending, and more complex financial instruments, such as securities, money market instruments, and re-insurance. SBP has identified several priority areas for financial development, with a heavy emphasis on the underserved, including SMEs and microfinance. The report picks up on some of those issues, as well as on the market for remittances, the rural and urban poor, gender and income dimensions of access, and informal finance. The data gathered do not focus on a specific set of institutions or financial instruments; instead, the approach is very much demand driven: via household surveys, the data permit us to elicit the exact set of institutions and instruments in demand and those in use by

---

Box 1.2   Household A2F Survey for Pakistan (Demand-Side Data)

The A2F household survey is a comprehensive national household survey of all the main financial services (transaction banking, savings, credit and insurance), needs, and usage among consumers, in both the formal and informal sectors. The survey design is based on a joint methodology developed by FinMark Trust (South Africa) and the World Bank, and rooted in economic fundamentals. The design has benefited from continuous improvements as the survey has been used in several large countries around the world, as well as from careful customization to Pakistan conditions via focus-group discussions and piloting. The aim of this demand-side study is to establish credible benchmarks and highlight opportunities for innovation in product and delivery, as well as suggest promising avenues for deepening and broadening access to finance. The data collected permit us to:

- Measure and track the landscape of access to financial services across all the main product categories—transaction banking, savings, credit, and insurance, in both the formal and informal sectors—and institutional categories—commercial banks, other regulated institutions, semiformal nonregulated institutions, including membership-based ones, and informal or village-based institutions;

- Understand characteristics of those who are financially excluded;

- Segment the market;

- Identify opportunities for expansion of financial services to the un- and underserved segments of the market;

- Understand the scope of the population of vulnerable poor whose needed financial transactions are too small for any financial institution to provide profitably.

The data also permit us to track the diverse patterns of access to financial services across such characteristics as age, gender, ethnic group, and area of residence. Further, the data extend over a spectrum of areas of financial usage and interest, from examining quality of life and poverty, to attitudes toward and the use of technology, as well as levels of financial literacy.

(continued)

different portions of the population (by income, region, rural/urban areas, gender, age, and so forth). In order to provide a complete picture, the report also reviews the supply data, to aid policy formulation and assist with the understanding of the Pakistan-specific financial system features.[1]

The A2F household survey coverage is nationally representative and reflects both rural and urban access to finance issues (box 1.2). In the case of rural areas, the report does not get into the technicalities of specialized agricultural finance instruments and their supply side, as this is a full topic in its own right. Farmer financing and insurance issues are significantly different from financing issues for other market participants, and a household survey would not be well suited to bring out the relevant problems and issues (consider, for example, the issue of weather-based insurance). The data do cover rural issues and differences, and the report elicits

> **Box 1.2   continued**
>
> The survey covers 10,305 households in all regions of Pakistan excluding the tribal areas. At an initial stage, the standardized questionnaire was customized to Pakistani conditions, to ensure high-quality data. Focus interviews were held in urban and rural areas of Sindh, Punjab, North West Frontier Province (NWFP), Balochistan, and Azad Jammu and Kashmir (AJK), for purposes of calibration and gathering of supplementary qualitative information. At a second stage, households were surveyed on the following topics in detail:
>
> - Basic household demographics;
> - Financial literacy;
> - Socioeconomic characteristics;
> - Psychographics/attitudes;
> - Household income;
> - Access to financial services; banks;
> - Provider differentiations;
> - Savings;
> - Loans/credit;
> - Insurance;
> - Money transfer/remittances;
> - Payment and receipts.
>
> Detailed descriptions of the survey design, methodology, sample, and data aspects, as well as the questionnaire itself, are presented in Appendix A.

issues of geographic and demographic access, as well as types of instruments used in rural formal and informal financing.

Finally, the A2F survey data were collected between October 2007 and March 2008, and the analysis in this report refers to this time frame. In particular, the analysis ignores subsequent events associated with the global financial crisis and its fallout within Pakistan.

Pakistan—A Brief Market Overview

Pakistan's financial system grew significantly in the past few years. At present, total financial assets have reached $215 billion (150 percent of GDP). While this ratio compares favorably with regional benchmarks (table 1.1), it is modest compared with countries like China (543 percent), India (298 percent), Malaysia (384 percent), and Thailand (211 percent). Nevertheless, Pakistan's banking sector has gained

Table 1.1 Basic Financial Indicators, International Comparison

	Credit to Private Sector (% of GDP)	Equity Market Capitalization (% of GDP)	Stocks Value Traded (% GDP)	Private, Bonds (% GDP)	Public Bonds (% GDP)	Total Financial Assets/GDP	GNI per Capita ($)
Bangladesh	37.7%	10.0%	7.1%	—	—	54.8%	470
Brazil	49.8%	104.3%	44.5%	2.9%	3.6%	205.1%	5910
China	114.5%	189.8%	237.5%	0.2%	0.4%	542.5%	2360
India	47.4%	155.4%	94.6%	0.7%	0.2%	298.3%	950
Indonesia	25.4%	48.9%	26.1%	2.1%	1.1%	103.6%	1650
Malaysia	108.8%	180.2%	83.0%	4.4%	7.1%	383.5%	6540
Pakistan	29.4%	48.9%	70.0%	0.6%	1.3%	150.2%	870
Philippines	23.8%	71.6%	20.3%	1.7%	11.3%	128.7%	1620
Sri Lanka	34.0%	23.3%	2.9%	0.3%	0.2%	60.8%	1540
Thailand	84.2%	79.8%	44.0%	1.4%	1.2%	210.6%	3400

Source: World Development Indicators 2008, data for 2007.

Note: GNI = gross national income. Total financial assets are defined in a simplified manner, based on aggregate of assets described in this table.

dynamism, profitability, and strength, with a deposit base reaching $62 billion and gross advances $47 billion nationally in August 2008. Supported by a growing financial intermediation process, banks' aggregate profitability rose to $1.8 billion in 2008. The banking system constituted 44.5 percent of the total assets of financial institutions on March 31, 2008.

Pakistan has successfully implemented significant financial sector reforms over about the past 15 years, starting with grant of licenses to a number of new private banks in the early 1990s and modernization of the governance and regulatory framework of the banking sector in the late 1990s, and the privatization of major public sector banks since the early to mid-2000s. The authorities have taken steps to phase out or reorganize most of the government-owned development finance institutions, have put in place several initiatives to promote the growth of the microfinance sector, and have allowed more freedom to insurance companies. The active pace of reform created a reasonably well-developed, diverse, and sophisticated financial market, given Pakistan's income level.

In line with these reforms, the private sector credit touched the figure of Rs 2,523 billion in May 2008, as compared with Rs 356.3 billion a year earlier. SME credit increased from Rs 18 billion in fiscal 2000 to Rs 403 billion on March 31, 2008, though the increase is entirely accounted for by medium, not small, enterprises (SBP 2008d). Consumer credit accounted for 14 percent of total outstanding advances at the end of March 2008. Agriculture credit rose from less than Rs 40 billion in fiscal 2000 to Rs 200 billion in fiscal 2008. The aggregate number of borrowers rose from 2.7 million in 2003 to about 5.5 million by December 2006. House building loans stood at Rs 64.94 billion in May 2008, whereas the total housing finance market of Pakistan stood at Rs 126 billion on December 31, 2007

(SBP 2008e), doubling its size from 2005. Microfinance loans (microcredit, microsavings, and microinsurance) worth Rs 22.6 billion were disbursed in 2007 through extension of 1.8 million microloans. Presently, the active clients of micro-credit are around 1.7 million.

In spite of recent achievements, access to financial services remains quite limited in Pakistan. The predominant share of the financial system, the banking sector, is mostly focused on large enterprise lending, with an increasing interest in consumer financing (though still on a very small scale), to the relative neglect of SMEs, rural areas, microfinance, and the poor. There is little understanding of the main barriers to wider provision of financial services, or the opportunities that exist for financial companies in underserved market segments. One of the reasons for the lack of improvements in access provision is the limited availability of data on patterns of access to and usage of financial services among different population groups.

Banking Sector

Total deposits (excluding interbank) stood at Rs 3,202 billion at the end of 2006 and Rs 3,779 billion in August 2008 (figure 1). The public sector banks accounted for 21 percent of deposits, domestic private banks for 74 percent, and foreign banks for 5 percent. The loan portfolio of the banking system is also growing and reached

Figure 1.1 Deposits, Loans, and Assets of the Banking System (Rs billion)

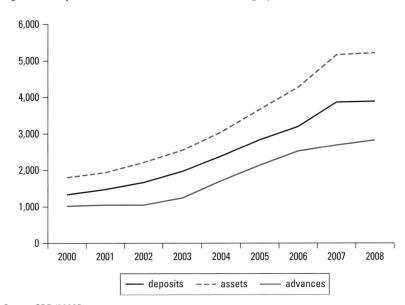

Source: SBP (2008f).

Note: 2008 data are for March 31, 2008.

Table 1.2 Breakdown of Loans (Domestic Operations) by Sector

	Loans Outstanding		Number of Borrowers	
	Amount (Rs Bn)	Share (%)	Number (Rs 000)	Share (%)
Corporate sector	1647.1	58.4%	25.9	0.6%
SMEs	409.5	14.5%	198.4	4.3%
Agriculture production	147.6	5.2%	1354.3	29.3%
Consumer finance	365.3	12.9%	2918.5	63.1%
Commodity operations	182.0	6.4%	3.0	0.1%
Staff loans	53.8	1.9%	92.0	2.0%
Other	17.1	0.6%	34.4	0.7%
Total	**2822.5**	**100.0%**	**4626.4**	**100.0%**

Source: SBP figures for March 2008.

Note: SBP regulations define SME loans as loans to enterprises or sole proprietors up to Rs 75 million.

Rs 2,336 billion in 2006. It stood at Rs 2,853 billion in August 2008. The major chunk of growth in loans portfolio could be attributed to local commercial private banks.

The banking system continues to grow, with its balance sheet size passing the level of Rs 5.2 trillion in March 2008.[2] The share of local commercial private banks in total assets increased to 74.8 percent. In contrast, the shares of public sector commercial banks, specialized banks, and foreign banks stood at 19.3 percent, 2.4 percent, and 3.6 percent, respectively.

Table 1.2 shows the limited access to bank finance of enterprises and individuals. Focusing only on the consumer side, according to latest (unpublished) SBP figures, there are only 16 million personal (nonbusiness) bank accounts and 5.5 million personal loans. Moreover, only 25 percent of the total bank deposits and 17 percent of the total borrowers are from rural areas. In value terms their shares are even smaller, 10 percent and 7 percent of the total value of deposits and advances, respectively (Akhtar 2008). The Pakistan Post Office manages 3.6 million savings accounts, through 12,343 branches, with 70 percent of such accounts holding savings below Rs 10,000 ($128). Most of the bank lending is concentrated in a few large manufacturing companies (figure 1.2). Aggregate data for all credit by borrower size shows a skewed distribution: 0.4 percent of bank borrowers account for 65 percent of all bank credit—and more than 5 million borrowers account for the remaining one-third of loans.

At the very top there is even more concentration; the largest 50 borrowers account for 37 percent of all credit outstanding. Limited access to services is captured by the low level of branch penetration, especially in rural areas, which has held back the growth of savings and impacted credit distribution systems (figure 1.3).

Consumer lending has been the fastest-growing segment in the past several years, by a wide margin, at 320 percent in terms of number of borrowers and slightly less

Figure 1.2 Bank Credit by Sector

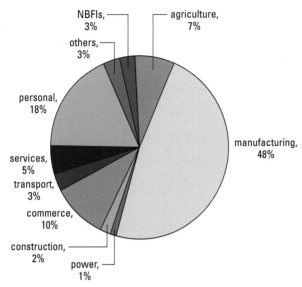

Source: SBP.

than 500 percent in loan amount, with 2.9 million clients between 2003 and 2007. Mortgage lending grew from Rs 4 billion in 2003 to Rs 67.4 billion in 2007. In tandem with growth, the sector has improved its efficiency dramatically. Application fees for start-up personal loans in Pakistan are found to be around 7 percent, one of the lowest in a broad spectrum of countries (World Bank 2008a). Similarly, Pakistan

Figure 1.3 Trends in Saving Rates

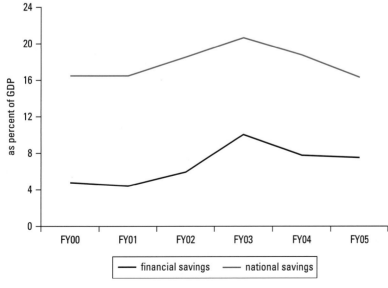

Source: SBP.

ranks well among the countries with very low complexity of personal loan applications, and ranks high among the countries with many free usage features for bank accounts.

Such positive effects of competition and efficiency improvements have not appeared yet in the SME lending sector, though the sector experienced a doubling of SME credit in 2004–7. Internationally, Pakistan compares unfavorably on business loan processing times and collateral to loan ratio, but does compete successfully on direct processing cost (Annex table A1.1). Similarly, 3.6 percent of firms use loans for investment (as compared with 12.7 percent for South Asia), and only 13.9 percent use them for expenses (versus 34.5 percent in South Asia). Overall, 37.6 percent of firms consider access to finance a constraint, as compared with 27.8 percent in South Asia (Annex table A1.1).

Agricultural disbursement has increased substantially (by 44 percent between 2003 and 2007, to 1.35 million borrowers) because of greater access, and holds considerable promise for medium-term development—commercial banks have aggressively lent, to the result of meeting SBP's target of Rs 200 billion set for fiscal 2008. Outstanding agriculture advances account for 6 percent of total advances and service 2 million clients. However, current credit meets only 45 percent of the agriculture requirements.

Banking Sector Penetration

Indicators of physical access to finance in Pakistan suggest a need to further improve the banking infrastructure (figure 1.4). Specifically, the number of automated teller machines (ATMs) is at less than 0.53 ATMs per 100,000 people. Compare this with the demographic ATM penetration figure for Sri Lanka, which is 4 ATMs per 100,000 people, and to the world median figure of 10. In terms of demographic penetration of bank branches, Pakistan is close to the world median levels at 5 branches per 100,000 people. This is still considerably lower than the figures of 6 for India and 7 for Sri Lanka.

The country records about 22 loan accounts per 1,000 people, compared with Bangladesh's 55 and the world median of 81. The use of deposit services is equally low—the country has 192 deposit accounts per 1,000 people, as compared with 229 in Bangladesh and 529 for the world median. A new focus is needed on a strategy to remove barriers to financial services access and actively encourage wider penetration by banks and other commercial providers. For this, better information is required on current levels of access to financial services as well as on impediments to wider access.

Doing Business 2008 indicators show that only 46 percent of adults in Pakistan are covered by the public registry (compared with 86 percent in countries of the Organisation for Economic Co-operation and Development [OECD] and 49 percent in China), while the private bureaus cover less than 1.4 percent (compared with 59 percent in OECD countries).

Figure 1.4 Banking Sector Penetration

Demographic branch penetration (number of branches per 100,000 people)

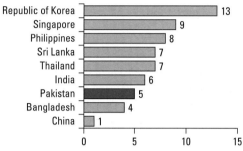

Geographic branch penetration (number of branches [ATMs] per 1,000 square km)

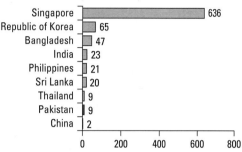

Demographic ATM penetration (number of ATMs per 100,000 people)

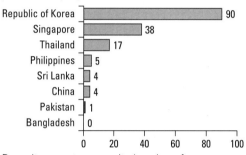

Geographic ATM penetration (number of ATMs per 1,000 square km)

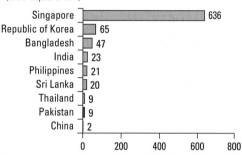

Deposit accounts per capita (number of deposits per 1,000 people)

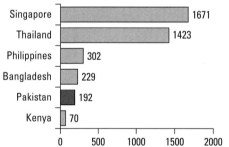

Loan accounts per capita (number of loans per 1,000 people)

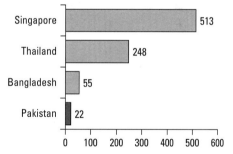

Percent of adults with access to an account with a financial intermediary

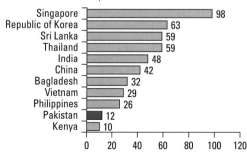

Source: WB Development Indicators 2008. ATM = Automated Teller Machine.

Banking Sector Performance

Pakistan's banking sector has gained dynamism, profitability, and strength with a deposit base reaching $62 billion and advances of $47 billion nationally. Supported by a growing financial intermediation process, banks aggregate profitability rose to $1.8 billion in 2008. Minimum capital requirements for banks were raised to Rs 1.5 billion by December 2004 and Rs 2 billion by December 2005. SBP has also required banks to increase their paid-up capital by Rs 1 billion a year, to reach Rs 6 billion by the end of December 2009. As a result, a consolidation of the banking market has taken place, and stronger banks have emerged. Banks capitalization and quality of assets have helped raise the risk weighted capital adequacy ratio to 13.2 percent. All banks maintain capital adequacy ratios well above the minimum international standard of 8 percent, except for state banks.

Growth of bank assets has picked up considerably since the late 1990s (Figure 1.5a), up to 18.8 percent and 17.25 percent most recently (December 2007 and March 2008, respectively). Nonperforming loans of the banking system have been declining overall, though they are still high for the specialized banks (Figure 1.5b). The capital adequacy ratios of the banking system show an increasing trend. They declined for all types of banks (except for specialized ones) over the period of 2002–3 but have shown an increasing trend since then. For public sector commercial banks, the capital adequacy ratio reached 15.2 in 2006 from −1.3 in 1997. Specialized banks, however, have been reporting negative capital adequacy ratios. In addition, the strengthening profitability of the banking sector can be assessed through increasing returns on assets (ROAs). As a group, all of the commercial banking groups except foreign banks have witnessed increase in ROA. Intermediation costs have stayed stable, while interest rate spreads have been on the increase.

Figure 1.5 Banking Sector Performance

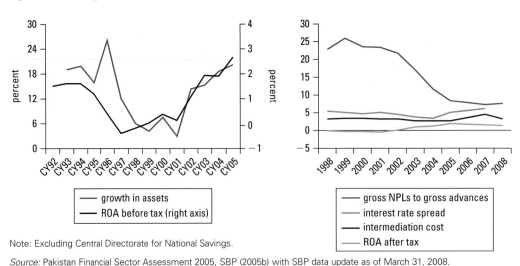

Note: Excluding Central Directorate for National Savings.

Source: Pakistan Financial Sector Assessment 2005, SBP (2005b) with SBP data update as of March 31, 2008.

Note: Interest rate spread defined as return on loans and advances minus cost of deposits.

Table 1.3 Comparative Position of Number of Branches in Pakistan (June 2008)

	Rural	Urban
Five big banks	2,247	3,315
Private banks	143	1,830
Specialized banks	179	360
Islamic banks	11	207
Foreign banks	—	51
Total	**2,580**	**5,763**

Source: SBP, September 2008.

Although the ROAs have been positive and growing for most of the period under consideration, return on equity of the banking system experienced a slight decline over 2005–6 due to the increase in capital to meet minimum capital requirement and the higher appropriation of profits by the banks. State-owned banks, however, have performed very poorly in terms of the profitability.

Overview of Market Players in the Banking Sector

The number of scheduled banks in Pakistan was 40 at end December 2007 (table 1.3). The number of commercial banks has declined from 41 to 26 through mergers, acquisitions, and closures. In the banking sector, specialized government-owned banks have made only a limited contribution in their niche markets. As of December 2007, there were 18 banks involved in Islamic banking, with a network of 288 branches in the country. Of these, 6 are full-fledged Islamic banks with 185 branches and 12 of the existing commercial banks have 103 branches that are offering Islamic banking services (SBP 2008i:2).

Pakistan Post Office

Another potentially major player in access to finance for the underserved is the Pakistan Post Office. It has a network of 13,419 branches throughout the country and is a significant provider of financial services, including savings, insurance, and remittances, through 7,276 bank branches. The Pakistan Post Savings Bank (PPSB) serves as an agent of the Ministry of Finance for a range of financial services, including savings mobilization, life insurance, postal giro accounts, and money transfers. It is present throughout the country and is the only banking service available in some remote areas. Pakistan Post has been able to upgrade the technology for its operations with help from the Islamic Development Bank. Internet services were launched in the late 1990s and are widely available at post offices, attracting the interest of small entrepreneurs and providing limited financial services. The PPSB offers several savings schemes, and in 2006 it had 3.6 million savings account holders. In addition, Pakistan Post acts as an agent to sell government-backed savings instruments. The

Postal Life Insurance offers 10 insurance options and had 252,810 active policies in 2004. Pakistan Post provides several options for national and international remittances in addition to hosting Western Union in some of its branches and acting as an agent to Western Union for international remittances.

Government policy has been to encourage financial institutions to use the extensive network of post office branches to extend outreach to more people. In recent years two MFBs, Khushhali Bank and First Micro Finance Bank, have linked up with the Pakistan Post to offer services at their branch offices. To date, though, the volume of this business has remained small. Given the significant developmental potential of Pakistan Post to enhance financial access, especially geographical penetration, it is important to pay specific attention to capacity building and strengthening of its performance and modernization, as well as standards. Since Pakistan Post dates back to the year 1873 when the Government Savings Bank Act, 1873 was promulgated, its financial services are not under SBP regulation, and thus have limited potential for technical supervision and performance improvement. A notable lesson from the East Asian Experience is the considerable advancement of postal financial operations once they move under central bank supervision and regulation. Box 3.2 presents successful experiences from Brazil and China and lessons learned from international case studies on postal financial systems.

Unmet Rural Credit Demand

Only 25 percent of the total bank deposits and 17 percent of the total borrowers are from rural areas. In value terms, their shares are even smaller, 10 percent and 7 percent of the total value of deposits and advances, respectively (Akhtar 2008). Only 15 percent of farmers are reached by the financial system as a whole (including the commercial banks, agricultural banks, and other financial institutions). Total credit to rural areas is Rs 130.7 billion, while rural credit demand is estimated as twice this volume (Rs 250 billion) (table 1.4). The bulk of rural finance volumes are in agricultural finance (Rs 108.7 billion), with a balanced share of farm and nonfarm credit. While microcredit volumes are skewed toward rural areas, rural microcredit currently represents merely 17 percent of total rural credit.

The access to finance gap is even starker in the case of farmers (table 1.5). The few upper-income large farmers enjoy almost 10 times higher access to formal finance (38.7 percent) than the farmers in the poorest quintile (6.5 percent). Large farmers get even more informal credit than their less fortunate counterparts—82 percent vs. 70.2 percent. Such skewed distribution of farm credit negatively affects the poverty level of agricultural households, and prevents faster development in rural areas.

Microfinance (Chapter 3)

Outside of the banking system, little financing is available for the underserved (table 1.6), though this is a promising area for long-term growth. Though access to finance has steadily improved over the years, it remains too low to make a real

Table 1.4 Rural Credit Market (Rs)

Total rural population of Pakistan	97.0 million
Total rural households	15.0 million
Farm	9.2 million
Nonfarm	5.8 million
Estimated credit demand	250.0 billion
Total agricultural credit supplied (Rs)	109.7 billion
Farm credit	51.5 billion
Nonfarm credit	58.2 billion
Total microcredit	28.4 billion
Total microcredit (rural)	22.0 billion
Total microcredit (urban)	6.4 billion

Source: www.pmn.org.pk/downloads/start.download.ruralperspective.php.

Table 1.5 Farmer Access to Finance

	Financially Included	Formally Included	Informally Included	Financially Excluded
Poorest	70.7%	6.5%	70.2%	29.3%
2nd quintile	81.8%	11.5%	80.6%	18.2%
3rd quintile	83.5%	13.2%	82.9%	16.5%
4th quintile	82.0%	24.9%	81.7%	10.0%
Richest	89.6%	38.7%	82.0%	10.4%

Source: Pakistan Access to Finance Database, 2008.

Table 1.6 Microfinance Outreach in Pakistan

	2007
No. of branches	1,343
Total no. of borrowers	1,471,295
Average loan size (Rs)	13,520
Average loan balance (Rs)	10,286
Gross loan portfolio (Rs in million)	15,134

Source: MicroWatch. Issue 6, Annual (2007).

difference in terms of the poverty impact of growth. Various estimates of potential market demand for microfinance place potential client figures in the tens of millions, as compared with actual client figures of 1.7 million currently (out of a total population of more than 160 million). Microfinance penetration in the region is higher, at 35 percent in Bangladesh, 25 percent in India, and 29 percent in Sri Lanka. Afghanistan has a relatively new microfinance industry, with about 437,000 active clients as of March 2008.

Currently, the network of microfinance providers is 1,343 branches with about Rs 15 billion portfolio. Among microfinance providers, Khushali Bank alone provides coverage in 86 districts, hence accounting for 47 percent of this network. The three microfinance entities, namely, National Rural Support Program (NRSP), Khushali Bank, and Kashf Foundation, accounted for approximately 70 percent of the sector's active clients. In the middle of 2008, total outreach measured by active borrowers was about 1.7 million in a market where it is estimated that there are 7 million poor households. In fact, based on experience in more mature microfinance markets like Bangladesh, the size of the potential market in Pakistan could be as high as 12–15 million since the vulnerable poor, those living above the poverty line but without access to most formal financial services, also use microfinance services. Some estimates of potential demand by women place the potentially viable savings clients at 35 million and viable borrowers at 22 million. Much remains to be done to capture a potential market of such proportions, including in terms of literacy improvement, awareness-raising, and cost reduction of access via technology improvements, as well as reliance on tried and tested low-tech solutions such as the Grameen model.

A second challenge for microfinance is for service providers to become profitable so that service provision to poor people can grow on a sustainable basis. A study of South Asian MFIs done in 2005 showed that only 42 percent of microcredit borrowers in Pakistan received services from profitable MFIs, the lowest percentage in South Asia (Microfinance Information Exchange, Consultative Group to Assist the Poor, and the World Bank (2006). Most microfinance providers rely on a combination of donor/noncommercial funding, and cannot claim commercial viability, with the exception of the recently formed microfinance banks (MFBs). Retail providers, such as the six recently licensed MFBs, operate on a sustainable footing and are expected to solidify their position further by increasing reliance on client deposits. The remaining microfinance providers are largely not expected to become sustainable as a class. Those include (1) the national and provincial rural support programs and charitable or specialized nongovernmental organizations (NGOs); (2) the wholesale apex institution, the principal being the Pakistan Poverty Alleviation Fund (PPAF), which relies on donor and government financing support to refinance community organization whose number has reached 60,000; and (3) the NGOs and the cooperatives, which are now mostly closed except for one principal operator, the Punjab Cooperative Bank, which has managed to be proactive but relies on SBP credit lines (quite an unsustainable approach) and provincial government support and has to be eventually restructured to be more financially viable.

A third challenge is that microfinance is almost exclusively focused on loans, while other financial services, savings, transfers/remittances, and insurance are often more in demand by poorer households. Indeed, this report finds that demand for savings, not credit, predominates, and is largely untapped. Unlike in most other

Table 1.7 Islamic Banking Players

	Dec-04	Dec-05	Dec-06	Dec-07
No. of Islamic banks	2	2	4	6
No. of branches	23	37	N.A.	185
No. of conventional banks offering Islamic banking	7	9	12	12
No. of conventional banks branches offering Islamic banking	21	33	N.A.	103
Total number of branches offering Islamic banking	**44**	**70**	**150**	**288**

Source: SBP Banking System Review for the year ending Dec. 2005.

countries, the microfinance sector has historically focused more on men than women, as product delivery methods have been poorly suited to women and established cultural mores.

Islamic Finance

In 2002, the first Islamic banking license was issued to Meezan Bank. Currently there are 6 licensed, full-fledged Islamic Banks and 12 conventional banks with stand-alone Islamic banking branches (table 1.7). As of December 31, 2007, the number of Islamic banking branches stood at 288 in 47 cities in all four provinces of the country. These also include international banks, such as ABN Amro and Standard Chartered. Applications for a few more players are under consideration. The most popular Islamic products currently include *murabaha*, *ijarah*, and diminishing *musharaka* financing.[3] The total assets portfolio in the Islamic Banking sector stands at Rs 200 billion as of March 31, 2008; deposits were at Rs 142 billion and financing and investment at Rs 114 billion. Total number of borrowers/finances is about 25,000.

Despite their rapid growth over the past few years, the Islamic banks are facing a number of problems, including the lack of liquidity management instruments,[4] specific Islamic-bank prudential regulations, depositor risk for Islamic depositors, and a certain lack of clarity with more complex financial instruments, such as foreign currency accounts, letters of credit, and assets to be generated in the future.

SME Finance (Chapter 4)

There are 3.2 million SMEs in Pakistan. SMEs account for more than 90 percent of all private enterprises, contribute to 30 percent of GDP, and account for 25 percent of exports of manufactured goods. In spite of their importance in the economy, lending to SME still accounts for only 16 percent of total lending in volumes and only 4 percent of total customers. While international comparisons of SME lending

Table 1.8 Credit to Private Sector and Growth in Lending

Sectors of the Economy	Credit to Private Sector (Dec. 2007, Rs billion)		Growth in % during Dec. CY03–Dec. CY07	
	Amount	Number of Borrowers	Number of Borrowers	Loans
Corporate sector	1,520.1	56.3	n.a.	n.a.
SMEs	437.4	16.2	101.9	103.4
Agriculture	150.8	5.6	0.3	43.6
Consumer finance	371.4	13.8	319.5	499.1
Total	2,700.9	100.0	114.9	599.7

Source: SBP.

are difficult because of inconsistent SME definitions, credit to Pakistani small enterprises has much potential to expand, relative to the international experience.

Lending to SMEs (as defined by the Prudential Regulations of SBP[5]), despite the importance of SMEs in the Pakistani economy, has shown a slightly downward trend over the period 2004–7. Although the development of the SME sector rests crucially on the availability and access to finance at an affordable cost, especially through the formal institutional setup, private sector credit to SMEs accounted only for 16.2 percent of total credit to the private sector in December 2007 (table 1.8). SME lending grew much more slowly than other lending market segments, such as consumer loans, especially credit to small, as opposed to medium, enterprises. One reason for such disappointing expansion of credit to SMEs is that the risk-assessment process for SMEs is more complex, especially in a dynamic business environment with little reliable information. Another reason is that banks consider SMEs as part of their business (corporate) finance activities, whereas SMEs should be part of their retail business, because SME lending will only work if less attention is paid to risk-assessment processes and more to efficiency and speed of delivery to produce scale of operations. In fact, many banks view SMEs as minicorporations and use more or less the same tools to assess risks. This proves to be too expensive as well as ineffective.

The reluctance of banks to perceive SMEs as a profitable business venture is compounded by the fact that many potential SME clients do not have immovable assets, which are the most-used form of collateral. Weaknesses in the existing collateral regime, especially for movable property, complicate matters further. Moreover, as the majority of the SMEs are sole proprietors, banks cannot secure their loans with movable assets either. In fact, on the basis of the existing law, only limited liability companies can register a lien over a movable asset in the company registry. Other reasons for the reluctance of banks to lend to SMEs are the general lack of reliable formal credit information, given that credit bureaus are still in an early stage of development, and the fact that most SMEs do not maintain proper books of accounts, making it difficult for traditional bankers to assess the viability of a going concern.

Remittances (Chapter 5)

International remittances have grown at impressive rates in Pakistan, in part because of a broad formalization effort by SBP, which has brought in more than 70 percent of international flows into the formal net. Not so the domestic remittance market, which has not enjoyed such policy attention, and on which official data are limited. Rough unofficial evidence exists that domestic flows are of considerable magnitude, and, as with international flows, most of the transfer happens in the informal sector.

Figures from the SBP indicate that international formal remittances into Pakistan for 2007–8 were $6.45 billion, up from $2 billion in 2002. Recent studies suggest that, in most cases, the macroeconomic benefits of remittances in a developing country are likely to be positive, and there are also considerable household-level benefits that have economic growth and poverty reduction effects. However, in Pakistan, remittances do not appear to make a significant portion of household income for the poorest quintile. Interestingly, domestic remittances constitute a larger share of income than international flows for poorer households, while the trend reverses among richer households. In part, this is because most migrant workers do not pertain to the lowest income groups. However, much more important, limited access to remittances by the poorest population is mostly to blame for the weakened poverty effect of remittances, in spite of the sector's spectacular recent growth and performance.

Remittances to Pakistan have been growing at an impressive rate in recent years (29 percent between fiscal 2001 and fiscal 2008). The largest amount remitted is from the United States (27.3 percent), followed by Saudi Arabia (19.4 percent). Increased remittances have supplemented foreign exchange earnings and have helped maintain the rupee exchange rate (though higher exchange rates also tend to suppress export-led growth). The steps taken by SBP to formalize the remittance market through formation of exchange companies (ECs), and reduction in the curb and interbank exchange rate, have helped increase formal remittance flows.

More than 80 percent of formal remittances comes through the formal banks, Habib Bank Limited and United Bank Limited being the two main players, while 17 percent comes through ECs and about 2.5 percent through the Pakistan Post Office. Western Union is very active in the market and has set up partnerships with various banks, ECs, and Pakistan Post. Fees for sending remittances from abroad vary from free transfer to more than $50, while the time taken for the transfer ranges from less than 10 minutes to more than 2 months.

The biggest challenge is to increase rural outreach of remittances. International success stories in this respect include mobile phone banking strategies based on the G-Cash model of the Philippines or the M-Pesa model of Kenya. Another strategy is to partner more closely with players who have better rural networks. While the current regulatory setup does not allow telecom operators to provide financial services, lessons can be learned from these telecom-led models and applied through partnership arrangements between banks and nonbanks. Other steps that can be taken include forming partnerships with banks abroad, as well as expanding the outreach of Pakistani banks abroad, informing, increasing awareness, and facilitating remittances by Pakistani workers aboard.

Financial Inclusion and the New Financial Regulatory and Technological Infrastructure

National Policies to Enhance Financial Inclusion

SBP has adopted a coordinating role with the Government of Pakistan (GOP) and private sector to implement a financial inclusion strategy, focusing on microfinance, SMEs, remittances, Islamic banking, agriculture finance, and insurance, among other areas. Many new SBP regulations have been issued to encourage financial development and inclusion, for example, electronic banking, branchless banking, the SME policy framework, and others.[6] The newly created Development Finance Group with SBP in September 2006 steers and helps policy implementation, in the areas of the legal and regulatory framework for SMEs, agriculture and rural credit, housing and infrastructure finance, and Islamic finance. The Financial Inclusion Program (FIP),[7] developed with considerable donor backing (from the UK Department for International Development, or DFID) and adopted in 2008, will constitute an important and promising initiative in this regard, over the long term.

SBP has further introduced the **Annual Branch Licensing Policy**[8] with a roadmap for 2008 and beyond. This policy requires commercial banks with 100 branches or more to open at least 20 percent of their branches outside big cities and set up branches in *tehsil* headquarters, where no branch of any bank exists. The five big banks have, as a result, more than 40 percent of their branches in rural areas. However, due to this policy, smaller banks are keeping the number of branches at less than 100—only after they make a conscious decision to go into rural areas do they exceed 100 branches. In addition, SBP has allowed banks to establish subbranches and booth and service centers of commercial banks in inner regions where it is costly to maintain a full-fledged branch. These subbranches can be managed by skeleton staff and can act as an extended arm of the nearby branch for performing limited banking functions such as deposits, withdrawals, issuance of demand drafts, and telegraphic transfers and to facilitate payment of home remittances to their beneficiaries. Other cautionary lessons should be taken into account while applying this policy. The recent World Bank study on *Banking the Poor* suggests that mandatory regional requirements for new branches may reduce the total number of branches (incremental costs might translate into increase in the cost of providing the additional services, thus making access prohibitively expensive even when the services are available), and while encouraging sub-branches or booths, may fall short of encouraging agency relationships or correspondents, where present mandates appear "unclear."

Since November 2005, all commercial banks operating in Pakistan are required to offer **Basic Banking Accounts**[9] to improve financing access for low-income Pakistanis. Such an account can be opened, for example, with a maximum deposit of Rs 1,000 carrying no fee, no minimum balance, and full ATM access. As of March 2007, about 120,000 basic accounts had been opened. Those are still associated with high transaction costs for banks and low demand from accountholders, who tend to stay with existing instruments in spite of low interest rates. Competition is expected to weaken these disadvantages in the longer term. Such regulatory measures should be treated with caution, however. The *Banking the Poor* study suggests that regulation in this area on its own is not enough and indeed there is a limited association with better access. However, in many places where banks have voluntarily offered commercial products of a basic banking character, there is a positive association with access.

The central bank with the support of its two principal training institutions, National Institute of Banking and Finance (NIBAF) and the Institute of Bankers Pakistan (IBP), is implementing an initiative for **financial literacy and capacity building** for financial institutions and the public, to leverage available financial services while building momentum for the community to appreciate the available lending opportunities. This agenda is important, and this report also finds low access to finance among individuals with lower levels of literacy. Causality has been debated by practitioners and policy makers, however. While financial literacy arguments are quite compelling, empirical evidence from Indonesia (Cole, Zia, and Sampson 2008) suggests that financial incentives (which remove or reduce affordability barriers of opening a bank account), not financial literacy, have an impact on the use and uptake of financial services among households. Nonetheless, this report contends that awareness of financial options and service providers, as well as development of trust in such providers, rather than literacy per se, hold the promise of increasing financial access nationwide. The evidence on SMEs also suggests that there may be an important role for business training—results of business development assistance have been very promising, per international experience.

In 2001, the *Microfinance Institutions Ordinance and Supportive Prudential Regulations* was adopted, allowing for the creation of national and regional MFBs. SBP published new guidelines in 2006 for commercial bank provision of microfinance services.[10] The microfinance ordinance was amended in 2007 (Finance Bill 2007–8) to ensure that minimum loan size is raised to Rs 150,000 to allow providers to tailor their services to microbusiness needs. Further, microfinance providers are now allowed to engage in the remittance sector. With a focus on expanding microfinance to 3 million borrowers by 2010, a strategy for Expanding Microfinance Outreach has been developed by the SBP and was approved by the GOP in February 2007. The strategy stresses commercialization of the sector as a key to financial and social sustainability, and benefits from extensive support by donors (DFID), via the overall FIP initiative, in terms of credit as well as capacity-building and technology initiatives support. While the long-term impact of the program, adopted in 2008, remains to be assessed, it will undoubtedly encounter short-term difficulties associated with the global financial turmoil and its fallout in Pakistan.

SBP introduced *Prudential Regulations for **Agricultural Financing** and Guidelines for Livestock and Fisheries Financing,* as well as simplified and standardized loan documents.[11] It has further focused on encouraging a revolving credit scheme for three years, under which farmers can borrow for one year and continue to borrow without providing documentation each year; guidelines have been issued on lending for livestock, fisheries, and horticulture subsectors, and programs are being launched for the dairy sector. In addition, a small farmer financing scheme has been promoted based on group lending and a crop loan insurance scheme has been structured that is now being offered by some insurance companies. SBP has further allowed banks to finance against market/realizable/forced sale value of the agriculture land, urban properties, gold/silver ornaments, and so forth, and also against two personal sureties (up to Rs 500,000,or $8,333), in addition to the passbook to the land, and so forth. These initiatives have contributed significantly to enhancing formal institutional agricultural credit disbursement for small borrowers.

SBP has also laid out an elaborate prudential regulatory and supervisory framework that conforms to the International Islamic Financial Service Board's (IFSB) framework, by way of enabling **Islamic finance**, which SBP expects will constitute almost 12 percent of the Pakistan financial system in the next five years. In 2004, SBP issued detailed criteria for (1) setting up of scheduled Islamic commercial banks based on the principles of *Shariah* (Islamic law) in the private sector, and (2) for setting up of Islamic banking subsidiaries by existing commercial banks. In the same year, SBP also issued guidelines for opening of standalone Islamic banking branches by existing banks. Islamic finance is still in its infancy worldwide and in Pakistan. Basic regulations are outstanding, as are estimates of potential demand among various population groups, and models for sustainable product delivery. The sector has much growth potential.

SBP has published new prudential guidelines for **SME financing**, wherein banks can issue unsecured loans to SMEs up to Rs 3 million.[12] A new SME Policy 2007 was launched in fiscal 2008, attempting to define uniformly SMEs in the manufacturing, trade, and services sectors for all the stakeholders. The policy document gives a broad framework for promotion of SMEs by improving the regulatory, fiscal, and business environment, as well as institutionalization of the support structure. The document further outlines a strategy for SME-led private sector growth, poverty reduction, and job creation. Sector Development Companies have already been set up for various industries, including gems and jewelry, marble and granite, furniture, dairy products, and the hunting and sporting arms sector. These companies work on a public-private partnership basis, with the private sector having a leading role in decision making. In parallel, there are several initiatives to extend financial services to small borrowers. These include SBP's SME financing strategy that advocates promotion of credit guarantee schemes and venture capital funds, establishment of SME training centers and capacity building of banks' SME loan officers, SME credit-risk scoring and competitiveness benchmarking, as well as a triennial survey on SMEs to estimate their finance demand.[13] Work is underway to develop an appropriate credit enhancement mechanism that will facilitate bank lending to the sector. SME credit policies have had mixed success, especially as concerns the small enterprises market, and more work is needed in the collateral and credit information aspects of SME lending.

While these initiatives are a step in the right direction, SBP needs to develop a strong and effective monitoring and evaluation system to monitor the impact of these initiatives and to bring mid-course corrections where needed to ensure that the ultimate objectives for which the initiatives have been taken are fully achieved. Other programs for financial inclusion in Pakistan are listed in box 1.3.

Box 1.3   **Other Programs in Pakistan for Financial Inclusion**

National Rural Support Program: Established in 1991, NRSP is the largest rural support program in the country in terms of outreach, staff, and development activities. It is a not-for-profit organization registered under Section 42 of Companies Ordinance 1984. NRSP's mandate is to alleviate poverty by harnessing people's potential and undertake development activities in Pakistan. It has a presence in 46 districts in all the four provinces including Azad Jammu and Kashmir. NRSP is currently working with more than half a million poor households organized into a network of more than 55,366 community organizations. With sustained incremental growth, it is emerging as Pakistan's leading engine for poverty reduction and rural development. NRSP manages one of the largest microcredit portfolios in Pakistan, with 282,421 active loans as of March 2007, and holds 25 percent of the microfinance market. NRSP provides various financial services to the community organization members in rural areas, to help them implement their microinvestment plans, including microcredit, microinsurance, and savings products.

Rozgar Scheme: The National Bank of Pakistan, the largest nationwide bank, is offering small loans to the unemployed and the poor to finance purchases of auto rickshaws, set up utility stores under franchise of the Utility Corporation, set up public call offices, and so forth. Interest on these loans is fixed at 12 percent: half of the interest charges are to be borne by the GOP and the remaining half by the borrowers. The government picks up first 10 percent of all losses and shares in the credit risk. External and internal verification of borrowers, references, and guarantees are handled by ICIL, a representative firm of Dun and Bradstreet. This scheme is anticipated to deliver about Rs 105 billion ($1.34 billion in lending) over a five-year period. Since its launch this year, the scheme has delivered Rs 2 billion to about 22,136 borrowers.

Pakistan Poverty Alleviation Fund: The PPAF was created in 2008 as a private sector apex fund to provide capacity building and loan funds to MFIs, primarily NGOs. By the end of 2005, it was supporting about 35 organizations, almost all NGOs that provide microfinance services. Sponsored by the GOP and funded by the World Bank and leading donors, the PPAF follows a model of public-private partnership through lending of wholesale funds to civil society organizations committed to community outreach programs for enhancing income and economic welfare of the disadvantaged. Specifically, the PPAF provides funding for projects that help generate income and improve the physical and social infrastructure and the skills of the vulnerable. On February 28, 2007, the PPAF had a resource base of Rs 49,560.2 million ($634.37 million).

Source: Akhtar (2007a).

Regulatory Framework for Branchless Banking

SBP has been working with the Consultative Group to Assist the Poor on using information and communications technology and new branchless banking models to reach massive numbers of presently unserved poor people.[14] Branchless banking is defined as the delivery of financial services outside conventional bank branches using information and communications technologies and nonbank retail agents. Industry players, particularly mobile network operators, see the enormous potential of branchless banking as a profitable value-added service. Branchless banking can help address the low point of sale infrastructure in Pakistan, in particular the very low ATM penetration. There are, however, considerable challenges to branchless banking posed by current regulation in Pakistan that need to be addressed, while paying due regard to the new and enhanced risks that branchless banking can carry. Some potentially viable paths include bank- and telcom-led models or a combination of models. Regulatory changes would be required, along the lines of some of the following: (1) the use of agents outside bank branches, thereby increasing the number of service points; (2) easier account opening (both onsite and remotely) while maintaining adequate know-your-customer standards; and (3) permission for a range of players to provide payment services and issue e-money, thereby enabling innovation from multiple sources.

These changes are considerable. For one, the legal framework restricts the use of agents for cash-in/cash-out activities and account opening, a major impediment to correspondent banking.[15] It is unclear whether it is legally possible for customers to withdraw money outside of bank branches, though an exception is provided for ATMs and withdrawals at "Authorized Merchant Establishments at Various Points of Sale" subject to a cash limit of Rs 10,000. However, MFBs are permitted to appoint agents and open booths for collection of cash or for making spot payments, yet those powers are restricted by regulation to specific circumstances. Further, SBP has granted permission for mobile banking (that is, the use of mobile vans and small service centers). ECs, which are also regulated by SBP, can make use of agents in remote areas; however, these agents currently are permitted to provide only one service: payment (in Pakistani rupees only) of remittances from foreign countries.

The current anti–money laundering/combating the financing of terrorism regime, which covers banks only, presents further obstacles to the potential introduction of branchless activities.[16] Examples include using the national identity card (approximately 20 percent of Pakistanis do not have one), as well as requirements for new customers to be introduced by existing ones, which is difficult in areas with low coverage. Other regulations on enhanced customer due diligence cause difficulties with remote account opening and other non–face-to-face transactions. The rules on establishing identity are more relaxed for MFBs, where in far-flung and remote areas where people, particularly women, do not have identity cards, the MFB may extend microcredit by establishing identity through other appropriate means.

Access to finance in Pakistan has lagged behind the country's growth and development needs, in spite of active policy support on the part of SBP. Part of this disappointing outcome can be explained by very high growth rates in access in the past five years, albeit from a very low client base. A second pertinent consideration suggests that financial policies alone are not sufficient to expand access, and a holistic approach linked to basic poverty reduction and financial awareness building would be more successful. In addition to financial access expansion, the task of strengthening financial provider sustainability, especially in the microfinance sector, is of paramount importance. Competition, efficiency improvements, and exposure of financial institutions to market discipline hold the promise of commercial viability and reliability for the microfinance sector. Competition and efficiency improvements are also needed if SME lending is to become profitable. New approaches suitable for smaller enterprises, such as bank downscaling, are workable tools to achieve sustainable SME lending products. In view of limited financial infrastructure and penetration, physical access can be stepped up using a two-pronged strategy, via existing agencies with higher penetration such as Pakistan Post, as well as via new technology solutions, such as branchless banking and mobile banking.

Notes

1. A word of caution: while the household survey collects a representative sample, including upper-income households that use more sophisticated consumer finance instruments, the report does not explicitly focus on the markets and access issues for such instruments as mortgage finance, automobile finance, consumer durables lending, credit cards, and sophisticated checking and saving accounts. On the other hand, it does attempt to convey best-practice and policy options as concerns simple instruments relevant for the underserved, such as debit cards, and very basic (limited) accounts, such as smart cards and simplified transaction accounts.

2. Provisional figure (SBP 2008g: table 5.3).

3. Murabaha financing is an investment partnership, as of 2007 at about 40 percent of the total financing by the Islamic banking institutions. Ijarah financing is an Islamic lease agreement, accounting for about 30 percent of the total financing. Diminishing musharaka financing is profit-and-loss sharing, where by the client purchases financier's share gradually, until all of financier's share is purchased by the client, making him sole owner, at about 17 percent of the total financing by the Islamic banking institutions.

4. The issuance of two *sukuks* (asset-backed Islamic bonds), both by the Water and Power Development Authority (WAPDA), have somewhat eased the situation for some of the Islamic banks, but there are no proper institutional arrangements available.

5. Prudential Regulations for Small and Medium Enterprises Financing: Banking Policy and Regulations Department, SBP (http://www.sbp.org.pk/publications/prudential/PRs-SMEs.pdf). The SBP data on SMEs provided in this section are based on this definition.

6. BPRD Circular No. 02 of 2008, Branchless Banking Regulations for Financial Institutions desirous to undertake branchless banking (http://www.sbp.org.pk/bprd/2008/Annex_C2.pdf), Prudential Regulations for Small and Medium Enterprises Financing: Banking Policy and Regulations Department, SBP (http://www.sbp.org.pk/publications/prudential/PRs-SMEs.pdf).

7. http://www.sbp.org.pk/MFD/FIP/inclusion.htm.

8. Annual Branch Licensing Policy, Banking Policy and Regulations Department, SBP (http://www.sbp.org.pk/bprd/2007/Annex_C15.pdf).

9. BPD Circular No. 30 of 2005 (http://www.sbp.org.pk/bpd/2005/C30.htm).

10. SMED Circular No. 11 of 2006 (http://www.sbp.org.pk/smfd/2006/C11.htm).

11. Prudential Regulations for Agriculture Financing, Banking Policy and Regulations Department, SBP (http://www.sbp.org.pk/publications/prudential/prs-agriculture.pdf); Guidelines for Fisheries Financing, Agricultural Credit Department, SBP (http://www.sbp.org.pk/acd/2007/Guidelines-for-Fisheries-Financing.pdf); Guidelines for Livestock Financing, Agricultural Credit Department, SBP (http://www.sbp.org.pk/acd/2006/Guidelines_Livestock_C1.pdf).

12. Prudential Regulations for Small and Medium Enterprises Financing: Banking Policy and Regulations Department, SBP (http://www.sbp.org.pk/publications/prudential/PRs-SMEs.pdf).

13. SME Policy 2007 (http://www.pakistan.gov.pk/ministries/industriesandproduction-ministry/media/SMEPolicyDevelopment.pdf).

14. BPRD Circular No. 02 of 2008, Branchless Banking Regulations for Financial Institutions Desirous to Undertake Branchless Banking (http://www.sbp.org.pk/bprd/2008/Annex_C2.pdf).

15. This section is closely based on Consultative Group to Assist the Poor (2007).

16. BPD Circular No. 20 of 2004 (http://www.sbp.org.pk/bpd/2004/C20.htm), Anti-Money Laundering Ordinance 2007 (http://www.sbp.org.pk/about/act/AML-Ordinance-2007.pdf).

Annex

Table A1.1 Indices of Financial Access: Mean Values by Region and Country

	All countries	S.Asia	E.Asia	Latin America	Africa	Pakistan
Domestic and Cross Border Payments Time indices						
Domestic Payments Time index (0-1)*	0.51	0.56	0.38	0.46	0.54	0.58
Cross Border Payments Time index (0-1)*	0.45	0.37	0.41	0.42	0.48	0.52
Retail Payments - Availability and Quality						
Range of payment services with standard bank account index (0-1)*	0.62	0.67	0.74	0.57	0.59	0.77
Mobile banking technologies index (0-1)*	0.27	0.36	0.38	0.22	0.24	0.32
Network quality and interoperability index (0-1)*	0.62	0.69	0.76	0.83	0.54	1.00
Retail payment channels index (0-1)*	0.47	0.43	0.65	0.50	0.43	0.48
Credit						
Business Loan Processing Time (days)	7.50	8.33	7.64	13.41	6.64	11.67
Start Up Loan Processing Fee (%)	1.20	0.70	0.85	1.33	1.35	0.71
Collateral to Loan Value Ratio (%)	88.07	88.48	74.43	73.82	92.49	136.67
Maximum Loan Terms for Start Up Loans (years)	4.42	4.41	3.31	6.25	4.40	5.33
Index of Business Loan Application Complexity*	0.73	0.68	0.73	0.77	0.74	0.58
Index of Collateral Flexibility*	0.71	0.66	0.78	0.57	0.71	0.80
Basic Banking						
No opening fee (average yes/no)	0.78	0.81	0.8	0.94	0.75	1
No Monthly Fee (average yes/no)	0.62	0.83	0.72	0.76	0.53	1
No min balance (average yes/no)	0.53	0.42	0.51	0.54	0.58	0.6
Package of free services (average yes/no)	0.56	0.61	0.57	0.66	0.53	1
No check writing fee (average yes/no)	0.57	0.61	0.47	0.49	0.6	0.8
Government policy (Commercial Bank response) (average yes/no)	0.57	0.7	0.62	0.36	0.55	1
Government: Offering Basic Banking*	0.23	0.33	0.25	0.20	0.22	1
Government: Exempting ID Requirements for Basic Accounts*	0.06	0.17	0.13	0.00	0.03	0
Basic Banking (0 to 1)*	0.60	0.67	0.64	0.59	0.58	0.90

(continued)

Table A1.1 Indices of Financial Access: Mean Values by Region and Country (continued)

	All countries	S.Asia	E.Asia	Latin America	Africa	Pakistan
Savings Schemes						
Doorstep Collection Schemes*	0.08	0.17	0.25	0.00	0.03	0
Govt Matched Savings Schemes*	0.02	0.00	0.13	0.00	0.00	0
Govt Tax Incentives for Savings*	0.43	0.33	0.75	0.40	0.38	0
Periodic Deposit Schemes*	0.41	0.53	0.48	0.46	0.36	0
Transparency and Consumer Protection						
Advising Applicants (0 to 1)*	0.46	0.58	0.56	0.40	0.42	0.5
Additional Document Requirements (0 to 1)*	0.10	0.17	0.13	0.13	0.08	0.13
Guidelines on Documents to Obtain Credit (0 to 1)*	0.70	0.67	0.72	0.90	0.68	0.75
Transparency Consumer Protection (0 to 1)*	0.39	0.60	0.50	0.40	0.33	0.67
Firms using Bank Loans (% all firms)						
Firms with Bank Loans	31.06	50.8	—	36.3	27.78	—
Firms that Use Loans for Investment	16.25	12.71	23.95	10.83	15.7	3.63
Firms that Use Loans for Expenses	28.2	34.47	33.27	28.16	25.58	13.99
Firms View Access to Finance as Constraint	35.61	27.76	15.11	22.06	46.17	37.55
Small and Micro firms using Bank Loans (% firms)						
Small Firms with Bank Loans	27	37	28	27	27	
Micro Firms with Bank Loans	20	34.00	21	22	19	
Small Firms that use Loans for Working Capital	10.76	13.63	13.18	12.41	9.82	—
Micro Firms that use Loans for Working Capital	8.97	10.48	9.55	11.19	8.35	—
Small Firms that use Loans for Investment	13.65	10.41	16.87	16.8	12.51	—

Micro Firms that use Loans for Investment	11.19	6.25	13.77	15.27	10.06	—
Small Firms that View Access to Finance as Constraint	75	34	53	74	81	—
Micro Firms that View Access to Finance as Constraint	60	18	34	56	67	—
Demographic and Socio-Economic Variables						
Per Capita GDP (USD)	2075.08	742.20	5485.00	3136.8	1334.40	810.00
Population (m)	53.25	292.20	63.38	27.2	20.51	159.00
Percentage of the population 15 years old and over	61.00	65.00	70.00	63.00	57.00	63.63
P. Density (/sq k)	249.47	437.40	920.63	124.00	87.14	206.00
Urban Population (%)	39.11	24.00	47.63	58	37.06	35.00
Literacy (15+)	64.80	53.50	85.88	79.6	59.34	45.00
Gini Coefficient	43.03	37.80	39.43	51	43.60	32.00
Private credit to GDP ratio	28.85	37.00	55.25	35	20.53	29.00
Banking assets covered (%)	68.35	68.67	64.88	49.8	72.06	60.00
Legal Rights Index	4.12	4.00	4.75	3.6	4.06	4.00
Credit Information Index	2.22	2.50	3.00	5.6	1.44	4.00

Source: World Bank (2008a).

*All the variables with an asterisk have a detailed explanation of their construction in the glossary.

Table A1.2 Weighted Average Lending and Deposit Rates, May 2008

Items	Gross Disbursements (% per Annum)		Outstanding Loans (% per Annum)		Fresh Deposits (% per Annum)		Outstanding Deposits (% per Annum)	
	Including Zero Markup	Excluding Zero Markup	Including Zero Markup	Excluding Zero Markup	Including Zero Markup	Excluding Zero Markup	Including Zero Markup	Excluding Zero Markup
Public	10.00	10.25	11.67	12.20	6.71	7.65	3.85	4.94
Private	11.56	11.60	11.50	11.87	6.58	7.81	4.26	5.69
Foreign	10.50	10.52	14.45	14.66	4.57	6.00	4.99	6.57
Specialized	9.40	9.40	9.02	9.61	0.95	2.18	4.85	7.16
All Banks	11.33	11.38	11.55	11.96	6.36	7.62	4.21	5.58

Source: State Bank of Pakistan. 2008. *Weighted Average Lending and Deposit Rates,* Economic Data section.

Table A1.3 Trends in Inflation

2007	Consumer Price Index		Wholesale Price Index	
	General	Food	General	Food
March	7.7	10.7	6.1	9.3
April	6.9	9.4	6.0	8.4
May	7.4	11.3	6.8	10.3
June	7.0	9.7	7.3	11.2
July	6.4	8.5	7.6	11.7
August	6.5	8.6	8.0	11.5
September	8.4	13.0	9.3	14.2
October	9.3	14.7	11.8	15.5
November	8.7	12.5	12.6	15.3
December	8.8	12.2	12.2	15.8
2008				
January	11.9	18.2	15.5	19.5
February	11.3	16.0	16.4	18.3
March	14.1	20.6	19.8	21.0

Source: Hussain, B., Ashfaq, M. et al. 2008. How to achieve food security. *DAWN Economic & Business Review, August 25–31, 2008. P II.* Published August 25, 2008.

Chapter 2

Access to Finance:
Evidence from the Demand Side

This chapter summarizes the detailed findings of the national household survey on individual and household interest, knowledge of, and usage of financial products, including savings, credit, insurance, payments, and remittance services, as well as informal financial products.[1] The average Pakistani household remains outside the formal financial system, saving at home, and borrowing from family or friends in cases of dire need. While only 14 percent is formally included, about 40 percent of the population is completely excluded from formal or informal financial systems. Disparate as formal access might be among rural and urban areas, men and women, income levels, as well as along education and employment lines, interest in financial services is virtually identical. The challenge is to translate financial interest into access. Income and financial literacy appear as key barriers to financial exclusion when controlling for all other characteristics. Other drivers of financial inclusion are employment (formal employment determining formal inclusion), age, education level, or status as the main household income earner. Mobile phone use and access reduce the chances of being financially excluded. The banked in addition enjoy access to collateral while distance is only a marginal deterrent to being banked. An analysis of perceptions of financial services links the popularity of informal finance to its minimum access requirements—in direct contrast to formal finance documentation, creditworthiness requirements, and associated fees that overburden population groups, such as women and low-income or rural populations.

Low Overall Access to Finance

The average Pakistani household saves at home, borrows from family or friends in cases of dire need, and does not use the formal financial system. About 14 percent have access to formal financial services,[2] as compared with 32 percent in Bangladesh, 48 percent in India, and 59 percent in Sri Lanka (World Bank, 2008c). Adding

Figure 2.1 Pakistan Access Strand

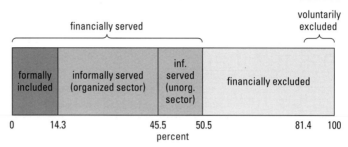

Source: Pakistan Access to Finance (A2F) Household Survey 2008.

informal finance, the proportion of financially serviced population rises close to 60 percent (figure 2.1). About 40 percent of the population is completely excluded from both the formal and informal financial system. Not all of these necessarily want to be served; in fact, 18.6 percent do not see the usefulness of being financially served. Of the remaining 22.3 percent, 6.3 percent are employed and could be profitably served, but have remained outside the financial system.

The survey data permit us to look at specific access and appeal issues along the lines of several basic financial products, in both the formal and informal sectors: banking, savings and investment, borrowing, informal finance and committees, insurance, and payments. The findings show low access to formal products overall. Islamic finance covers less than 1 percent of individuals, mostly high-income urban males. There are 2.5 percent formal borrowers as per the Access to Finance (A2F) Household Survey, and the corresponding State Bank of Pakistan (SBP) figure for the number of accounts (not clients) per adult population is 6.3 percent (4.9 million).[3] About 1.7 million of the adult population are serviced by the microfinance sector (SBP data)—this is about 1 percent of the population and about 2 percent of adults. About 2.3 percent of people send or receive remittances, and 1.9 percent are insured. Less than 1 percent of the population benefited from mortgages (but 3.5 percent used a loan for those purposes). Pakistan is a cash-based economy—even in the formal sector, income is primarily received in cash.

Few households are formally served, especially rural and lower-income groups and women. Within the informal finance sector, 35 percent of individuals save at home, 21 percent in livestock, and 14 percent use committees[4] to place their savings. A third of individuals hold loans or credits, mostly in the informal sector (33.7 percent, which includes 19 percent who borrow from family and friends). Overall, a little over half of the population have formal or informal savings/investments, and 35 percent have credit (table 2.1). Close to 13 percent of individuals (10.4 percent rural and 17.2 percent urban) have bank accounts. Banking with Pakistan Post, however, is almost equally used among rural and urban households. Another notable exception is in accessing savings for investment in productive activities, stronger in rural than in urban areas.

Table 2.1 Access to Financing, by Service

Service	% Population Using	Rural	Urban
Savings/Investment	55.4%	55.7%	54.8%
Loan and credit	35.0%	38.7%	28.6%
Banked	12.9%	10.4%	17.2%
Money transfers	2.3%	1.9%	3.2%
Insurance	1.9%	1.7%	2.3%

Source: Pakistan A2F Household Survey 2008.

Several patterns of financial access in Pakistan come out of the national household survey and are presented methodically in the subsequent sections below:

- Rural areas are underserved and less financially literate but display an equal or higher level of interest in financial services.

- Males have better access to financial services than females, though decision making is joint and willingness to learn about financial matters is comparable.

- There are wide provincial differences in financial services, literacy, and access.

- Lower-income groups display significantly lower awareness of and access to financial products, though only mildly lower interest in financial services.

Disparate as formal access might be among rural and urban areas, men and women, lower- and upper-income people, as well as along education and employment lines, interest in financial services is virtually identical. The challenge is to translate financial interest into access. The analysis goes on to suggest specific avenues for capitalizing on the considerable promise for financial expansion. Strong growth rates of financial access measures also point to the country's potential, though they also return the analyst to the current status quo with very limited levels of access.

The chapter reviews (1) financial access patterns by income, provinces, gender, and other individual characteristics; (2) financial literacy and interest issues; (3) informal finance and committees; (4) banking; (5) savings and investment; (6) borrowing; (7) insurance; and (8) payment and check services.

Considerable Variability of Financial Access across Rural/Urban Areas, Provinces, Income, Gender, and Other Population Characteristics

For the median individual, a 32-year-old with education up to 4th grade of elementary school, living in a rural area, and employed, joining the government or becoming a farmer reduces his or her chances of remaining financially excluded by a whopping 10 and 9 percentage points, respectively, whereas joining the corporate sector improves those chances by only 1 percentage point (Annex table A2.2). Being a woman, on the other hand, reduces one's chance of being informally served by

3 percentage points, and respectively increases the chances by as much to be financially excluded, though gender has no marginal effect on formal inclusion of any economic magnitude (-0.003 percentage points). Every 10 years of age adds one percentage point to the chances of leaving the ranks of the unserviced and joining the formally included, though there is no significant effect of age on informal inclusion. Completing primary school improves one's chances of joining the formal financial market by 0.6 percentage points. Moving into urban areas improves one's chances to join the informally served by 8 percentage points but does not affect the chances for formal inclusion. Mobile phone use and access reduce the chances of being financially excluded by 5 and 10 percentage points, respectively.

What are the critical factors for improving access to finance? We segment our findings by analyzing rural-urban, state, gender, and other individual differences.

Lower access to finance in rural areas might be determined by an indirect income and literacy effect, rather than such factors as time/cost of access, though differences in accessibility are clearly considerable, between urban and rural areas (Annex tables A2.1, A2.6–A2.10). Interestingly, location in rural areas alone would not hurt or improve one's chances for financing, and an urban address would not improve them either. While formal sources are much more ubiquitous in urban areas, controlling for the effects of income, education, and employment, both locations are equally well served by formal and informal financing.

This suggests that there is nothing inherently "unserviceable" about rural areas. In fact, informal and some formal channels are providing access there quite successfully and can be easily imitated by various microfinance institutions (MFIs) to emulate their success in access provision. Post office access (and, interestingly, insurance) is significantly higher for the rural population. What is perhaps inherently harder with rural areas is access to certain instruments, such as credit/debit cards, and, curiously, Islamic products and committees.

Wide provincial differences emerge as to the likelihood of being financially served (formally and informally), as well as banked. Overall, Baluchistan and the North West Frontier Province (NWFP) show lower interest, awareness, and access than other regions. Punjab and Azad Jammu and Kashmir (AJK) lead other provinces (figure 2.2). Econometric analysis shows that, while provincial effects are observed, income is the main driver of financial inclusion observed in Pakistan states. Half of the population in NWFP and Baluchistan are among lowest two quintiles, while Punjab has the highest population (48.9 percent) among all provinces in the highest two quintiles. However, provincial differences persist after controlling for income. Bank accessibility in Baluchistan might be one reason for low access, though time and cost to getting to a bank are high in AJK as well. There are significant differences among provinces regarding requirements prior to receiving a formal loan. While 79 percent in Baluchistan and 21 percent in NWFP have to provide a coguarantor, this requirement is quoted by around 50 percent in Punjab, Sindh, and AJK. Differences in financial and banking access are significant (Annex table A2.3, Panel A).

Women have dramatically less access to the financial sector, with the exception of formal borrowing. There are fewer women with access to banking services (5.5 percent vs. 21.1 percent men), money transfers (1.4 percent vs. 3.3 percent men),

Figure 2.2 Share of Banked, by Province

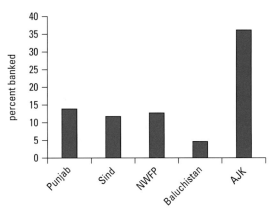

Source: Pakistan A2F Household Survey 2008.

and insurance (0.6 percent vs. 3.3 percent men).[5] The same pattern holds for other financial products—generally, women are disadvantaged in access, with the consistent exceptions of Pakistan Post and committee services (Annex tables A2.9 and A2.10). Women remain significantly less likely than men to have access to the financial sector overall, after accounting for the effect of income and other socioeconomic differences (Annex tables A2.1 and A2.6). This overall disadvantage belies a complex picture, however. Women enjoy significantly less access to borrowing (24.7 percent vs. 46.4 percent men), except to formal borrowing. In contrast, women have almost equal access to savings (52.6 vs. 58.5 percent men), though they are significantly more likely to save informally (Annex tables A2.7 and A2.8).[6]

In the South Asia region, in contrast to Pakistan, microfinance providers have tended to focus on female clients (figure 2.3). Evidence has accumulated of the link between microfinance for and empowerment of women. Further, financial institutions also tend to find women to be better credit risks. Segmenting female clients by offering them tailor-made products is a promising strategy for catching up with regional neighbors in terms of female access to finance (box 2.1). Out of roughly

Figure 2.3 Women and Microfinance

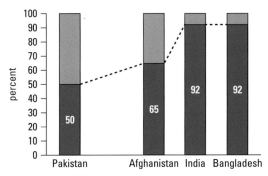

Source: Competitiveness Support Fund (2008).

| Box 2.1 | **Facts about Segmenting Pakistani Female Clients** |

Women around the globe have been observed to better manage their debt responsibilities. There is no evidence that women offer a less-attractive business proposition than men from the same income category. Women tend to be net savers, and although the average size of a woman's deposit tends to be less than that of a man, women tend to maintain their account with a specific bank for longer while men may shift their patronage for marginal gains. Thus, by ignoring women as a potential and separate market segment with unique demand dynamics, financial institutions may be forgoing potential revenue and profits.

Women tend to have preferences that are distinct from men's. Women's attitudes toward savings are consistent with their desire to learn: women are more likely to follow a budget than men. They are also more reluctant to take debts and are more risk-averse than male respondents. In addition, women tend to prefer convenience above all. Indicative of this may be the fact that the banks think that the share of women among their total borrowing clients increased after the introduction of credit cards. Pakistani women also tend to avoid going to bank branches; thus, many women bank through their close relatives. Given the banks' criteria for lending credit only to those (men and women) who are either salaried or have business income, many women including those who may have a secure source of rent income are precluded from the banks' financing including credit cards. Women might also be facing more difficult loan requirements—more women than men (59.8 percent vs. 45.3 percent, respectively) cite the co-guarantor/cosigner as a condition to receiving formal credit. Being less-experienced banking clients than men, women tend to be more anxious about banking procedures; thus, simplified procedures can be an effective selling proposition to women. Finally, women are rarely the main income earners (only 3.6 percent of Paskistani women are) and are largely more exposed than men to receiving irregular income. More than 85 percent of women, being housewives, only receive pocket money as income. It is therefore unsurprising that the poorest quintile in terms of personal (not household) income is three-quarters composed of women and only a quarter by men. As a result, women's transactions will in general be smaller than men's. Women's equal access to mobile communications make mobile phones a promising channel to reach women in terms of mobile banking products but also awareness campaigns on the benefits of access to finance.

Bank Al-Falah is currently marketing a "women's" credit card promoted as "A Credit Card Exclusively for Women." Though a laudable effort to attract a dormant market segment, this card does not differ from a regular credit card offered by the bank itself or any other bank in terms of either the features or the eligibility criteria.

Source: Bank Af Falah Website (2008).

(continued)

47 million females over the age of 16, it is estimated that potentially 35 million are viable savings clients, and 22 million are viable borrowers.

Access increases with **age, an employed status, and education.**[7] **Household heads** are found to have better access to financial services.[8]

The **sector of employment** also affects access to formal and informal finance, to the extent that government and corporate sector employment augment the probability of financial access, and laborer status diminishes it. Farmers have worse access to the for-mal sector, but, unlike laborers, have better chances of accessing the informal sector than remaining unserved. Government employment is negatively associated with Islamic product use. Surprisingly, laborers and farmers have weaker access to commit-tees than other (better-employed) groups. Belonging to the formal sector in general improves access to financing, especially formal financing. If formal finance specifically is what one is after, add a government job, or employment in the formal/corporate sec-tor, and higher income. A more surprising finding is that the positive effect of age on financial access disappears in the case of Islamic products and committees.

Personal and household income is strongly associated with access to finance, though they have roughly comparable levels of interest in financial matters (45.2 percent of the poorest quintile are interested vs. 51.2 percent of the population on average). The share of the banked population increases sixfold with income lev-els, from very low levels (3.8 percent) among the lowest income quintile to 25.5 per-cent for the wealthiest quintile (Figure 2.4). Yet microfinance and informal finance are by no means a privilege of lower-income groups. Microfinance is used four times as much by the richest quintile than the poorest quintile. The lowest income group faces on average four times longer delay in reaching a bank than the highest income

Figure 2.4 Product Penetration

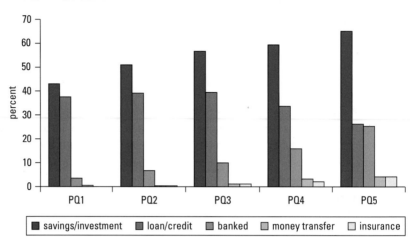

Source: Pakistan A2F Household Survey 2008.

quintile (though medians differ less). The lowest income quintile faces higher absolute costs than the highest (median of Rs 36 vs. Rs 26).

The upper-income, especially male, population has much higher access to various formal financial products, including such products as basic banking accounts. Less than 1 percent of the poorest and second poorest have a basic banking account, as compared with 4.3 percent among the highest income quintile. Credit cards, debit cards, or Islamic finance are reserved for the richer, as almost no one in the two poorest quintiles had access to these products.

The top three income quintiles have a significantly higher access to finance than the lower quintiles. Interestingly, though the top three quintiles do not differ significantly among themselves in the case of access to formal and informal finance, they fare quite distinctly in terms of banking access, which each higher quintile obtaining markedly better access. The bottom two quintiles are never significantly different from each other (Annex table A2.3, panel B).

Availability of **collateral** is positively associated with the probability of being financially served, as well as banked. Interestingly, it also has a significant positive effect on access to savings. There might be a substitution effect between access to collateral and access to Islamic products and insurance as collateral access is significantly negatively associated with access to both Islamic products and to insurance.

High Interest in Financial Services and Low Financial Literacy Among Rural, Lower-income, and Female Groups

Rural areas are more likely to express interest in financial matters than urban areas, controlling for income. The same is true for those with more education, with employed status, heading the household, in the formal sector, and regularly using a

Table 2.2 Financial Literacy

	Mean	Rural	Urban
Interested or strongly interested in financial matters (%)	51.2	51.7	50.2
Follows what is written/said on financial matters (%)	60.6	59.0	63.5

Source: Pakistan A2F Household Survey 2008.

cell phone. Age and gender do not impact interest in financial matters, though they are significant determinants of the willingness to attain access to finance, along with education. The availability of collateral and a government job also significantly positively affect motivation to join the financially served. These findings[9] have important policy implications for financial awareness campaigns, in terms of the selection of relevant audience given limited resources.

In fact, 51.2 percent of the population expresses interest or strong interest in financial matters (51.7 percent in rural areas; Table 2.2). Nearly two-thirds (60.6) of households follow what is written or said about financial matters, equally in urban and rural areas. Pakistani households get their financial information predominantly from family (41.1 percent) and the media (24.5 percent). Rural areas rely much less on media than urban (18.3 percent as against 35.1 percent), but much more on family (42.1 percent vs. 39.3 percent). This is true also for lower-income groups. Lower-income groups have much less access to and awareness of financial products, though they have roughly comparable levels of interest in financial matters (45.2 percent of the poorest quintile are interested vs. 51.2 percent of the population on average). The most interest in further learning, across income groups and rural/urban areas, focuses on preparation of a household/personal budget for 33.2 percent of the population, opening of a bank account (26.9 percent), and savings methods (18.3 percent). Interestingly, insurance is not a focus area of interest.

The bulk of Pakistanis make financial decisions with family or spouse, not alone (78.1 percent). The effect is even more pronounced in rural and lower-income groups. While women represent a group that is consistently less financially literate and more reliant upon informal financial sources than men, they express a strong desire to learn about saving and budget planning. Close to 44 percent of women show an interest in financial services, albeit less than men (59.4 percent). The concepts of profit and loans, as well as committees and moneylenders, seem closer to females than other topics. Males enjoy better access to all sources of information. Women get their news primarily from family members, while men rely on the media twice as much as women. In addition, women express a stronger desire than men to be educated in areas that include preparing a personal budget effectively and learning about ways to save money. Women follow a budget and are more likely to save regularly, begging the question of their relative exclusion as savings clients as compared to men. They are also more reluctant to take on debt (59.8 percent) than men (48.2 percent) and are more risk averse (63.2 percent) than males (51.3 percent).

Household understanding of specific products is fair, with common financial terms being familiar to more than half to 90 percent of the population (table 2.3).

Table 2.3 Literacy Measures in Rural and Urban Areas

Heard and do understand (percent)	Mean	Rural	Urban
Loans	89.1	89.2	89.1
Committees	87.9	85.2	92.5
Profit	75.9	76.2	75.4
Interest	74.6	71.8	79.4
Bank	72.8	69.5	78.6
Moneylender	70.6	68.7	73.7
Collateral	43.7	40.7	48.8
Post office saving accounts	21.7	16.1	31.4
Microfinance	21.1	17.7	26.9
PLS/savings account	19.2	12.4	31.0
Insurance premium	15.2	10.0	24.2
Credit card	12.6	6.2	23.6
Islamic banking	11.6	6.6	20.3
Automated Teller Machine (ATM)	11.3	4.7	22.8
Mobile banking	3.5	1.7	6.5
Swift transfer	3.3	1.9	5.7
Mobile phone banking	3.1	1.2	6.4

Source: Pakistan A2F Household Survey 2008.

Rural areas have lower understanding, consistently, with the exception of the concepts of profit and loans. Only 17.7 percent in rural areas understand microfinance (versus 26.9 percent in urban areas). Rural awareness of post office savings accounts follows a similar pattern. The largest differentials between rural and urban areas are in the understanding of more complex products such as profit loss sharing (PLS)/savings accounts, insurance premium, credit card, automated teller machine (ATMs), Islamic banking, mobile banking, and swift transfers.

Low Bank Access Nationwide, Driven by Income Constraints and the Lack of Information and Financial Education

Of all adults in Pakistan, only 12.9 percent are banked. This ranks low in the region compared, for example, with 66 percent in India and 51 percent in Nepal. More than 87 percent are not banked, yet 42 percent of those would like to be.

Older, more educated, employed persons, and main income earners, have a higher chance of being banked.[10] Positive effects on bank access are also at work for individuals who have collateral, are employed in the formal/corporate sector, and enjoy regular cell phone use. Similarly, the three highest household income quintiles are more likely to be banked than poorer households.

Location in rural areas does not have a significant effect on the probability of being banked. In contrast, provinces differ significantly in the probability of their population being financially served, even when informal financing is included. Baluchistan, due to income, geography, and cultural reasons, lags behind in terms of offering its inhabitants financial access.

Income constraints caused by poor opportunities for productive employment/ entrepreneurial activities are indeed the main reason for not being banked, followed by lack of information/literacy/awareness. Other reasons (sociocultural, religious, mobility, high fees, unfriendly staff, product complexity, or delays) are much less cited than personal reasons. Lack of information is more acute among women and the poor nonbanked. While savings are well understood (by 86.3 percent of the population), 83.8 percent do not consider bank accounts essential.

Demand-side evidence points to three main banks by market share: National Bank of Pakistan followed by Habib Bank Limited and Muslim Commercial Bank are the most popular among people with bank accounts, all generating higher usage in urban areas and among men. This suggests a considerable potential for rapid expansion of access to banking.

Cash-based Economy with High Willingness of the Nonbanked to Gain Access to Bank Services

About 41.6 percent of the nonbanked population expressed a high desire to own individual bank accounts, growing with income. It is also stronger among men (51.4 percent) and in urban areas. Saving money appears to be the main reason for the nonbanked to desire a bank account, equally for men and women (cited by 26.7 percent of the population), and cited twice as often in urban areas (9.4 percent). The security of being able to withdraw money as needed is a stronger concern for women than men (11.4 percent vs. 9.7 percent). Guarding against theft is cited by 3.9 percent on average (twice as much in urban areas). Accessing a loan is still three times less cited than saving as a motive to access the banking sector, and is mostly of interest to men (11.4 percent vs. 4.8 percent women). Making deposits from income is the third most popular reason, again much more popular in urban areas.

Cash dominates income received in the formal and informal sectors (figure 2.5). Ten percent of the population receive income in kind. Nearly 16 percent put all or most of their income into their bank accounts. Almost a third don't put any there, in particular women (almost 39.2 percent) and people in rural areas (32.5 percent). The poorest are three times more likely than the richest to not save any income at the bank. New delivery infrastructure represented by electronic transfers represents a nonnegligible share of government salary payments.

Currently, 10.8 percent of government salary payments and 3 percent of payments for pensions are made through electronic transfers. Collecting pensions or salary payments are strong drivers for opening an account. Independently of income and other characteristics, being a government worker increases one's chances to be formally included by 7.5 percent.

Figure 2.5 Cash-based Income across Sectors

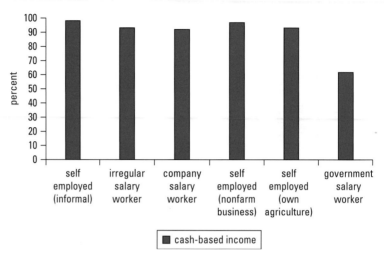

Source: Pakistan A2F Household Survey 2008.

More than half of working Pakistanis are self-employed, in particular among the poor.[11] Adding other informally engaged groups (such as housewives), we find that a considerable majority of the population receives irregular and/or informal earnings. This is a significant barrier to being banked, given current bank service procedures and approach. Credit information availability could permit the use of credit scoring techniques, which would eliminate such barriers to access. Outside of borrowing, such barriers arise due to the small size of the transactions and the high per-account cost to the banking institution. Yet technology advances have gone along way toward resolving this issue—Microfinance Banks (MFBs) internationally report up to 12 percentage points of reduction in intermediation costs attributable to technology improvements.

Usage and Penetration of Financial Products Is Limited in Range, and not well Suited to Different Market Segments

The main products used by the majority of banked population are basic savings and checking accounts (figure 2.6; savings and borrowing products are discussed in more detail later in this chapter). Yet different population segments, such as women, might require products more attuned to their needs, as illustrated in box 2.1. Saving accounts are held by 8.2 percent of the population and current/checking accounts by 6.5 percent. Card penetration is low (2 percent), with a tenfold higher penetration of both credit and ATM cards in urban households. These findings are closely associated with the undeveloped ATM infrastructure highlighted in Chapter 1. Cards and savings account are also much more frequent among higher-income males than lower-income groups or women, with the exception of Pakistan Post savings accounts and committees.

Figure 2.6 Product Penetration (as % of banked)

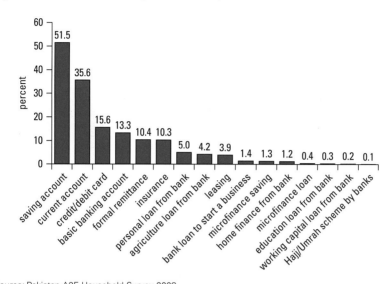

Source: Pakistan A2F Household Survey 2008.

A closer look at the determinants of access to specific products, such as **credit/debit cards, checks, savings accounts, and current accounts**, further informs the analysis. The probability of holding varying banking instruments increases with age, education levels, and other characteristics that include being the main income earner and being employed. Bank product users are unlikely to be located in rural areas. A position with government, but not with the formal corporate sector, increases the probability of being banked.

There is a positive association between specific product usage and the upper income quintiles. Just like for access to banking services, women generally have less access to specific banking products (Annex table A2.9).

The national household survey data results suggest that **Islamic finance** is a high-end product: the population that is male, richer, urban, household head, more educated, and part of the formal sector is significantly more likely to use Islamic products (Annex table A2.10, regression V). Interestingly, Islamic finance is inversely associated with age, employment, and availability of collateral, as well as with employment in the corporate sector. Only a fifth of the population are willing to pay more for Islamic products than a conventional banking product. Women are less willing than men to do so (14.7 percent vs. 26.6 percent).

Access to **Pakistan Post and insurance** services is determined by much the same characteristics as standard banking products—age, education, employment, heading a household, being employed by government, and being part of the formal sector. However, location in a rural area is positively associated with both insurance and post office access, as opposed to standard banking (nonpostal) product access.

Informal finance via committees also differs significantly from standard banking access in terms of determining factors. The positive effect of employment is about the only common factor we observe. The committees are oriented toward women, who are significantly more likely to gain access to finance via a rotating saving and credit association (ROSCA)-type scheme. They are further not focused on older groups, and do not cater to other underserved groups, such as farmers and laborers. These effects are rooted in the culture and tradition of maintaining committees among married women as a social undertaking.

Chief Obstacles to Access Include Heavy Documentation, and Lack of Income and Information

The most frequently cited perceptions of formal financial service providers pertain to **requirements for becoming a customer** (associated with 53.8 percent of the population).[12] Commercial banks require an identity document, a permanent address, credit references, and a guarantor. The current requirements for two identity documents on average to open an account in a commercial bank in Pakistan,[13] while not appearing to be a serious hurdle for the population in general, may realistically represent a significant obstacle to being banked for certain population groups, such as women or low-income groups. This places Pakistan as number one in South Asia, better than the South Asia average (2.65 documents required), though below top performers such as Thailand.[14] According to the World Bank (2006a), more-competitive banking sectors are less bureaucratic because banks that are vigorously competing against each other tend to simplify procedures.

The second most important cluster of issues defining perceptions of formal finance are **personal reasons,** cited by 50.7 percent of the population, including awareness limitations and self-exclusion.[15] Baluchistan highlights the lack of product information as its major obstacle. Lack of information is also more cited by non-banked women and is much higher among the poor. In addition, 5 percent more women than men express no need for a bank account, making it the biggest reason among women for not banking. This perception decreases with income and might also be related to the awareness of the benefits of financial products, especially among women ("if I don't work, why would I need financial instruments?").

Perceptions on **accessibility issues,** while a minor obstacle overall (4.9 percent),[16] are more acute in rural areas. Whereas an average of 23.2 percent of the population consider that commercial banks are too far away, one-third in rural areas perceive this issue. Committees and informal moneylenders on the other end do not prompt accessibility issues. Very few (6.5 percent) of urban households travel more than an hour to the nearest bank, as opposed to 34.5 percent in rural areas who travel one hour or more (up to two days).[17] Cost to reach a bank is also more cited by rural areas (2.8 percent of nonbanked vs. 2.5 percent of nonbanked in urban areas). While close to half of the urban population spend Rs 20 ($0.26) or less on a one-way trip to the bank, more than half in rural areas (50.6 percent) have to spend Rs 21–80 ($0.26 to $1) and 14.9 percent incur more than $1 each way to reach a bank (figure 2.7).[17]

Service-related reasons for not being banked seem less pronounced (5.1 percent).[18] Fees and lengthy procedures, cited on average by 1.9 percent of the nonbanked population, do not appear as a strong block to being banked. Only about 3.5 percent

Figure 2.7 Cost of Bank Access

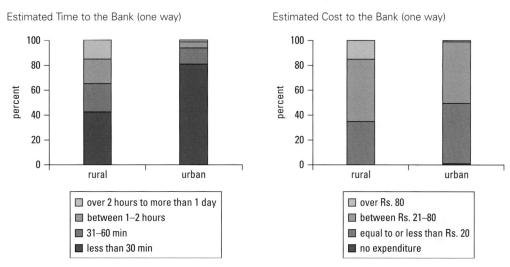

Estimated Time to the Bank (one way)

Estimated Cost to the Bank (one way)

Legend (left):
- over 2 hours to more than 1 day
- between 1–2 hours
- 31–60 min
- less than 30 min

Legend (right):
- over Rs. 80
- between Rs. 21–80
- equal to or less than Rs. 20
- no expenditure

Source: Pakistan A2F Household Survey 2008.

of the nonbanked point to low returns as a reason for not having a bank account, while about the same proportion of the banked (3.6 percent) list earning income as a reason for being banked. This suggests a weak association between having an account and earning interest on it, consistent with surveys in other parts of the world.[19] The slow service and somewhat onerous documentation requirements of Pakistan Post banks are also frequently cited.

Pakistan ranks near the top for the world in terms of highest opening fees (application fees and other types of fees). While it takes minutes to open an account in many developing countries, Pakistan is among the countries where it takes longer, on average 2.8 days, much beyond the South Asia average of 1.21 days (World Bank 2008a).[20] Whereas developing-country banks are more likely to charge fees, that tends to result in lower financial access, even after adjusting for income.

Sociocultural reasons such as trust, religion, and cultural barriers to access are also not important overall (8.5 percent of the population) but are very strongly skewed toward women and Baluchistan. Such reasons for not banking are cited by 11.9 percent of the nonbanked women (compared with a marginal 1.3 percent among nonbanked men) and more than 9 percent of the nonbanked population of Baluchistan and Sindh. This reason does not appear strongly correlated with income. Religious reasons such as issues with paying or receiving interest, bank mistrust, and issues with corruption are cited by only 2.5 percent of the nonbanked.

Informal Financial Services—More Accessible and Less Complex

Informal financial services are perceived as more geographically accessible and less complex, and they are the only financial instruments that the majority of Pakistanis will ever know and use. Informal financial markets are discussed from a supply standpoint in Chapter 3. Informal services have fewer requirements and are easier to understand. As noted, informal savings are pervasive (63.6 percent of all savers), be it at home (in cash, gold, or jewelry) or in assets (livestock, land). Ninety-seven percent of borrowers also borrow informally, be it from shopkeepers (77.9 percent of all borrowers) or from friends and family (53.5 percent of all borrowers). Groups that are less targeted by the formal sector—rural areas, women, and the poor—have a higher share of informal savings in total savings. There is a detailed discussion of supply issues for informal finance in Chapter 3, while this section focuses on distinguished characteristics or the informal sector relative to the informal sector and on another popular informal vehicle, the committee.[21]

What can be learned from informal financial systems? Using access to credit as a benchmark, the perception of borrowers is that the informal sector operates with much lower service requirements than the formal sector, in particular in terms of co-guarantor (cited by 4.8 percent vs. 46.5 percent), immovable collateral (1 percent vs. 27.5 percent) and minimum balance (0.3 percent vs. 10.3 percent) conditions (figure 2.10). More than a quarter (27.5 percent) of the population cite immovable collateral as a condition for formal credit. In rural areas 36 percent cite immovable collateral requirements.

As discussed in Chapter 3, informal sources might have some advantages over formal sources. In general, informal sources of credit are more expensive than formal sources, and there is much evidence to suggest that they exploit poor people, but they have the advantages of being available all the time, not requiring documentation, operating outside the purview of formal authorities, and not requiring collateral. Informal markets deal effectively with the higher risk they face from clients, substituting social contracts and client information for immovable collateral that is often not available to the poor, lending only for productive uses (cash lending is frequently done at a 300–400 percent premium) and on average charging only a small premium over the formal sector (23 percent vs. 19 percent, Qadir 2005).

Perceptions of service providers give a striking perspective of gaps between formal and informal institutions. Positive perceptions, such as absence of legal formalities, of service charges, and of documentation rank are frequently associated with committees or informal moneylenders. Conversely, negative perceptions and constraints are most frequently cited about formal financial institutions, in particular the need for credit references, documentation, and a co-guarantor.

Focus on committees. Although the concept of committees is widely understood by 87.9 percent of the population, committees rank only as the third savings channel, far behind home saving and saving in assets. They are also only the third most popular borrowing channel, behind shopkeeper loans and family/friends. This is surprising, especially compared with previous studies of limited sample sizes that suggest the majority of Pakistanis are involved in such group schemes. Ballot committees are much more frequently used than other committees (named by 87 percent of committee users) among the committee users.

Committees are not used significantly more by women (14 percent) than men (14.5 percent). They do not cater to other underserved groups, such as farmers and laborers. Finally, committees are used more than twice as much in urban areas than in rural areas, particularly in Punjab and Sindh. Their use also increases with income.

Women and urban areas are significantly more likely to participate in committees (last regression in Annex table A2.9). The incidence of committee participation is also found to increase with education levels and decrease with age. While being employed in the formal or informal sector has a positive incidence on using committees, the professional profile effect on the likelihood of committee participation reinforces their urban nature. Committee participants are more likely to be formal corporate workers.

Committees are mostly used to save as well purchase household goods. Few participate in committees to purchase fixed assets (7.3 percent) or invest into business (12.1 percent) (figure 2.8), although a slightly larger share than overall formal or informal savers (10.76 percent) list business investment as a savings motive.

Most users participate in only one committee (84.1 percent). Contributions to committees are made monthly. Change in income has the highest impact on changes in payments to committees, with the exception of Baluchistan, where family reasons have the highest impact on amounts paid to committees. While perceptions expressed on the service of committees are very positive, and involve trust, good service, and ease of use, women have an even better perception of committees than the average individual.

Figure 2.8 Reasons for Participating in a Committee

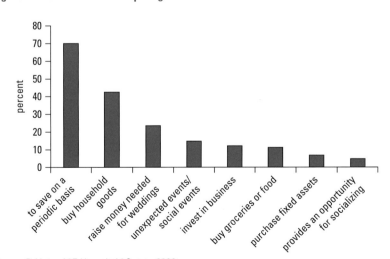

Source: Pakistan A2F Household Survey 2008.

Savings and Investment—Popular but Mostly Informal

Among financial products, savings and investments, by far the most popular, are used by two-thirds of the population followed by loans and credits, used by one-third. Among those who save, savings are mostly done informally (only 14.9 percent of savers go to formal financial institutions). About 63.6 percent of savers save at home. Committees are the second most popular informal savings channel (25.7 percent) for the savers, as much among women as men (26.6 percent and 24.8 percent, respectively).[22] Saving with family and friends (6.7 percent) is done equally among rural and urban areas, across income groups. Three-quarters of formal savers were also saving informally. This topic will be explored in more detail below and in the following two sections, which discuss the interaction of the formal and informal sectors in general and in terms of borrowing specifically.

Demand-side evidence links higher income levels to a higher probability of saving, formally or informally (Annex table A2.8). Rural areas are more likely to hold savings accounts overall, and in the informal sector, while urban areas hold more formal savings accounts. While women's attitudes toward financial services suggest higher savings motives than men, women are excluded from access to most savings channels; all characteristics held constant, women are found less likely than men to be savings account holders. Women are found to be more likely than men to use informal savings channels than not save at all.

The other characteristics associated with an increased likelihood of saving include employment, education, and status us the main household income earner. While age is important for formal savings, it plays if anything a negative role in the probability for informal savings. Government workers are positively associated with savings (and mainly formal savings), while farmers are also positively associated with savings accounts, but upon disaggregating, the effect mainly comes from the informal sector accounts. Finally, laborers have a lower probability to access savings instruments. Regular cell phone users are also more likely to be savings account users.

Only a small share of the saving volume is captured in the commercial banking sector. The most popular savings product, the PLS/savings account, is used by only 11.2 percent of savers (figure 2.9). This proportion increases with income levels (2.1 percent for lowest quintile vs. 19.6 percent for the highest), men (18.6 percent vs. 3.8 percent for women), and urban areas (16.2 percent vs. 8.4 percent for rural). The penetration of post office savings is appreciably less than that of post office remittance products (discussed in detail in Chapter 5). Despite its presence throughout Pakistan and its existing remittance customer base, the Pakistan Post Bank may not be leveraging its relative proximity in some provinces to diversify further into banking and saving products. Post offices and State Life Insurance are the most-used nonbank formal financial institutions for saving, used by 0.7 percent and 0.6 percent, respectively, of those who save, although well behind the banks. Microfinance savings (0.2 percent) and Islamic savings (0.1 percent) represent minor savings channels.

Within the formal sector, government savings (provident funds, pension funds, prize bonds, and government savings certificates) and private savings (PLS/saving

Figure 2.9 Government/Private Savings Accounts

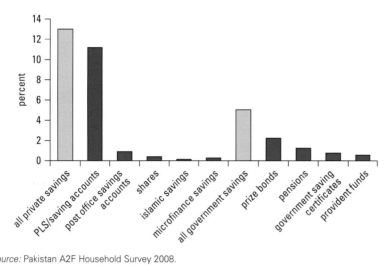

Source: Pakistan A2F Household Survey 2008.

account, post office savings account, microfinance, Islamic savings, and shares) products are both popular among Pakistan households who save. Among the private and government saving products, PLS/savings are the most popular with more than 11 percent of people using them. While the penetration of pensions in annuity grows as income levels increase, the product is most popular in AJK and among men.

Savings is for smoothing consumption, not investment, though rural areas invest more. Reasons for saving seem to revolve around immediate needs, such as food, household goods, and medical and schooling costs, in rural and urban areas alike. Marriage and death/disability rank high among saving motives. Longer-term prospects, such as retirement, and future buying prospects, such as land, are marginally cited, in particular among the poorest. Saving to invest in or start a business, on the other hand, although overall low, is more common in rural areas (12.5 percent vs. 7.8 percent), irrespective of income. The bulk of rural savers use money to invest in cattle (54.4 percent) or farm land (19 percent). Close to 1.3 percent of savers invest in working capital, such as machinery or buying inputs for small businesses. Retirement, pension fund, and life insurance investments are marginal, at 1.2 percent of savers on average.[23]

Mostly Informal Borrowing, Strong Aversion to Debt

A third of the population (35 percent) has a loan or credit, but only 1 in 14 received it from the formal sector. Almost half of the Pakistanis (44.9 percent) have never contracted a loan (55.5 percent of women and 33 percent of men). A strong aversion to debt and associated bias against borrowing is observed and shared across gender, rural areas, and income levels (61.3 percent). Religious objections to borrowing, while expressed by a third of the population, do not represent such a significant effect on borrowing as the aversion bias, and come out insignificant in regressions (Annex table A2.10). To gain an understanding of the extent of borrowing aversion among the population, consider that the most widespread form of borrowing (77.9 percent of all borrowers) is getting goods on credit interest-free from a shop-keeper, which is more a culturally determined practice than a financial transaction. Borrowing interest free from friends and family (53.5 percent) comes in a close second. The use of shopkeepers, as well as family friends, as an informal source of borrowing is substantial among rich and poor and urban and rural areas alike.

All other types of borrowing are rare (including moneylenders, interestingly, at 2.9 percent on average). Personal loans from a bank are cited by 1.8 percent of the borrowers and agricultural loans are cited by only 2.1 percent of rural borrowers. Credit cards usage is reserved to the highest income quintile. Islamic and microfinance loans are sparsely used—0.03 percent of borrowers held an Islamic loan at the time of the survey.[24] About one-fifth of the population is willing to pay more for Islamic than traditional products, less so women than men (14.7 percent vs. 26.6 percent). *Hajj/Umrah* schemes are used only by 0.2 percent of Pakistanis. Furthermore, 3.5 percent of the population bought, built, or renovated their houses with a mortgage or a formal or informal loan.

World Bank (2002) notes the considerable literature that examines the interaction of the informal and formal credit sectors. Some borrowers are found to be simultaneously active in both markets, either because they are unable to get all the credit they need from one sector alone, or because formal lenders might condition their lending on the borrower's obtaining cofinancing from other (presumably informal) sources. This is the case in Pakistan, both in terms of savings, and borrowing (table 2.4). Borrowers use their dual access more in rural areas (one-third of urban formal borrowers also access the informal sector vs. more than half of formal borrowers in rural areas), confirming the trend discussed in Chapter 1 suggesting a more credit-constrained rural market.

Access to credit increases with age, employed status, and education (Annex table A2.7). The three highest income quintiles are likely to borrow more than poorer groups. Interestingly, and consistent with previous findings, rural location alone does not exert a negative effect on access to loans. Women are less likely to contract an informal loan, though more likely to contract a formal loan, presumably because women's responsible money management habits are taken into consideration

Table 2.4 Formal and Informal Borrowing

	Urban	Rural	Total
Formal credit holders	2.9	2.3	2.5
Informal credit holders	26.6	37.9	33.7
Formal and informal credit holders	0.9	1.4	1.3

Source: Pakistan A2F Household Survey 2008.

Table 2.5 Purpose of the Loan (% of all borrowers)

	Formal			Informal		
	Urban	Rural	Total	Urban	Rural	Total
Personal loans	1.7	2.2	*3.9*	24.2	61.8	*86.0*
Business/farm loans	0.4	2.4	*2.8*	3.5	13.5	*17.0*

Source: Pakistan A2F Household Survey 2008.

Notes: Personal loans include loans to buy food or goods; meet expenses of a dowry, wedding, Hajj/Umrah, or unforeseen emergency costs (hospital, childbirth, funeral); buy or build a house; travel; buy luxury items/durables; and pay utility bills. Business loans include loans to buy goods for agriculture or business, productive assets, meet expenses of business.

in the formal financial sector. Overall, women seem to be less likely to borrow than men, mainly as a self-expressed preference. Heading a household also improved one's chances to access financial services. Positive effects on access are also at work for groups that have collateral and are employed in the government or as a farmer. Laborers face significantly lower access to loans. Those who enjoy regular cell use or have access to a cell phone are significantly associated with borrowing. It is worth noting that informal borrowers are likely to have access to a mobile phone but not regularly use it, as opposed to formal borrowers, who tend to be significantly associated with regular cell phone usage.

Like saving, borrowing is used in a majority of cases to attend to personal needs (decreasing as income increases) rather than to invest in a business. Rural areas borrow much more than urban, and tend to use the loan much more for productive purposes than for consumption (table 2.5).[25] While formal borrowers take loans for various investment purposes (agricultural, nonfarm, and housing investment), informal clients borrow exclusively for household needs. Borrowing for personal needs decreases as income increases, while borrowing to invest is positively correlated to income. Relative to their borrowing portfolio, men borrow more for productive activities than women. On average, one-fifth of those who borrowed (19.1 percent) missed a payment, the poorest more than twice as frequently as the richest (25.9 percent vs. 11.9 percent).

In addition to credit requirements, chief obstacles for borrowing include a general aversion to debt, religious bias, and a significant likelihood of getting rejected. Almost a third of Pakistanis consider that interest rates go against religious principles (twice as many as those who think that interest rates are not a problem). These views, although shared throughout income groups, are strongest among the highest income groups and men (43.8 percent vs. 25.2 percent for women), suggesting that they are not the major obstacle where financial access enhancement is relevant—among the poor and women. In addition, religious attitudes are only one part of the negative perceptions toward credit, dwarfed by the general aversion to being in debt, which is pervasive across gender (58.1 percent for men and 64.2 percent for women), location, and income divides.

Figure 2.10 Requirements before Receiving a Loan

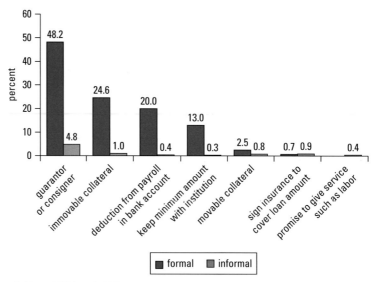

Source: Pakistan A2F Household Survey 2008.

Onerous and complex credit requirements are a considerable obstacle to formal credit. The most frequently cited formal loan requirements are a guarantor (46.5 percent), movable collateral (27.5 percent), and automatic payroll deduction (20.3 percent). Informal requirements are minimal to nonexistent (Figure 2.10). Over a quarter (27.5 percent) of the population cite immovable collateral as a condition for formal credit. In rural areas, 36 percent cite immovable collateral requirements. Collateral conditions are much less cited than for informal loans.

The likelihood of being approved is an important factor considered before taking a personal long-term formal loan. Diverse as formal and informal loans are, borrowers are preoccupied with the same issues: successful outcome, speed, affordability, and rates, in that order (table 2.6).

Table 2.6 Factors Considered before Taking a Personal Long-term Loan

(% of formal, respectively informal, borrowers)	Formal Loan	Informal Loan
Likelihood that the loan will be granted in the amount needed	51.4	28.0
Getting the loan approved as soon as possible	43.0	16.6
The affordability of the monthly installment	36.4	14.5
Their interest rate charges	28.4	10.4

Source: Pakistan A2F Household Survey 2008.

Table 2.7 Rejection Rates for Existing Borrowers (% of all formal borrowers)

	Population	Urban	Rural	Men	Women
Existing borrowers with loan application in past 12 months	76.6	81.9	74.0	76.9	75.8
Share of loan applications in past 12 months that were rejected	7.8	6.6	8.4	6.2	12.9
Rejection rates	10.2	8.1	11.4	8.1	17.0

Source: Pakistan A2F Household Survey 2008.

Three-quarters of formal borrowers applied within the past 12 months (76.6 percent). Rejection rates were at about 10 percent, and higher for rural areas (11.4 percent) and for women (17 percent) (table 2.7). About 41.4 percent of the existing formal borrowers whose applications were rejected are confused about the reason for their unsuccessful applications, suggesting service issues on the part of the banks. Other reasons cited for unsuccessful applications include existing overindebtedness, absent credit history, insufficient assets, and lack of existing accounts.

Emergency payments are a feature of the lives of urban and rural, rich and poor; informal borrowing is the usual response to such exigencies. Emergency payments not covered by regular income affect rural and urban areas equally. The poorest households (15.4 percent) as well as the richest ones (12.1 percent) had to make an unanticipated emergency payment in a 12-month period prior to the survey. Emergency payments are more than twice as often linked to involuntary than voluntary payments (70.1 percent vs. 35 percent of emergency payments). Involuntary payments linked to health issues dominate (48.9 percent of the population had emergency medical expenses in the previous year). Religious and social purposes (wedding celebrations were financed by 22.4 percent of Pakistanis in the previous year), score the highest among voluntary payments. Households that made an emergency payment used informal borrowing most often, such as loans from friends/relatives for more than half of the affected households (67.1 percent), loans from shopkeepers (10.3 percent) or cash from home (13.4 percent) for an emergency payment (figure 2.11). Formal borrowing sources were little mentioned by these households. Savings are also a way to mitigate emergency expenses and are ranked second in sources of funding (17.1 percent) after loans from friends/relatives.

Insurance

Insurance is used by only 1.9 percent of the population, though demand is high for life insurance and viable crop insurance products. Its penetration is higher in urban areas (2.3 percent vs. 1.7 percent in rural areas) and among the upper-income groups (4.6 percent vs. 0.3 percent for the lowest-income quintile). Formal insurance

Figure 2.11 Sources of Funding of Emergency Payment

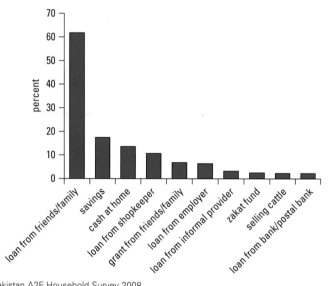

Source: Pakistan A2F Household Survey 2008.

channels are more used than informal ones. Life insurance is virtually the only product (used by 90.8 percent of insurance beneficiaries). Reasons for not having insurance point more toward literacy issues about its benefits rather than about using insurance (figure 2.12). State Life Insurance is the most popular entity among insurance companies (serving 71.4 percent of clients), followed by employer insurance schemes (11 percent), Adamjee Insurance (5.2 percent), EFU General Insurance (3.4 percent), and New Jubilee Insurance (1.4 percent).

Insurance is reserved for higher-income groups. Age, education, employed status, a government job, and belonging to the two highest-income quintiles all individually increase the incidence of being an insurance holder. Interestingly, rural areas are significantly positively associated with being insured, though of course they also profess the highest insurance needs (for crop and life insurance).

Little Use of Check Services beyond Government Payments

More than twice as many people in urban areas know how to write a check when compared to rural areas, and three times as many men as women. Baluchistan appears to be the least proficient province, corroborating earlier financial literacy results.

About a third of the check-proficient population (33 percent) had cashed a check in the month prior to being interviewed. Rural/urban and gender divides are consistent through proficiency and usage. Eighty-four percent of check users have cashed checks themselves at a bank or a Pakistan Post bank, while 17.2 percent have cashed checks through someone else. Possible reasons for the weak uptake of checks

Figure 2.12 Reasons for Not Having Insurance (% of uninsured)

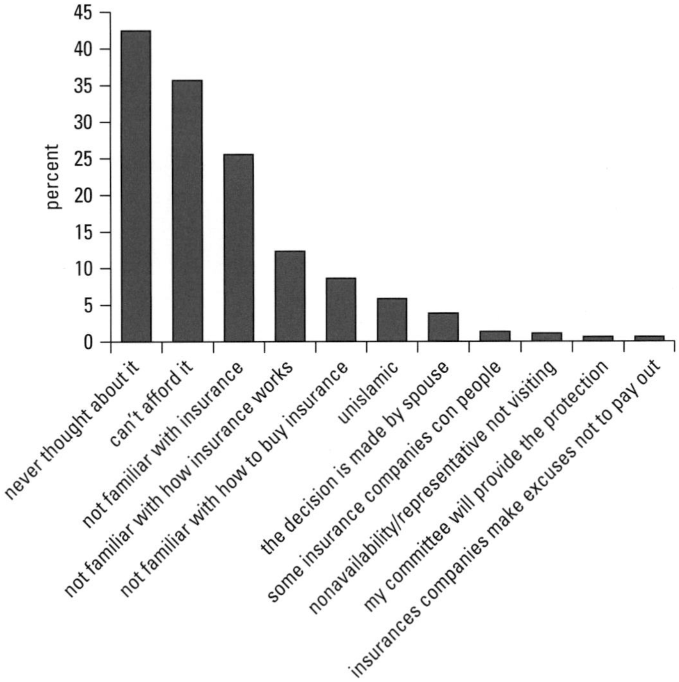

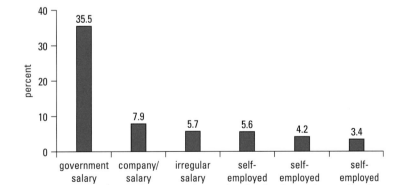

Source: Pakistan A2F Household Survey 2008.

Figure 2.13 Means of Receiving Income

Source: Pakistan A2F Household Survey 2008.

as payment infrastructure include widespread fees: a third of those who cashed a check in the month preceding the survey paid fees for this service. Wide province differences exist—ranging from 20 percent in NWFP to 38.1 percent in Sindh who pay fees for check-related services.

Income and education, employed status, age, availability of collateral, heading the household, and working in government are significant determinants of using checks. Figure 2.13 highlights the percentage of checks and income according to employment. Check users also tend to be regular mobile phone users. Women are less likely to use checks.

The little uptake of checks can be linked to the cash-based nature of the Pakistani economy. The literature finds that other factors underlying little check usage internationally include high fees, delays in check clearance, physical distance from bank branches, and reliability of check as a payment instrument given the inherent disincentive to write bad checks, as well as trust in the system. Existing measures set by SBP to encourage check usage include provisions in the Negotiable Instruments Act to categorize bounced checks as a criminal offense, as well as tax measures involving the withdrawal taxes on cash. Recommended next steps would include that SBP launch further awareness campaigns on these new provisions.

Suggested Strategies for Expanding Access to Finance for the Underserved

A major drive to enhance financial inclusion would involve a joint effort of SBP, the national government, private sector, the community, and donor efforts. The best bet for a rapid scaling up of access is to rely on technology, literacy gains, financial reengineering of processes and products, and an enabling legal and institutional framework.

Way Forward for the Private Sector

Diversifying the product range to increase outreach: The road ahead certainly also lies in **product diversification**, with more services and fewer requirements catering to the mass population of lower-income capacity. Smaller size of products, and bulk service, might better attract lower-income groups. Market segmentation and product diversification can also lower costs and help banks' risk management. Policy makers and banks would note the importance of the market for financial products targeting heads of households, given the finding that being a household head has a significant impact on financial access. This potential is particularly of interest in rural areas as well as clusters of urbanized rural migrants into bigger cities.

Reaching out to the female client: **Women present an untapped potential financial client base for Pakistan.** Better managers of their debt responsibilities and more loyal clients, women are also more assiduous savers. Yet products and procedures are not customized to the specificity of women's needs. Focusing on women has been a profitable proposition in international microfinance experience. The private sector has started to segment female clients in Pakistan by offering them tailor-made products. This is a promising business proposition and strategy for increasing access to finance.

Learning from the informal financial sector's success: The gap between the popularity of informal finance and limited formal financial sector outreach, combined with the perception gap between a heavy procedure-driven formal sector and informal sector with minimum requirements, calls for **learning from informal financial systems and developing linkages with the informal sector.** Strengthening financial infrastructure, by expanding credit information bureaus and other payment systems, would allow banks to lower binding requirements, such as guarantors and immovable collateral, therefore attracting new customers among women, the poor, and residents of rural areas.

Reaching out to the rural client: **Household survey evidence suggests that there is nothing unserviceable about rural areas.** In fact, the larger use of savings for productive use in rural areas and positive association with insurance and post office financial products represent an untapped opportunity for commercial services.

Leveraging technology: **Technology can be used** as an enabler of cost reductions within financial institutions as well as for innovative applications for service delivery. Further cost reductions thanks to the use of technology within banks would allow expansion of the customer base by decreasing fees and increasing the quality of product and services. The positive association between access to formal financing and regular mobile phone use carries potential for new services among an existing customer base. The significant association between the informally served and mobile phone access unleashes opportunities to tap into a new formal customer base already operating in the informal sector.

Way Forward for the Public Sector

Creating awareness of the benefits of access to financial services: **Further gains in financial literacy are critical.** Awareness-creation and trust-building could be forged through **social mobilization and mass media.**

Stronger institutions (including SECP and Credit Information Bureau) are a major part of a rapid increase in financial inclusion. More efficient post office banking is a must (following the successful examples of Brazil and China). Pakistan Post, given its significant developmental potential to enhance financial access, needs modernization in operations and regulations. Following most success cases in East Asia, as well as other continents, PPSB should be placed under the supervision of SBP. This is the case in China, Philippines, Thailand, and Sri Lanka,[26] as well as about half of the countries with a separate postal bank in Africa, almost all countries in Europe and Central Asia, and a considerable number of countries in Latin America, including Argentina and Brazil.

Creating an enabling environment for expanding access to the underserved: Regulations should keep up with the needs of the sector and technological developments, to enable expansion. Simultaneously, an enabling environment should go hand in hand with a carefully chosen government presence. Indiscriminate subsidies, especially of the interest-rate variety, can be detrimental to the expansion of the sector, as they not only distort prices but crowd out efficient institutions and products. The government should resist populist perceptions that low interest-rate funding can serve a developmental purpose. Even more detrimental are state-owned institutions created to promote financial access. In addition to weak evidence in the case of Pakistan that such institutions actually improve access (for example, SME Bank), these efforts waste valuable public resources that could more usefully be deployed elsewhere, and eliminate the level playing field for market participants.

In sum, while financial access is low, and mostly limited to informal financial services, interest in finance outstrips effective access rates considerably. Poverty and lack of information on financial services predicate lack of interest—the perception of irrelevance of the financial system to the everyday lives of a considerable share of the Pakistani population. Several groups seem particularly excluded, though market studies suggest they could be viable customers if the formal financial sector adopts appropriate services and instruments to reach these groups—residents of rural areas and women in particular. In testimony to the commercial viability of these client segments, informal finance seems to be capable of profitably serving such groups at a reasonably lower premium than formal services. Income, employment, education, and status as the head of the household have a significantly positive impact on financial access, a finding with significant policy implications. The following chapters will focus on three such services, and attempt to point to potential areas of development and access expansion, putting information on demand and supply together—microfinance, small enterprise finance, and remittance flows.

Notes

1. What this chapter identifies as "demand" is the potential demand arising from characteristics captured through the national household survey and analyzed though an econometric analysis model. It should not be understood as effective demand.

2. Seventeen percent per SBP figure (Akhtar 2007).

3. "SBP Statistical Bulletin June 2008." The differences between SBP statistics and the Pakistan A2F survey statistics are discussed in detail in Appendix A (Calibration). Some differences arise due to clustering of financial services in specific areas, which a nationwide household survey of this size (10,305 households) cannot adequately address. This is the case for microfinance clients and committees (particularly the business committees in bazaars). Other differences are caused by multiple accounts maintained by clients and some double counting of clients among financial institutions (this is the case for bank lending), as well as some stale or inactive accounts (this is the case for Pakistan Post). Differences can further be explained by shortcomings on the part of literacy and understanding on part of respondents.

4. Committees, an informal mechanism for group saving and lending, are explained later in this chapter.

5. Supply-side data show a similar picture. Penetration of the market for credit to women is estimated at 4 percent. The penetration in savings is slightly higher at 9 percent. Response from banks suggests that around 4 percent of the small and medium enterprise (SME) clients and 5 percent of consumer credit clients are women. Approximately 19 percent of long-term interest

earning deposit accounts and 1 percent of total current accounts are owned by women. The most recent available financial sector outreach estimate suggests there are currently 4 million women accessing formal financial services (credit and/or savings). Of these, about 3 million women are banking with the traditional financial institutions and about 1 million access services from MFIs.

6. Specifically note the positive and significant coefficients in table A2.6 in the regressions of formal versus informal and nonborrowers, and formal versus informal borrowers only. Note also the positive and significant coefficients in table A2.7 in the regressions of formal versus informal and nonsavers, and formal versus informal savers only.

7. The regression analysis on which the discussion is based is in Annex table A2.2 and more generally in Annex tables 1–6. These tables are also discussed in further detail in the following sections of this chapter. The probit and multinomial logit regression frameworks follow the specification of Kumar et al. (2005).

8. Except in the case of informal financing (see, for example, the significantly negative association with informal borrowing in Annex table A2.3 and the significantly negative association of age with informal savings in Annex table A2.4).

9. See Annex table A2.4 for econometric results supporting this evidence.

10. Demand-side regression analysis introducing a number of explanatory variables to the probability of being banked shows positive significant effect of age, education level, being employed, and status as the main income earner on the probability of being banked (Annex table A2.6). The regressions follow the specification of Kumar (2005).

11. The self-employed are predominantly male (see Annex table A2.10), with a lower level of education than the average individual. Those informally employed also tend to be younger and live in urban areas. The formally self-employed tend to regularly use cell phones, not so the informally self-employed.

12. Specifically, respondents felt that they did not have enough collateral, too much documentation was involved, references were hard to obtain, they did not have an identity document, or did not have enough money, regular income, or sufficient minimum balance to open an account.

13. World Bank (2008a). While identification documentation penetration is high (80.2 percent on average, though lower for female and poorer income groups), other documents are extremely hard to come by. Electricity bills and household ownership documents are a distant second and third in penetration (12.1 percent and 8.3 percent on average, respectively) and are more frequently possessed by higher-income households (with a large gender divide in favor of men in both instances).

14. With its top three banks making up less than 45 percent of the banking system assets and, on average, only one document required to open an account, Thailand is an example of a vibrant banking sector.

15. Personal reasons include lack of information about bank products, preference to deal in cash, no perceived need for being banked, lack of self-confidence, uneasiness in the bank environment, no time to go to the bank, and no knowledge of how to open an account.

16. Accessibility issues include the cost and time to reach a bank.

17. Walking is the most common mode of transportation to reach a financial institution in urban areas (38.9 percent) vs. public transport in rural areas (48.5 percent rural respondents commute to their financial institution by train, rickshaw, tonga, bus, or van). About 43.9 percent of respondents combine other activities while going to the bank; this is true across the income spectrum, though with women a little less, at 36.3 percent vs. 45.9 percent men.

18. Service-related issues explored include: charges and fees are too high; returns are low; hours of operation are inconvenient; long lines at the bank; and staff are condescending, unhelpful, speak in complicated terms, do not understand client needs, and do not give importance to the client.

19. A survey covering 2,000 urban individuals in Brazil also highlighted a weak association between rates of returns and making deposits. See Access to Financial Services in Brazil, p. 39.

20. World Bank (2008a). Banks in South Asia are least likely to charge a monthly maintenance fee for a bank account or charge annual debit card fees, which encourages more access. Eighty-six percent of banks surveyed opened the account within a few minutes of the application or on the same day (World Bank 2006a).

21. Committees, also called ROSCA, are groups through which participants join contributions to lend to a single member. Members take turns to access committee loans, through an order determined by list, lottery, or auction. By aggregating individual funds and channeling them in a predetermined order to individual members, committees play an important intermediation function, based on revolving funds. Committees do not require physical capital as collateral. Instead, repayment is based on reciprocity and social pressure.

22. The figure includes group savings schemes.

23. Regression results confirm and enrich these findings (Annex table A2.12). While both formal and informal savers are motivated by investment motives, education, and socioreligious reasons, only informal savers are further driven by household needs and medical, accident, emergency, and old-age provisions. Presumably, formal savers have covered these motives by other financial products. Female, rural, younger individuals, household members other than the household head, farmers, and less educated individuals are more likely to save informally. In contrast, government employees and regular cell phone users are more likely to save formally.

24. We do not quote microfinance loan figures due to a suspected survey bias as discussed in Appendix A (Calibration). Instead we go with official SBP figures, which put microfinance clients at 1.7 million.

25. Regression analysis demonstrates similar patterns (Annex table A2.13).

26. Not in Indonesia, where half of postal services are under private sector provision.

Annex

Table A2.1 Determinants of Access to Formal and Informal Financial Services, Probits

	Financially Served vs. Financially Excluded					Formally Served vs. All Others			Formally Served vs. Informally Served			Informally Served vs. Financially Excluded		
	Model I	Model II	Model III	Model IV	Model V	Model I	Model II	Model III	Model I	Model II	Model III	Model I	Model II	Model III
Female	−0.096 (0.092)	−0.134[b] (0.069)	−0.133[c] (0.069)	−0.128[c] (0.069)	−0.132[c] (0.068)	−0.124 (0.108)	−0.155[a] (0.090)	−0.145 (0.090)	−0.102 (0.124)	−0.125 (0.110)	−0.115 (0.109)	−0.072 (0.101)	−0.113 (0.078)	−0.113 (0.077)
Age	0.005[a] (0.002)	0.004[a] (0.001)	0.004[a] (0.001)	0.004[a] (0.001)	0.004[a] (0.001)	0.017[a] (0.002)	0.015[a] (0.002)	0.017[a] (0.002)	0.017[a] (0.003)	0.017[a] (0.003)	0.018[a] (0.002)	0.001 (0.002)	0.000 (0.001)	0.001 (0.001)
Education	0.033[c] (0.020)	0.040[a] (0.014)	0.040[a] (0.014)	0.035[a] (0.013)	0.034[a] (0.013)	0.179[a] (0.020)	0.157[a] (0.019)	0.145[a] (0.019)	0.188[a] (0.019)	0.165[a] (0.020)	0.152[a] (0.021)	−0.016 (0.017)	0.000 (0.014)	−0.003 (0.013)
Rural	0.182[a] (0.068)	0.197[a] (0.061)	0.197[a] (0.061)	0.191[a] (0.061)	0.194[a] (0.060)	−0.060 (0.090)	−0.009 (0.081)	−0.028 (0.082)	−0.133 (0.102)	−0.141 (0.090)	−0.151 (0.093)	0.212[a] (0.076)	0.216[a] (0.068)	0.215[a] (0.067)
Employed	0.318[a] (0.083)	0.376[a] (0.063)	0.365[a] (0.079)	0.377[a] (0.063)	0.380[a] (0.063)	0.420[a] (0.116)	0.253[a] (0.091)	0.397[a] (0.094)	0.339[a] (0.127)	0.127 (0.113)	0.294[a] (0.112)	0.259[a] (0.090)	0.365[a] (0.090)	0.331[a] (0.073)
Household head	0.137[b] (0.058)	0.179[a] (0.046)	0.179[a] (0.046)	0.182[a] (0.047)	0.187[a] (0.048)	0.241[a] (0.080)	0.274[a] (0.060)	0.292[a] (0.060)	0.217[b] (0.092)	0.210[a] (0.064)	0.230[a] (0.064)	0.067 (0.064)	0.104[b] (0.045)	0.110[b] (0.047)
Collateral	0.061 (0.068)	0.136[b] (0.061)	0.135[b] (0.062)	0.139[b] (0.062)	0.137[b] (0.062)	0.074 (0.103)	0.107 (0.086)	0.114 (0.084)	0.052 (0.141)	0.079 (0.094)	0.089 (0.093)	0.044 (0.091)	0.122[c] (0.064)	0.121[c] (0.065)
Corporate	0.051 (0.098)	0.165[c] (0.085)	0.157[c] (0.090)	0.156[c] (0.084)	0.160[c] (0.083)	0.133 (0.134)	0.232[c] (0.128)	0.268[b] (0.116)	0.133 (0.156)	0.183 (0.137)	0.225[c] (0.122)	0.029 (0.109)	0.101 (0.093)	0.071 (0.087)
Government	0.821[a] (0.129)	0.767[a] (0.131)	0.760[a] (0.146)	0.764[a] (0.129)	0.768[a] (0.128)	1.138[a] (0.180)	1.083[a] (0.161)	1.144[a] (0.143)	1.063[a] (0.194)	1.025[a] (0.175)	1.099[a] (0.154)	0.268 (0.182)	0.281 (0.185)	0.276 (0.172)
Farmer	0.210[b] (0.103)	0.332[a] (0.075)	0.326[a] (0.081)	0.335[a] (0.076)	0.331[a] (0.076)	−0.044 (0.121)	−0.092 (0.104)	−0.037 (0.092)	−0.117 (0.126)	−0.188[c] (0.112)	−0.122 (0.101)	0.275[a] (0.097)	0.422[a] (0.084)	0.397[a] (0.078)
Laborer	−0.074 (0.125)	0.016 (0.097)	0.026 (0.116)	0.022 (0.097)	0.031 (0.094)	−0.257[b] (0.131)	0.060 (0.124)	−0.043 (0.128)	−0.280[c] (0.144)	0.066 (0.129)	−0.070 (0.138)	−0.014 (0.123)	0.010 (0.118)	0.053 (0.094)
Type of house	−0.105[c] (0.060)	−0.097[b] (0.044)	−0.097[c] (0.044)	−0.104[b] (0.043)	−0.108[b] (0.043)	0.188[b] (0.096)	0.080 (0.059)	0.053 (0.060)	0.236[b] (0.097)	0.122[c] (0.065)	0.098 (0.067)	−0.154[b] (0.062)	−0.124[a] (0.046)	−0.132[a] (0.046)
Type of latrine	−0.114 (0.071)	−0.071 (0.072)	−0.071 (0.072)	−0.077 (0.072)	−0.082 (0.072)	0.176[c] (0.096)	0.011 (0.085)	0.001 (0.085)	0.220[b] (0.097)	0.016 (0.092)	0.013 (0.093)	−0.131[c] (0.071)	−0.062 (0.075)	−0.068 (0.075)

(continued)

Table A2.1 Determinants of Access to Formal and Informal Financial Services, Probits (continued)

	Financially Served vs. Financially Excluded					Formally Served vs. All Others			Formally Served vs. Informally Served			Informally Served vs. Financially Excluded		
	Model I	Model II	Model III	Model IV	Model V	Model I	Model II	Model III	Model I	Model II	Model III	Model I	Model II	Model III
Household income Q2	0.147[b] (0.075)					−0.006 (0.137)			−0.015 (0.165)			0.169[b] (0.082)		
Household income Q3	0.159[b] (0.073)					0.289[b] (0.145)			0.290[c] (0.169)			0.136 (0.084)		
Household income Q4	0.201[b] (0.085)					0.448[a] (0.134)			0.460[a] (0.150)			0.125 (0.096)		
Household income Q5	0.243[a] (0.077)					0.491[a] (0.160)			0.498[a] (0.177)			0.141[c] (0.083)		
Personal income Q2		0.043 (0.079)	0.042 (0.079)	0.034 (0.080)	0.027 (0.080)		0.079 (0.091)	0.049 (0.094)		0.063 (0.097)	0.041 (0.098)		0.048 (0.085)	0.036 (0.085)
Personal income Q3		0.253[a] (0.087)	0.252[a] (0.087)	0.245[a] (0.088)	0.235[a] (0.089)		0.232[a] (0.082)	0.200[b] (0.087)		0.160[c] (0.087)	0.137 (0.090)		0.253[a] (0.087)	0.238[a] (0.089)
Personal income Q4		0.246[b] (0.117)	0.245[b] (0.116)	0.228[c] (0.119)	0.213[c] (0.119)		0.471[a] (0.110)	0.418[a] (0.111)		0.441[a] (0.107)	0.395[a] (0.111)		0.204[c] (0.115)	0.176 (0.118)
Personal income Q5		0.229[b] (0.100)	0.227[b] (0.100)	0.202[b] (0.102)	0.184[c] (0.103)		0.624[a] (0.108)	0.564[a] (0.107)		0.655[a] (0.120)	0.614[a] (0.119)		0.110 (0.108)	0.073 (0.110)
Formal sector			0.020 (0.097)				0.216[b] (0.113)			0.263[b] (0.121)			−0.068 (0.103)	
Cell use				0.120[a] (0.043)	0.184[a] (0.045)			0.409[a] (0.053)			0.362[a] (0.064)			0.118[b] (0.047)
Cell access					0.212[a] (0.060)			0.121 (0.076)			0.037 (0.086)			0.224[a] (0.062)
Punjab	−0.201 (0.161)	−0.447[a] (0.120)	−0.446[a] (0.121)	−0.492[a] (0.126)	−0.534[a] (0.130)	−3.042[a] (0.279)	−2.964[a] (0.178)	−3.184[a] (0.185)	−2.734[a] (0.305)	−2.566[a] (0.201)	−2.757[a] (0.208)	0.007 (0.161)	−0.291[b] (0.122)	−0.352[a] (0.129)

	(1)	(2)	(3)	(4)	(5)	(6)	(7)	(8)	(9)	(10)	(11)	(12)	(13)	(14)
Sind	−0.099 (0.164)	−0.432[a] (0.127)	−0.431[a] (0.128)	−0.460[a] (0.130)	−0.495[a] (0.132)	−3.223[a] (0.251)	−3.080[a] (0.175)	−3.250[a] (0.183)	−2.980[a] (0.279)	−2.731[a] (0.197)	−2.876[a] (0.209)	0.142 (0.159)	−0.258[b] (0.126)	−0.303[b] (0.130)
NWFP	−0.378[b] (0.186)	−0.752[a] (0.158)	−0.751[a] (0.159)	−0.794[a] (0.161)	−0.838[a] (0.166)	−2.727[a] (0.298)	−2.956[a] (0.191)	−3.144[a] (0.195)	−2.336[a] (0.346)	−2.530[a] (0.220)	−2.686[a] (0.226)	−0.299 (0.193)	−0.631[a] (0.165)	−0.693[a] (0.173)
Baluchistan	−1.066[a] (0.171)	−1.331[a] (0.145)	−1.331[a] (0.145)	−1.343[a] (0.146)	−1.373[a] (0.150)	−3.756[a] (0.308)	−3.592[a] (0.213)	−3.692[a] (0.216)	−3.124[a] (0.336)	−2.924[a] (0.232)	−2.992[a] (0.233)	−0.802[a] (0.168)	−1.143[a] (0.138)	−1.178[a] (0.143)
AJK	0.339[c] (0.182)	−0.038 (0.163)	−0.038 (0.164)	−0.074 (0.164)	−0.134 (0.169)	−2.054[a] (0.323)	−2.019[a] (0.243)	−2.212[a] (0.246)	−1.763[a] (0.346)	−1.622[a] (0.261)	−1.785[a] (0.267)	0.362[b] (0.182)	−0.077 (0.165)	−0.154 (0.171)
Number of observations	5941	10288	10288	10288	10288	5941	10288	10288	3,939	5,967	5,967	4,829	8,698	8,698
F(k, d)	43.28	52.55	51.59	48.58	45.19	133.44	171.75	124.02	61.22	125.21	84.12	23.7	21.56	19.37

Standard errors in parenthesis (a = Significant at 1% level; b = Significant at 5% level; c = Significant at 10% level).

Table A2.2 Determinants of Access to Formal and Informal Financial Services, Multinomial Logits, Marginal Effects

	Model I			Model II			Model III			Model IV			Model V		
	Marginal Effects Financially Excluded	Marginal Effects Informally Served	Marginal Effects Formally Included	Marginal Effects Financially Excluded	Marginal Effects Informally Served	Marginal Effects Formally Included	Marginal Effects Financially Excluded	Marginal Effects Informally Served	Marginal Effects Formally Included	Marginal Effects Financially Excluded	Marginal Effects Informally Served	Marginal Effects Formally Included	Marginal Effects Financially Excluded	Marginal Effects Informally Served	Marginal Effects Formally Included
Female	0.030 (0.037)	−0.026 (0.038)	−0.003 (0.003)	0.046 (0.031)	−0.045 (0.031)	−0.001 (0.001)	0.047 (0.031)	−0.046 (0.031)	−0.001 (0.001)	0.044 (0.031)	−0.044 (0.031)	0.000 (0.001)	0.046 (0.030)	−0.046 (0.031)	0.000 (0.001)
Age	−0.001 (0.001)	0.000 (0.001)	0.001[a] (0.000)	0.000 (0.001)	0.000 (0.001)	0.000[a] (0.000)	0.000 (0.001)	0.000 (0.001)	0.000[a] (0.000)	0.000 (0.001)	0.000 (0.001)	0.000[a] (0.000)	0.000 (0.001)	0.000 (0.001)	0.000[a] (0.000)
Education	0.004 (0.006)	−0.010 (0.006)	0.006[a] (0.002)	−0.001 (0.006)	−0.001 (0.006)	0.002[a] (0.001)	−0.001 (0.006)	−0.001 (0.006)	0.002[a] (0.001)	0.000 (0.005)	−0.001 (0.005)	0.001[b] (0.001)	0.001 (0.005)	−0.002 (0.005)	0.001[b] (0.001)
Rural	−0.081[a] (0.029)	0.081[a] (0.029)	0.000 (0.002)	−0.086[a] (0.026)	0.086[a] (0.026)	0.000 (0.001)	−0.086[a] (0.026)	0.086[a] (0.026)	0.000 (0.001)	−0.085[a] (0.026)	0.084[a] (0.026)	0.000 (0.001)	−0.084[a] (0.025)	0.084[a] (0.025)	0.000 (0.001)
Employed	−0.100[a] (0.035)	0.094[a] (0.035)	0.005 (0.004)	−0.133[a] (0.028)	0.129[a] (0.029)	0.004 (0.003)	−0.145[a] (0.035)	0.144[a] (0.035)	0.001 (0.002)	−0.133[a] (0.029)	0.130[a] (0.029)	0.003 (0.002)	−0.135[a] (0.029)	0.132[a] (0.029)	0.003 (0.002)
Household head	−0.026 (0.023)	0.025 (0.024)	0.001 (0.003)	−0.044[b] (0.019)	0.043[b] (0.019)	0.001 (0.001)	−0.044[b] (0.019)	0.043[b] (0.019)	0.001 (0.001)	−0.044[b] (0.019)	0.043[b] (0.019)	0.000 (0.001)	−0.046[b] (0.019)	0.045[b] (0.019)	0.000 (0.001)
Collateral	−0.013 (0.034)	0.017 (0.035)	−0.004 (0.005)	−0.047[c] (0.026)	0.047[c] (0.025)	0.000 (0.001)	−0.047[c] (0.025)	0.047[c] (0.025)	0.000 (0.001)	−0.048[c] (0.025)	0.048[c] (0.025)	0.000 (0.001)	−0.046[c] (0.025)	0.046[c] (0.025)	0.000 (0.001)
Corporate	−0.010 (0.040)	0.015 (0.039)	−0.005 (0.005)	−0.029 (0.036)	0.029 (0.035)	0.000 (0.002)	−0.040 (0.038)	0.041 (0.038)	−0.001 (0.002)	−0.028 (0.035)	0.028 (0.035)	0.000 (0.001)	−0.030 (0.035)	0.030 (0.035)	0.000 (0.001)
Government	−0.108[a] (0.054)	0.032 (0.066)	0.075[c] (0.046)	−0.112[c] (0.067)	0.086 (0.066)	0.026[c] (0.016)	−0.121[c] (0.072)	0.098 (0.072)	0.023 (0.014)	−0.109 (0.067)	0.088 (0.067)	0.021[c] (0.012)	−0.117[c] (0.067)	0.095 (0.067)	0.022[c] (0.013)
Farmer	−0.093[a] (0.033)	0.103[a] (0.032)	−0.010[b] (0.004)	−0.161[a] (0.032)	0.164[a] (0.032)	−0.003[b] (0.001)	−0.170[a] (0.033)	0.173[a] (0.033)	−0.003[b] (0.002)	−0.162[a] (0.032)	0.164[a] (0.032)	−0.002[b] (0.001)	−0.162[a] (0.032)	0.165[a] (0.032)	−0.002[b] (0.001)
Laborer	0.009 (0.046)	−0.004 (0.045)	−0.005 (0.005)	−0.017 (0.039)	0.016 (0.039)	0.002 (0.003)	−0.007 (0.048)	0.002 (0.048)	0.004 (0.003)	−0.018 (0.039)	0.017 (0.039)	0.001 (0.002)	−0.021 (0.037)	0.020 (0.037)	0.001 (0.002)
Type of house	0.052[b] (0.023)	−0.066[a] (0.025)	0.014[b] (0.007)	0.047[a] (0.018)	−0.049[a] (0.018)	0.002 (0.001)	0.047[a] (0.018)	−0.049[a] (0.018)	0.002 (0.001)	0.048[a] (0.018)	−0.049[a] (0.018)	0.001 (0.001)	0.049[a] (0.018)	−0.051[a] (0.018)	0.001 (0.001)
Type of latrine	0.044[c] (0.026)	−0.049[b] (0.025)	0.005[c] (0.003)	0.023 (0.030)	−0.023 (0.030)	0.001 (0.001)	0.023 (0.030)	−0.024 (0.030)	0.001 (0.001)	0.024 (0.030)	−0.024 (0.030)	0.001 (0.001)	0.026 (0.030)	−0.026 (0.030)	0.001 (0.001)
Household income Q2	−0.061[b] (0.027)	0.057[b] (0.028)	0.004 (0.005)												
Household income Q3	−0.050[c] (0.028)	0.044 (0.030)	0.007 (0.007)												

2

	(1)	(2)	(3)	(4)	(5)	(6)	(7)	(8)	(9)	(10)	(11)	(12)	(13)	(14)	(15)
Household income Q4	−0.048 (0.032)	0.038 (0.035)	0.011 (0.008)												
Household income Q5	−0.055[c] (0.028)	0.031 (0.033)	0.024[c] (0.013)												
Personal income Q2				−0.020 (0.035)	0.018 (0.034)	0.002 (0.002)	−0.020 (0.034)	0.018 (0.034)	0.002 (0.002)	−0.018 (0.035)	0.017 (0.035)	0.001 (0.001)	−0.015 (0.034)	0.014 (0.034)	0.001 (0.001)
Personal income Q3				−0.103[b] (0.036)	0.100[a] (0.035)	0.003[b] (0.002)	−0.104[a] (0.035)	0.101[a] (0.035)	0.003[c] (0.002)	−0.102[a] (0.036)	0.100[a] (0.036)	0.004[c] (0.002)	−0.098[a] (0.036)	0.096[a] (0.036)	0.002 (0.001)
Personal income Q4				−0.085[c] (0.048)	0.078[c] (0.046)	0.007[c] (0.004)	−0.087[c] (0.047)	0.080[c] (0.046)	0.004[c] (0.002)	−0.081[c] (0.048)	0.077 (0.047)	0.004[c] (0.002)	−0.075 (0.048)	0.070 (0.047)	0.005[c] (0.003)
Personal income Q5				−0.045 (0.044)	0.037 (0.044)	0.009[a] (0.003)	−0.047 (0.044)	0.039 (0.044)	0.008[a] (0.003)	−0.040 (0.045)	0.035 (0.045)	0.005[b] (0.002)	−0.032 (0.045)	0.027 (0.044)	0.005[b] (0.002)
Formal sector							0.023 (0.042)	−0.027 (0.042)	0.004 (0.003)						
Cell use										0.016 (0.017)	−0.019 (0.017)	0.004[b] (0.002)	−0.047[a] (0.018)	0.044[b] (0.019)	0.003[b] (0.002)
Cell access													−0.092[a] (0.025)	0.093[a] (0.025)	−0.001 (0.001)
Punjab	0.313[a] (0.027)	0.593[a] (0.042)	−0.906[a] (0.039)	0.462[a] (0.040)	0.343[a] (0.051)	−0.805[a] (0.069)	0.462[a] (0.039)	0.341[a] (0.051)	−0.803[a] (0.069)	0.480[a] (0.038)	0.351[a] (0.049)	−0.830[a] (0.062)	0.503[a] (0.037)	0.329[a] (0.050)	−0.832[a] (0.061)
Sind	−0.044 (0.054)	0.057 (0.054)	−0.013[a] (0.005)	0.105[b] (0.047)	−0.101[b] (0.048)	−0.004[b] (0.002)	0.106[b] (0.047)	−0.101[a] (0.048)	−0.005[a] (0.002)	0.109[a] (0.047)	−0.105[b] (0.048)	−0.003[a] (0.001)	0.119[a] (0.046)	−0.115[a] (0.046)	−0.004[b] (0.001)
NWFP	0.122 (0.078)	−0.109 (0.078)	−0.013[a] (0.005)	0.229[a] (0.048)	−0.224[a] (0.048)	−0.004[b] (0.002)	0.228[a] (0.047)	−0.224[a] (0.047)	−0.005[a] (0.002)	0.231[a] (0.046)	−0.228[a] (0.046)	−0.003[a] (0.001)	0.235[a] (0.043)	−0.232[a] (0.043)	−0.004[b] (0.001)
Baluchistan	0.321[a] (0.062)	−0.308[a] (0.063)	−0.013[a] (0.005)	0.345[a] (0.030)	−0.341[a] (0.030)	−0.004[b] (0.002)	0.345[a] (0.029)	−0.340[a] (0.029)	−0.005[a] (0.002)	0.342[a] (0.029)	−0.339[a] (0.029)	−0.003[a] (0.001)	0.332[a] (0.027)	−0.328[a] (0.027)	−0.004[b] (0.001)
AJK	−0.109[b] (0.053)	0.122[b] (0.053)	−0.013[a] (0.005)	0.040 (0.065)	−0.036 (0.066)	−0.004[b] (0.002)	0.041 (0.066)	−0.036 (0.066)	−0.005[a] (0.002)	0.045 (0.065)	−0.042 (0.065)	−0.003[a] (0.001)	0.069 (0.064)	−0.066 (0.064)	−0.004[b] (0.001)
Number of observations	5,166			9,221			9,221			9,221			9,221		
F(k, d)	85.05			81.59			84.68			162.64			147.3		

Standard errors in parenthesis (a = Significant at 1% level; b = Significant at 5% level; c = Significant at 10% level).

Table A2.3 F-Statistic Comparisons of Likelihood for Financial Access

Panel A F-statistic comparisons of likelihood for financial access among provinces

	Banked				Financially Served			
	Sindh	NWFP	Baluchistan	AJK	Sindh	NWFP	Baluchistan	AJK
Punjab	2.25	0.24	21.0[a]	36.92[a]	0.07	8.14[a]	82.17[a]	12.99[a]
Sindh		2.91[c]	13.5[a]	42.48[a]		7.58[a]	67.52[a]	10.74[a]
NWFP			21.3[a]	31.09[a]			16.76[a]	2235[a]
Baluchistan				64.62[a]				83.55[a]

Source: Pakistan A2F Household Survey 2008; a = Significant at 1% level; b = Significant at 5% level; c = Significant at 10% level.

Panel B F-statistic comparisons of likelihood for financial access among income quintiles

	Banked				Financially Served			
	Personal income Q2	Personal income Q3	Personal income Q4	Personal income Q5	Personal income Q2	Personal income Q3	Personal income Q4	Personal income Q5
Personal income Q1	0.89	10.11[a]	1592[a]	34.71[a]	0.29	8.45[a]	4.42[b]	5.24[b]
Personal income Q2		6.59[b]	1425[a]	49.82[a]		8.79[a]	4.29[b]	5.85[b]
Personal income Q3			3.45[c]	24.14[a]			0	0.1
Personal income Q4				3.74[c]				0.05

Source: Pakistan A2F Household Survey 2008; a = Significant at 1% level; b = Significant at 5% level; c = Significant at 10% level.

Table A2.4 Determinants of Interest in Financial Matters

	Interested in Financial Matters vs. Others	
	Model I	Model II
Female	0.085	0.035
	(0.096)	(0.073)
Age	0.003	0.002
	(0.002)	(0.001)
Education	0.041[a]	0.029[b]
	(0.014)	(0.013)
Rural	0.224[a]	0.170[a]
	(0.060)	(0.044)
Employed	0.198[b]	0.280[a]
	(0.083)	(0.070)
Household head	0.252[a]	0.324[a]
	(0.061)	(0.052)
Collateral	0.009	0.031
	(0.091)	(0.065)
Corporate	0.039	0.061
	(0.109)	(0.096)
Government	0.126	0.101
	(0.177)	(0.123)
Farmer	−0.082	−0.085
	(0.108)	(0.081)
Laborer	0.060	0.030
	(0.115)	(0.084)
Formal sector	0.215[a]	0.121[c]
	(0.082)	(0.069)
Cell use	0.147[a]	0.249[a]
	(0.055)	(0.042)
Household income and house/latrine effects	Yes	
Personal income and house/latrine effects		Yes
Province effects	Yes	Yes
Number of observations	5,941	10,288
F(k, d)	17.99	19.07

Standard errors in parenthesis (a = Significant at 1% level; b = Significant at 5% level; c = Significant at 10% level).

Table A2.5 Determinants of Willingness to Enter the Financial Sector

	Those Wanting to Have Their Own Bank Account vs. Others	
	Model I	Model II
Male	0.245[b]	0.467[a]
	(0.118)	(0.100)
Age	−0.009[a]	−0.011[a]
	(0.002)	(0.002)
Education	0.083[a]	0.072[a]
	(0.017)	(0.012)
Rural	−0.040	−0.036
	(0.068)	(0.052)
Employed	−0.002	0.146[c]
	(0.094)	(0.079)
Household head	0.016	0.016
	(0.083)	(0.066)
Collateral	−0.178[c]	−0.155[b]
	(0.102)	(0.072)
Corporate	0.216[c]	0.113
	(0.121)	(0.104)
Government	0.616[a]	0.566[a]
	(0.200)	(0.166)
Farmer	0.215[c]	0.046
	(0.121)	(0.095)
Laborer	0.197[b]	0.090
	(0.096)	(0.096)
House	−0.007	−0.079
	(0.068)	(0.054)
Latrine	−0.054	−0.044
	(0.069)	(0.061)
Household income	−0.018	
	(0.028)	
Personal income		0.118[a]
		(0.022)
Formal sector	0.156	0.057
	(0.097)	(0.090)
Cell phone use	0.208[a]	0.211[a]
	(0.056)	(0.049)
Male * Household income	−0.007	
	(0.015)	
Male * Personal income		−0.004[c]
		(0.002)
Province effects	Yes	Yes
Number of observations	4,611	7,878
F(k, d)	15.34	57.69

Note: This regression is run on a subset of the sample who do not presently have a bank account. Standard errors in parenthesis (a = Significant at 1% level; b = Significant at 5% level; c = Significant at 10% level).

Table A2.6 Determinants of Access to Banking

Banked vs. Unbanked	Model I	Model II	Model III	Model IV	Model V
Female	−0.115	−0.154[c]	−0.144[c]	−0.134[c]	−0.135[c]
	(0.099)	(0.080)	(0.081)	(0.079)	(0.080)
Age	0.017[a]	0.015[a]	0.015[a]	0.017[a]	0.017[a]
	(0.003)	(0.002)	(0.002)	(0.002)	(0.002)
Education	0.188[a]	0.166[a]	0.165[a]	0.154[a]	0.154[a]
	(0.021)	(0.019)	(0.019)	(0.019)	(0.019)
Rural	−0.008	0.043	0.039	0.020	0.021
	(0.090)	(0.078)	(0.077)	(0.078)	(0.078)
Employed	0.431[a]	0.442[a]	0.295[a]	0.440[a]	0.443[a]
	(0.110)	(0.095)	(0.102)	(0.095)	(0.095)
Household head	0.211[a]	0.269[a]	0.267[a]	0.281[a]	0.283[a]
	(0.081)	(0.068)	(0.067)	(0.067)	(0.067)
Collateral	0.053	0.129[c]	0.123[c]	0.129[c]	0.128[c]
	(0.105)	(0.070)	(0.072)	(0.074)	(0.073)
Corporate	0.157	0.339[a]	0.273[b]	0.308[a]	0.308[a]
	(0.136)	(0.122)	(0.135)	(0.120)	(0.120)
Government	1.203[a]	1.208[a]	1.145[a]	1.206[a]	1.206[a]
	(0.176)	(0.147)	(0.161)	(0.142)	(0.142)
Farmer	−0.020	−0.009	−0.066	−0.007	−0.011
	(0.108)	(0.083)	(0.100)	(0.084)	(0.083)
Laborer	−0.310[c]	−0.071	0.050	−0.060	−0.056
	(0.166)	(0.144)	(0.139)	(0.149)	(0.150)
Type of house	0.181[b]	0.089	0.087	0.062	0.060
	(0.081)	(0.056)	(0.057)	(0.056)	(0.056)
Type of latrine	0.181	0.020	0.022	0.011	0.012
	(0.111)	(0.099)	(0.098)	(0.098)	(0.099)
Household income Q2	−0.026				
	(0.139)				
Household income Q3	0.271[c]				
	(0.141)				
Household income Q4	0.375[a]				
	(0.145)				
Household income Q5	0.447[a]				
	(0.169)				
Personal income Q2		0.094	0.087	0.059	0.056
		(0.100)	(0.099)	(0.100)	(0.102)
Personal income Q3		0.281[a]	0.268[a]	0.240[a]	0.237[a]
		(0.088)	(0.087)	(0.090)	(0.092)
Personal income Q4		0.467[a]	0.449[a]	0.401[a]	0.397[a]
		(0.117)	(0.116)	(0.118)	(0.119)
Personal income Q5		0.658[a]	0.627[a]	0.575[a]	0.571[a]
		(0.112)	(0.110)	(0.110)	(0.111)

(continued)

Table A2.6 Determinants of Access to Banking (continued)

Banked vs. Unbanked	Model I	Model II	Model III	Model IV	Model V
Formal sector			0.219[c]		
			(0.120)		
Cell use				0.365[a]	0.393[a]
				(0.052)	(0.051)
Cell access					0.091
					(0.079)
Punjab	−3.163[a]	−3.235[a]	−3.210[a]	−3.394[a]	−3.417[a]
	(0.306)	(0.214)	(0.214)	(0.215)	(0.222)
Sind	−3.331[a]	−3.340[a]	−3.314[a]	−3.450[a]	−3.473[a]
	(0.275)	(0.203)	(0.202)	(0.204)	(0.210)
NWFP	−2.798[a]	−3.198[a]	−3.180[a]	−3.333[a]	−3.356[a]
	(0.320)	(0.219)	(0.219)	(0.218)	(0.223)
Baluchistan	−3.812[a]	−3.789[a]	−3.774[a]	−3.843[a]	−3.865[a]
	(0.325)	(0.239)	(0.240)	(0.239)	(0.244)
AJK	−2.144[a]	−2.225[a]	−2.200[a]	−2.352[a]	−2.380[a]
	(0.347)	(0.263)	(0.263)	(0.261)	(0.267)
Number of observations	5,941	10,288	10,288	10,288	10,288
F(k, d)	84.72	119.05	129.16	108.89	104.77

Standard errors in parenthesis (a = Significant at 1% level; b = Significant at 5% level; c = Significant at 10% level).

Table A2.7 Determinants of Access to Formal and Informal Borrowing

	Borrowers vs. Nonborrowers			Formal Borrowers vs. Others			Formal Borrowers vs. Informal Borrowers			Informal Borrowers vs. Nonborrowers		
	Model I	Model II	Model III	Model I	Model II	Model III	Model I	Model II	Model III	Model I	Model II	Model III
Female	-0.243[a] (0.085)	-0.293[a] (0.066)	-0.298[a] (0.066)	0.349[b] (0.165)	0.162 (0.146)	0.156 (0.145)	0.653[a] (0.221)	0.416[b] (0.196)	0.396[b] (0.189)	-0.303[a] (0.086)	-0.327[a] (0.067)	-0.331[a] (0.067)
Age	0.003 (0.002)	0.002 (0.001)	0.002 (0.001)	0.009[b] (0.005)	0.009[b] (0.004)	0.009[a] (0.004)	0.010[b] (0.005)	0.010[a] (0.004)	0.011[a] (0.004)	0.002 (0.002)	0.001 (0.001)	0.001 (0.001)
Education	-0.025[c] (0.013)	-0.011 (0.013)	-0.012 (0.013)	0.169[a] (0.031)	0.137[a] (0.028)	0.126[a] (0.025)	0.224[a] (0.033)	0.181[a] (0.030)	0.170[a] (0.029)	-0.051[a] (0.015)	-0.028[b] (0.013)	-0.029[b] (0.013)
Rural	0.102 (0.071)	0.083 (0.061)	0.086 (0.060)	-0.021 (0.088)	0.053 (0.084)	0.052 (0.087)	-0.097 (0.132)	-0.041 (0.104)	-0.025 (0.107)	0.105 (0.077)	0.080 (0.064)	0.083 (0.063)
Employed	0.260[a] (0.085)	0.328[a] (0.088)	0.313[a] (0.066)	0.637[a] (0.242)	0.331 (0.251)	0.500[b] (0.213)	0.719[b] (0.302)	0.291 (0.299)	0.451[c] (0.263)	0.212[b] (0.088)	0.311[a] (0.090)	0.283[a] (0.067)
Household head	0.136[b] (0.068)	0.173[a] (0.051)	0.178[a] (0.052)	0.145 (0.129)	0.199[c] (0.111)	0.213[c] (0.110)	0.114 (0.150)	0.124 (0.125)	0.149 (0.125)	0.120[c] (0.070)	0.154[a] (0.051)	0.159[a] (0.052)
Collateral	0.118[c] (0.065)	0.071 (0.066)	0.070 (0.065)	0.251 (0.182)	0.144 (0.135)	0.126 (0.133)	0.167 (0.245)	0.060 (0.163)	0.051 (0.160)	0.094 (0.065)	0.056 (0.064)	0.054 (0.064)
Corporate	-0.030 (0.124)	-0.015 (0.091)	-0.023 (0.093)	0.236 (0.197)	0.098 (0.166)	0.123 (0.151)	0.267 (0.209)	0.120 (0.186)	0.155 (0.165)	-0.076 (0.123)	-0.031 (0.090)	-0.046 (0.092)
Government	0.254[a] (0.092)	0.265[a] (0.094)	0.253[a] (0.086)	0.568[a] (0.140)	0.469[a] (0.143)	0.503[a] (0.135)	0.599[a] (0.170)	0.466[a] (0.171)	0.517[a] (0.162)	0.098 (0.100)	0.162 (0.102)	0.144 (0.094)

(continued)

Table A2.7 Determinants of Access to Formal and Informal Borrowing (continued)

	Borrowers vs. Nonborrowers			Formal Borrowers vs. Others			Formal Borrowers vs. Informal Borrowers			Informal Borrowers vs. Nonborrowers		
	Model I	Model II	Model III	Model I	Model II	Model III	Model I	Model II	Model III	Model I	Model II	Model III
Farmer	0.185[a] (0.060)	0.182[a] (0.064)	0.166[a] (0.053)	0.236 (0.145)	0.271[c] (0.157)	0.306[c] (0.157)	0.205 (0.161)	0.271 (0.173)	0.318[c] (0.176)	0.172[a] (0.058)	0.169[a] (0.067)	0.146[a] (0.055)
Laborer	−0.002 (0.095)	−0.013 (0.090)	0.012 (0.074)	−0.277 (0.181)	−0.058 (0.177)	−0.185 (0.167)	−0.373[c] (0.226)	−0.091 (0.224)	−0.226 (0.201)	0.014 (0.100)	−0.014 (0.097)	0.022 (0.077)
Formal sector		−0.034 (0.087)			0.222 (0.202)			0.265 (0.221)			−0.057 (0.088)	
Cell use			0.082[c] (0.047)			0.356[a] (0.112)			0.314[a] (0.118)			0.055 (0.044)
Cell access			0.269[a] (0.058)			0.302[b] (0.131)			0.160 (0.147)			0.261[a] (0.060)
Household income and house/latrine effects	Yes			Yes			Yes			Yes		
Personal income and house/latrine effects		Yes	Yes		Yes	Yes		Yes	Yes		Yes	Yes
Province effects	Yes	Yes	Yes	Yes	Yes	Yes	Yes	Yes	Yes	Yes	Yes	Yes
Number of observations	5,941	10,288	10,288	5,941	10,288	10,288	2,359	3,503	3,503	5,742	10,013	10,013
F(k, d)	13.41	34.76	36.51	329.19	255.4	268.4	92.45	127.47	132.34	12.19	34.81	40.37

Standard errors in parenthesis (a = Significant at 1% level; b = Significant at 5% level; c = Significant at 10% level).

Table A2.8 Determinants of Access to Formal and Informal Savings

	Savers vs. Nonsavers			Formal Savers vs. Others			Formal Savers vs. Informal Savers			Informal Savers vs. Nonsavers		
	Model I	Model II	Model III	Model I	Model II	Model III	Model I	Model II	Model III	Model I	Model II	Model III
Female	0.306[a]	0.244[a]	0.245[a]	−0.261[c]	−0.346[a]	−0.335[a]	−0.462[a]	−0.531[a]	−0.523[a]	0.383[a]	0.341[a]	0.340[a]
	(0.092)	(0.073)	(0.073)	(0.144)	(0.098)	(0.097)	(0.165)	(0.119)	(0.117)	(0.100)	(0.076)	(0.076)
Age	−0.003	−0.004[a]	−0.003[b]	0.020[a]	0.018[a]	0.019[a]	0.024[a]	0.022[a]	0.023[a]	−0.007[a]	−0.007[a]	−0.007[a]
	(0.002)	(0.001)	(0.001)	(0.003)	(0.003)	(0.002)	(0.003)	(0.003)	(0.003)	(0.002)	(0.001)	(0.001)
Education	0.045[b]	0.038[a]	0.031[b]	0.190[a]	0.166[a]	0.157[a]	0.195[a]	0.172[a]	0.165[a]	0.011	0.005	−0.001
	(0.019)	(0.013)	(0.013)	(0.020)	(0.019)	(0.019)	(0.019)	(0.018)	(0.019)	(0.018)	(0.012)	(0.012)
Rural	0.209[a]	0.260[a]	0.256[a]	−0.183[b]	−0.132[b]	−0.150[b]	−0.274[a]	−0.287[a]	−0.297[a]	0.249[a]	0.291[a]	0.287[a]
	(0.074)	(0.060)	(0.058)	(0.086)	(0.068)	(0.069)	(0.098)	(0.072)	(0.073)	(0.081)	(0.063)	(0.061)
Employed	0.220[a]	0.279[a]	0.354[a]	0.197[c]	0.048	0.159	0.098	−0.093	−0.001	0.239[a]	0.349[a]	0.403[a]
	(0.068)	(0.073)	(0.067)	(0.117)	(0.122)	(0.116)	(0.133)	(0.163)	(0.150)	(0.072)	(0.081)	(0.074)
Household head	0.114[b]	0.135[a]	0.142[a]	0.212[b]	0.220[a]	0.232[a]	0.181[c]	0.167[b]	0.179[b]	0.054	0.072	0.078
	(0.056)	(0.051)	(0.052)	(0.106)	(0.086)	(0.084)	(0.101)	(0.080)	(0.079)	(0.052)	(0.048)	(0.048)
Collateral	0.125	0.270[a]	0.273[a]	−0.079	0.063	0.062	−0.077	−0.021	−0.028	0.137	0.266[a]	0.270[a]
	(0.092)	(0.068)	(0.068)	(0.085)	(0.107)	(0.109)	(0.101)	(0.110)	(0.113)	(0.096)	(0.067)	(0.066)
Corporate	−0.001	−0.015	0.022	0.125	0.149	0.171	0.161	0.193	0.197	0.014	−0.029	0.000
	(0.085)	(0.092)	(0.076)	(0.184)	(0.176)	(0.177)	(0.220)	(0.224)	(0.226)	(0.107)	(0.121)	(0.106)
Government	0.350[a]	0.357[a]	0.396[a]	0.769[a]	0.826[a]	0.864[a]	0.799[a]	0.887[a]	0.918[a]	−0.001	−0.023	0.013
	(0.106)	(0.115)	(0.098)	(0.160)	(0.142)	(0.129)	(0.180)	(0.167)	(0.156)	(0.137)	(0.135)	(0.122)

(continued)

Table A2.8 Determinants of Access to Formal and Informal Savings (continued)

	Savers vs. Nonsavers			Formal Savers vs. Others			Formal Savers vs. Informal Savers			Informal Savers vs. Nonsavers		
	Model I	Model II	Model III	Model I	Model II	Model III	Model I	Model II	Model III	Model I	Model II	Model III
Farmer	0.205[b]	0.243[a]	0.282[a]	−0.121	−0.099	−0.061	−0.218	−0.188[c]	−0.156	0.272[a]	0.312[a]	0.343[a]
	(0.101)	(0.079)	(0.072)	(0.131)	(0.105)	(0.098)	(0.140)	(0.114)	(0.108)	(0.104)	(0.081)	(0.074)
Laborer	−0.220[b]	−0.172[c]	−0.223[a]	−0.267	−0.006	−0.094	−0.229	0.088	0.001	−0.181[c]	−0.180[c]	−0.212[a]
	(0.099)	(0.095)	(0.079)	(0.183)	(0.181)	(0.156)	(0.205)	(0.206)	(0.188)	(0.100)	(0.096)	(0.082)
Formal sector		0.125			0.168			0.144			0.091	
		(0.086)			(0.130)			(0.151)			(0.089)	
Cell use			0.222[a]			0.317[a]			0.238[a]			0.197[a]
			(0.058)			(0.060)			(0.071)			(0.056)
Cell access			0.177[b]			0.045			−0.019			0.186[b]
			(0.075)			(0.107)			(0.119)			(0.077)
Household income and house/latrine effects	Yes			Yes			Yes			Yes		
Personal income and house/latrine effects		Yes	Yes		Yes	Yes		Yes	Yes		Yes	Yes
Province effects	Yes	Yes	Yes	Yes	Yes	Yes	Yes	Yes	Yes	Yes	Yes	Yes
Number of observations	5,941	10,288	10,288	5,941	10,288	10,288	3,767	5,643	5,643	5,278	9,332	9,332
F(k, d)	23.09	27.21	25.41	97.85	162.12	160.42	67.82	85.49	83.16	11.65	25.46	27

Standard errors in parenthesis (a = Significant at 1% level; b = Significant at 5% level; c = Significant at 10% level).

Table A2.9 Determinants of Access to Specific Formal and Informal Financial Products

	Credit/Debit Card Users vs. Nonusers		Check Users vs. Nonusers		Savings Account Users vs. Nonusers		Current Account Users vs. Nonusers		Islamic Clients vs. Others		Post Office Clients vs. Others		Insurance Users vs. Nonusers		Committee Users vs. Nonusers	
	Model I	Model II	Model I	Model II	Model I	Model II	Model I	Model II	Model I	Model II	Model I	Model II	Model I	Model II	Model I	Model II
Female	−.269 (.242)	−.336[b] (.146)	−.272 (.169)	−.336[a] (.109)	−.282[c] (.147)	−.359[a] (.100)	−.126 (.121)	−.154 (.097)		−1.778[a] (.376)	.054 (.156)	.135 (.185)	−.128 (.180)	−.148 (.150)	.320[a] (.111)	.235[a] (.089)
Age	.000 (.006)	.004 (.006)	.014[a] (.003)	.013[a] (.003)	.021[a] (.003)	.018[a] (.003)	.010[a] (.003)	.010[a] (.003)	−.039[a] (.008)	−.020[a] (.007)	.005 (.004)	.003 (.003)	.010[b] (.004)	.007[b] (.003)	−.003 (.003)	−.004[b] (.002)
Education	.218[a] (.055)	.189[a] (.052)	.228[a] (.026)	.185[a] (.022)	.193[a] (.020)	.170[a] (.019)	.197[a] (.024)	.179[a] (.024)	−.008 (.048)	.036 (.075)	.117[a] (.036)	.102[a] (.031)	.111[a] (.024)	.098[a] (.024)	.049[a] (.019)	.021 (.018)
Rural	−.412[a] (.145)	−.428[a] (.125)	.047 (.119)	.035 (.095)	−.194[b] (.087)	−.146[b] (.069)	−.110 (.103)	−.040 (.086)	−1.403[a] (.392)	−1.468[a] (.460)	.209[b] (.095)	.170[b] (.074)	.275[a] (.084)	.253[a] (.094)	−.323[a] (.075)	−.299[a] (.058)
Employed	.505[a] (.177)	.535[b] (.255)	.432[a] (.124)	.412[a] (.140)	.190 (.119)	.045 (.125)	.511[a] (.131)	.449[a] (.150)		−1.661[a] (.449)	.104 (.185)	.134 (.207)	.603[a] (.154)	.134 (.126)	.351[a] (.105)	.396[a] (.109)
Household head	.139 (.180)	−.090 (.145)	.237[a] (.087)	.146[b] (.062)	.209[c] (.108)	.224[a] (.088)	.171 (.111)	.203[b] (.082)	1.356[a] (.318)	.889[a] (.257)	.229[b] (.115)	.312[b] (.145)	.170 (.206)	.150 (.173)	.068 (.087)	.024 (.075)
Collateral	−.192 (.169)	−.071 (.175)	.041 (.147)	.203[b] (.104)	−.086 (.085)	.054 (.107)	.136 (.172)	.101 (.101)	−.803[a] (.143)	−.508[a] (.118)	−.102 (.169)	.002 (.148)	−.231 (.160)	−.240[b] (.117)	−.042 (.085)	.029 (.064)
Corporate	−.011 (.199)	.448[a] (.102)	.167 (.179)	.130 (.171)	.132 (.187)	.153 (.179)	.091 (.094)	.226[c] (.117)	−2.976[a] (.719)	−2.527[a] (.655)	.055 (.225)	.164 (.220)	−.044 (.170)	−.183 (.176)	.140 (.101)	.185[b] (.081)

(continued)

Table A2.9 Determinants of Access to Specific Formal and Informal Financial Products (continued)

	Credit/Debit Card Users vs. Nonusers		Check Users vs. Nonusers		Savings Account Users vs. Nonusers		Current Account Users vs. Nonusers		Islamic Clients vs. Others		Post Office Clients vs. Others		Insurance Users vs. Nonusers		Committee Users vs. Nonusers	
	Model I	Model II	Model I	Model II	Model I	Model II	Model I	Model II	Model I	Model II	Model I	Model II	Model I	Model II	Model I	Model II
Government	.208 (.187)	.339ᵃ (.132)	1.111ᵃ (.205)	.977ᵃ (.183)	.767ᵃ (.162)	.825ᵃ (.144)	.765ᵃ (.201)	.742ᵃ (.182)	−.854 (.601)	−.903 (.563)	.292ᶜ (.175)	.210 (.170)	.376ᵇ (.148)	.375ᵃ (.134)	.169 (.144)	.146 (.118)
Farmer	−.217 (.177)	−.128 (.141)	−.202 (.153)	−.209 (.146)	−.102 (.133)	−.079 (.108)	.108 (.112)	−.073 (.096)	−.204 (.605)	−.160 (.405)	−.036 (.122)	−.094 (.139)	−.118 (.208)	−.224 (.194)	−.353ᵃ (.092)	−.344ᵃ (.073)
Laborer	.036 (.128)	.251 (.248)	−.177 (.208)	.044 (.170)	−.281 (.187)	.000 (.187)	−.135 (.110)	.083 (.141)			−.250 (.265)	−.199 (.244)	−.005 (.173)	.259 (.178)	−.270ᶜ (.143)	−.253ᵇ (.120)
Formal sector	−.037 (.176)		.167 (.127)		.172 (.134)		.150 (.116)			1.420ᵇ (.564)		.208ᶜ (.125)		.424ᵃ (.112)		−.013 (.081)
Household income and house/latrine effects	Yes		Yes		Yes		Yes		Yes		Yes		Yes		Yes	
Personal income and house/latrine effects		Yes		Yes		Yes		Yes		Yes		Yes		Yes		Yes
Province effects	Yes	Yes	Yes	Yes	Yes	Yes	Yes	Yes	Yes	Yes	Yes	Yes	Yes	Yes	Yes	Yes
Number of observations	5,941	10,288	5,941	10,288	5,941	10,288	5,941	10,288	5,943	10,288	5,941	10,288	5,941	10,288	5941	10288
F(k, d)	106.74	623.49	72.65	78.46	100.00	16.88	169.32	336.63	47.7	351.18	162.06	475.2	706.77	428.54	102.65	173.04

Standard errors in parenthesis (a = Significant at 1% level; b = Significant at 5% level; c = Significant at 10% level).

Table A2.10 Religious Considerations as a Determinant of Access to Finance, for a Range of Products

	Borrowers vs. Nonborrowers	Formal Borrowers vs. Others	Formal Borrowers vs. Informal Borrowers	Informal Borrowers vs. Nonborrowers	Credit/Debit Card Users vs. Nonusers	Check Users vs. Nonusers	Savings Account Users vs. Nonusers	Current Account Users vs. Nonusers	Islamic Clients vs. Others	Post Office Clients vs. Others	Insurance Users vs. Nonusers	Committee Users vs. Nonusers
Female	−0.075 (0.114)	0.342[c] (0.196)	0.442[c] (0.268)	−0.128 (0.118)	−0.225 (0.233)	−0.188 (0.152)	−0.213 (0.134)	−0.145 (0.124)		0.474[b] (0.232)	0.079 (0.179)	0.208[c] (0.126)
Age	0.001 (0.002)	0.009[b] (0.004)	0.011[b] (0.004)	0.000 (0.002)	−0.001 (0.008)	0.014[a] (0.004)	0.018[a] (0.004)	0.009[b] (0.004)	−0.027[a] (0.007)	0.006[c] (0.003)	0.016[c] (0.005)	−0.006[c] (0.003)
Education	0.007 (0.020)	0.123[a] (0.036)	0.143[a] (0.034)	−0.012 (0.021)	0.215[a] (0.059)	0.140[a] (0.028)	0.159[a] (0.033)	0.161[a] (0.027)	0.094 (0.073)	0.077[b] (0.037)	0.179[a] (0.041)	−0.028 (0.024)
Rural	0.062 (0.087)	0.086 (0.130)	−0.033 (0.138)	0.046 (0.090)	−0.343[b] (0.168)	0.138 (0.105)	−0.092 (0.087)	0.023 (0.116)	−1.520[a] (0.463)	0.294[b] (0.132)	0.246 (0.153)	−0.079 (0.084)
Employed	0.327[a] (0.118)	0.587[b] (0.247)	0.547[c] (0.324)	0.279[b] (0.120)	0.415 (0.262)	0.477[a] (0.150)	0.083 (0.162)	0.555[a] (0.144)	−0.216 (0.220)	0.575[b] (0.200)	0.705[a] (0.160)	0.351[b] (0.152)
Household head	0.281[a] (0.073)	0.315[b] (0.152)	0.203 (0.157)	0.239[a] (0.073)	0.060 (0.091)	0.131 (0.094)	0.253[b] (0.121)	0.187[b] (0.091)	1.475[a] (0.347)	0.328[c] (0.183)	0.090 (0.192)	−0.002 (0.111)
Collateral	0.057 (0.111)	0.154 (0.136)	0.061 (0.158)	0.043 (0.112)	0.015 (0.163)	0.243 (0.175)	0.236 (0.184)	0.190 (0.135)	−0.695[a] (0.172)	0.197 (0.231)	−0.478[b] (0.202)	−0.032 (0.112)
Corporate	0.072 (0.128)	0.012 (0.212)	−0.003 (0.223)	0.077 (0.123)	0.650[a] (0.133)	0.215 (0.203)	0.198 (0.205)	0.278[b] (0.113)	−2.656[a] (0.713)	0.353 (0.251)	−0.079 (0.193)	0.231 (0.143)

(continued)

Table A2.10 Religious Considerations as a Determinant of Access to Finance, for a Range of Products (continued)

	Borrowers vs. Nonborrowers	Formal Borrowers vs. Others	Formal Borrowers vs. Informal Borrowers	Informal Borrowers vs. Nonborrowers	Credit/Debit Card Users vs. Nonusers	Check Users vs. Nonusers	Savings Account Users vs. Nonusers	Current Account Users vs. Nonusers	Islamic Clients vs. Others	Post Office Clients vs. Others	Insurance Users vs. Nonusers	Committee Users vs. Nonusers
Government	0.236[c]	0.494[a]	0.474[a]	0.116	0.124	0.873[a]	0.811[a]	0.587[a]	-1.157	0.072	0.340[b]	0.207
	(0.132)	(0.138)	(0.175)	(0.153)	(0.140)	(0.205)	(0.184)	(0.202)	(0.759)	(0.217)	(0.163)	(0.189)
Farmer	0.270[a]	0.420[b]	0.398[b]	0.240[b]	-0.510[a]	-0.190	0.014	-0.139	0.444	-0.497[a]	-0.261	-0.463[a]
	(0.096)	(0.186)	(0.195)	(0.097)	(0.191)	(0.170)	(0.144)	(0.097)	(0.399)	(0.181)	(0.203)	(0.122)
Laborer	0.039	-0.367	-0.420[c]	0.079	0.007	-0.165	-0.089	-0.346[b]		-0.191	0.206	-0.333[b]
	(0.129)	(0.241)	(0.256)	(0.124)	(0.236)	(0.222)	(0.198)	(0.156)		(0.335)	(0.232)	(0.134)
Anti-Islamic	-0.073	-0.185	-0.130	-0.051	0.007	0.129	0.050	0.055	-0.151	0.071	-0.362[a]	0.092
	(0.070)	(0.120)	(0.139)	(0.073)	(0.172)	(0.099)	(0.100)	(0.114)	(0.183)	(0.127)	(0.141)	(0.077)
Personal income and house/latrine effects	Yes	Yes	Yes	Yes	Yes	Yes	Yes	Yes	Yes	Yes	Yes	Yes
Province effects	Yes	Yes	Yes	Yes	Yes	Yes	Yes	Yes	Yes	Yes	Yes	Yes
Number of observations	4,199	4,199	1,937	3,989	4,199	4,199	4,199	4,199	4,199	4,199	4,199	4,199
F(k, d)	9.13	160.02	50.64	9.07	419.86	58.72	119.96	98.84	138.33	166.32	441.69	81.04

Standard errors in parenthesis (a = Significant at 1% level; b = Significant at 5% level; c = Significant at 10% level).

Table A2.11 Determinants of Access to Finance of the Self-Employed

	Self-employed in Formal Sector vs. Others		Self-employed in Informal Sector vs. Others	
	Model I	Model II	Model I	Model II
Male	1.675[a]	1.843[a]	1.276[a]	1.382[a]
	(0.113)	(0.086)	(0.136)	(0.120)
Age	0.002	0.001	−0.005[c]	−0.006[b]
	(0.002)	(0.002)	(0.003)	(0.003)
Education	−0.039[b]	−0.067[a]	−0.037	−0.039[b]
	(0.017)	(0.017)	(0.026)	(0.020)
Household head	0.077	0.125[c]	0.212[b]	0.197[b]
	(0.077)	(0.069)	(0.088)	(0.089)
Cell use	0.177[a]	0.156[a]	−0.145[b]	−0.142[a]
	(0.053)	(0.047)	(0.065)	(0.048)
Cell access	0.006	0.035	0.057	0.029
	(0.101)	(0.083)	(0.109)	(0.100)
Urban	−0.245	−0.337[a]	0.136	0.117
	(0.161)	(0.115)	(0.178)	(0.140)
Urban * male	−0.434[b]	−0.409[a]	0.093	0.099
	(0.183)	(0.124)	(0.200)	(0.148)
Household income and house/latrine effects	Yes		Yes	
Personal income and house/latrine effects		Yes		Yes
Province effects	Yes	Yes	Yes	Yes
Number of observations	5,943	10,297	5,943	10,297
F(k, d)	70.35	144.23	101.27	241.26

Standard errors in parenthesis (a = Significant at 1% level; b = Significant at 5% level; c = Significant at 10% level).

Table A2.12 Reasons for Saving

	Formal Savers vs. Others		Informal Savers vs. Nonsavers	
	Model I	Model II	Model I	Model II
Female	−0.408[b]	−0.486[a]	1.032[a]	0.809[a]
	(0.167)	(0.119)	(0.224)	(0.159)
Age	0.025[a]	0.022[a]	−0.025[a]	−0.023[a]
	(0.003)	(0.003)	(0.007)	(0.006)
Education	0.173[a]	0.157[a]	−0.089[b]	−0.129[a]
	(0.016)	(0.018)	(0.045)	(0.033)
Rural	−0.283[a]	−0.289[a]	0.331[a]	0.302[a]
	(0.087)	(0.070)	(0.093)	(0.112)
Employed	−0.078	−0.088	−0.293	−0.165
	(0.176)	(0.162)	(0.262)	(0.203)
Household head	0.214[c]	0.174[b]	0.207	0.024
	(0.118)	(0.083)	(0.175)	(0.179)
Collateral	−0.168[c]	−0.068	−0.294	−0.076
	(0.095)	(0.111)	(0.235)	(0.152)
Corporate	0.148	0.201	0.354	0.219
	(0.181)	(0.208)	(0.354)	(0.297)
Government	0.738[a]	0.807[a]	−0.524[c]	−0.655[a]
	(0.145)	(0.139)	(0.285)	(0.245)
Farmer	−0.262[c]	−0.170	0.325	0.465[b]
	(0.138)	(0.112)	(0.214)	(0.184)
Laborer	−0.089	0.090	0.123	0.316
	(0.271)	(0.207)	(0.397)	(0.344)
Formal sector	0.115	0.082	−0.201	−0.059
	(0.220)	(0.158)	(0.181)	(0.233)
Cell use	0.346[a]	0.231[a]	−0.622[a]	0.430[a]
	(0.074)	(0.063)	(0.141)	(0.110)
Food and household needs	−0.037	−0.046	0.458[a]	0.418[a]
	(0.058)	(0.065)	(0.146)	(0.109)
Medical needs	0.060	0.047	0.386[b]	0.253[c]
	(0.085)	(0.072)	(0.172)	(0.134)
Education needs	−0.035	0.087	0.414	0.345[c]
	(0.085)	(0.058)	(0.279)	(0.187)
Investment needs	0.251[b]	0.169[c]	0.720[a]	0.545[b]
	(0.110)	(0.099)	(0.135)	(0.258)
Provision for accident and death	−0.134[b]	0.059	0.422[b]	0.407[a]
	(0.065)	(0.068)	(0.177)	(0.150)
Social and religious needs	0.166[c]	0.073	0.810[a]	0.678[a]
	(0.087)	(0.068)	(0.236)	(0.158)
Old age needs	0.090	0.113	1.309[a]	0.620[b]
	(0.109)	(0.100)	(0.352)	(0.259)

(continued)

Table A2.12 Reasons for Saving (continued)

	Formal Savers vs. Others		Informal Savers vs. Nonsavers	
	Model I	Model II	Model I	Model II
Household income and house/latrine effects	Yes		Yes	
Personal income and house/latrine effects		Yes		Yes
Province effects	Yes	Yes	Yes	Yes
Number of observations	3,854	5,773	3,191	4,817
F(k, d)	74.28	105.23	284.55	244.46

Standard errors in parenthesis (a = Significant at 1% level; b = Significant at 5% level; c = Significant at 10% level).

Table A2.13 Reasons for Borrowing

	Formal Borrowers vs. Others		Informal Borrowers vs. Nonborrowers	
	Model I	Model II	Model I	Model II
Female	0.586[a]	0.313	1.092[a]	1.695[a]
	(0.211)	(0.208)	(0.342)	(0.252)
Age	0.009[c]	0.010[a]	0.039[a]	0.023[a]
	(0.005)	(0.004)	(0.010)	(0.006)
Education	0.113[a]	0.094[a]	−0.202[b]	−0.246[b]
	(0.024)	(0.023)	(0.094)	(0.121)
Rural	0.016	0.071	1.869[a]	1.027[a]
	(0.139)	(0.132)	(0.615)	(0.309)
Employed	0.225	0.071	0.791[a]	0.919[a]
	(0.327)	(0.349)	(0.306)	(0.229)
Household head	0.215	0.188	−0.863[a]	−0.264[c]
	(0.179)	(0.152)	(0.217)	(0.142)
Collateral	0.145	0.096	0.758[a]	0.547[a]
	(0.244)	(0.134)	(0.231)	(0.159)
Corporate	0.120	0.099	0.656	−0.545[c]
	(0.233)	(0.213)	(0.615)	(0.329)
Government	0.834[a]	0.754[a]	0.352	0.573
	(0.204)	(0.219)	(0.605)	(0.670)
Farmer	−0.087	0.130	−0.060	−0.323
	(0.163)	(0.176)	(0.268)	(0.252)
Laborer	−0.242	−0.068	−0.395[a]	−0.185
	(0.242)	(0.242)	(0.155)	(0.231)
Formal sector	0.504[b]	0.339	−0.078	0.209
	(0.222)	(0.287)	(0.427)	(0.365)

(continued)

Table A2.13 Reasons for Borrowing (continued)

	Formal Borrowers vs. Others		Informal Borrowers vs. Nonborrowers	
	Model I	Model II	Model I	Model II
Cell use	0.280[b]	0.234[b]	−0.184[a]	−0.201
	(0.113)	(0.103)	(0.187)	(0.188)
Food and household needs	−0.848[a]	−0.772[a]	1.092[a]	1.009[a]
	(0.148)	(0.110)	(0.198)	(0.270)
Medical, accident, funeral needs	−0.433[c]	−0.595[a]	0.318	0.397
	(0.235)	(0.226)	(0.328)	(0.466)
Agricultural investment needs	0.451[a]	0.406[a]		
	(0.140)	(0.134)		
Nonfarming investment needs	0.214	0.263[c]	0.531	0.466
	(0.207)	(0.152)	(0.438)	(0.412)
Social and religious needs	−0.174	−0.039	0.855	1.242
	(0.171)	(0.140)	(0.609)	(0.793)
Home investment and improvement	0.294	0.390[c]		
	(0.257)	(0.235)		
Household income and house/latrine effects	Yes		Yes	
Personal income and house/latrine effects		Yes		Yes
Province effects	Yes	Yes	Yes	Yes
Number of observations	2,357	3,506	2,183	3,267
F(k, d)	54.69	72.65	212.46	818.00

Standard errors in parenthesis (a = Significant at 1% level; b = Significant at 5% level; c = Significant at 10% level).

Access to Finance for the Underserved

Microfinance services in Pakistan are offered both formally and informally. Informal markets are generally characterized by high interest rates, widespread rationing, segmentation, and a sizeable gap between lending and deposit rates. Still, the informal sector can be competitive for clients with alternative options, and it has good lessons to offer to its formal counterpart. Formal markets are growing fast (at 40 percent), but from a negligible base. Microfinance banks (MFBs) accounted for 31 percent of the microfinance lending portfolio and 85 percent of its growth. Profitability and performance in the microfinance sector are low but improving. A key challenge is the sustainability of microfinance institutions (MFIs), which still rely considerably on noncommercial funding (commercial liabilities are barely 21 percent of total lending portfolio). In the formal sector, 1.7 million microfinance clients are reported, in a population of more than 160 million. The total lending portfolio of all MFIs in Pakistan stood at $340 million in 2007 (0.2 percent of the financial system assets). There is still considerable room for growth of microfinance in Pakistan—the estimated potential market size is at least 10–20 million active borrowers, and some estimates place the number as high as 35 million. Women are a poorly explored clientele with tremendous potential, as noted in chapter 2. While microfinance policy and services have focused on credit, there is a considerable potential for other products, such as insurance, payments, and, above all, savings.

There are several avenues that can deliver expanded outreach and address the demand gap for microfinance: encouraging strong sustainable MFIs, improving literacy and public awareness, and employing technology (smart cards, automated teller machines (ATMs), point of sale (POS) devices, branchless banking, and mobile telephone networks). Two approaches have been used internationally to address high transaction costs due to low population density, small average loans, and low household savings— the Grameen and BRAC low-tech, low-cost, high-volume models of microfinance, and the Philippines/Kenya high-tech, low-cost, high volume approach. Cell phones, used by more than half of the population, hold much promise to increase access. Informal services could be co-opted into the formal financial system, learning for their competitive aspects. Product diversification toward more savings products is a promising strategy as well, as is focusing on women clients and tailoring products to their specific needs. In 2000, microfinance was elevated to a core aspect of the government's poverty reduction program. In spite of State Bank of Pakistan (SBP) encouragement, commercial banks have shown little desire to service microfinance clients. The SBP strategy of offering a bank license to stronger MFIs has proven more successful, though the hoped-for deposit mobilization has not materialized with the speed expected, and MFB outreach remains small.

The Microfinance Sector

The microfinance sector has emerged over the past 20 years (box 3.1), and has focused hopes for expanded service provision to underserved population. While there is a long way still to go to match the outreach of informal services, or even what is being

---

Box 3.1   The Story of Microfinance in Pakistan

Development of the microfinance sector in Pakistan was initiated by not-for-profit development organizations in the early 1980s. The most influential of these NGO experiences began in 1982 when the Aga Khan Rural Support Program was established and subsequently spawned the rural support program (RSP) movement. The Aga Khan Rural Support Program was also the first NGO to transform its microfinance program into a MFB. Although two other RSPs were formed in 1989 and 1992 and other players also began to enter the market in the 1990s, the microfinance movement remained small and not very visible. Network Leasing Company was established as a listed leasing company in 1994 and with some donor support it began a microleasing program. The first commercial bank to begin a separate microfinance division, in 1995, was the Bank of Khyber, owned by a provincial government. At about the same time, the government established the First Women's Bank. In addition to supporting the needs of women entrepreneurs, the bank tried to establish a microfinance program, although it has not been particularly successful. More NGOs began to offer microcredit services during the 1990s, the most significant being the Kashf Foundation, which was the first NGO established exclusively to provide microfinance services and the first to be managed by women and have only women clients.

A major shift began in the late 1990s with the establishment the PPAF, a wholesale funding and capacity-building apex that became the main source of funding for NGOs engaged in microfinance. In 2000, the government established Khushhali Bank, a MFB set up through a special ordinance. This was followed in late 2001 by the MFI Ordinance that allowed for the creation of MFBs under SBP supervision. First Microfinance Bank was set up by the Aga Khan Development Network in early 2002, and over the next few years, four more MFBs began operations. In 2008 the two largest NGO microfinance organizations managed by NRSP and Kashf Foundation applied for licenses to establish MFBs. These banks are expanding rapidly and now account for almost half of the outreach of the microfinance sector.

Table 3.1 Microfinance Penetration across Asia

Country	Microfinance Penetration	Coverage of Poor Families
Bangladesh	17%	35%
Sri Lanka	7%	29%
India	—	25%[1]
Vietnam	7%	25%
Cambodia	4%	12%
Indonesia	3%	11%
Nepal	3%	8%
Philippines	2%	6%
Pakistan	**1%**	**2%**

Source: World Bank (forthcoming).[2]

provided by the other formal financial service providers, the general view is that the microfinance sector has the potential to eventually reach most poor people with a range of financial services through sustainable institutions. In Pakistan, 1.7 million microfinance clients are reported, as against a population of more than 160 million. Microfinance penetration in the South Asia region is higher, at 35 percent in Bangladesh, 25 percent in India, and 29 percent in Sri Lanka (see table 3.1). The total lending portfolio of all MFIs stood at $340 million in 2007 (0.2 percent of the financial system assets).

Chapter 3 looks at (1) microfinance providers, (2) products, (3) clients and growth trends, (4) sources of funding, (5) MFI performance, (6) regulatory issues, (7) the informal financial sector, and (8) the role of technology and the regulatory framework for further growth of the sector.

Providers of Financial Services

The microfinance sector is made up of several types of key players. **Microfinance banks** are licensed and regulated by SBP under the MFI Ordinance 2001. Licenses can be granted for district, regional, provincial, and national-level banks. Loan sizes are currently restricted to a maximum of Rs 150,000, savings can be mobilized from any individual or organization, and in-country remittance services can be provided. By early 2008 there were eight MFBs (with National Rural Support Program (NRSP) Bank and KASHF most recently) and another two to four parties planning to establish a bank including BRAC (table 3.2).

Specialized nongovernmental organizations (NGO) MFIs provide only microfinance services. Like all NGOs, they can provide loans but cannot mobilize deposits. By early 2008, there were five such organizations.

RSPs are a particular type of not-for-profit rural development organization that together have a large presence throughout the country. Of these, five also provide microfinance services.

Table 3.2 Market Players

Largest Providers of Microcredit (Active Borrowers)				MFPs with Largest Geographic Spread		
	MFP	Active Borrowers (30-Sep)	Market Share (% of Active Borrowers)		MFP	Geographic Spread (No. of Districts)
1	NRSP	604,776	32.3	1	KB	89
2	KB	377,486	20.2	2	NRSP	51
3	Kashf	322,669	17.2	3	FMFBL	45
4	FMFBL	185,202	9.9	4	Kashf	24
5	PRSP	76,938	4.1	5	PRSP	20

Source: Microwatch, Issue 9 Quarter 3, 2008.

Other NGO MFIs, possibly 50 or more, provide some microcredit services as one part of their multidimensional development programs. Twelve of these organizations, representing almost 100 percent of the total outreach for this type of organization, are included in the analysis provided in the next section.

There are some **commercial financial institutions with separate microfinance departments**. Two of these, Bank of Khyber and Orix Leasing Company, are included in the analysis below. But the relative contribution of these institutions has been declining, and they now represent a very small part of the microfinance sector.

Another potentially major player in access to finance for the underserved is the **Pakistan Post Office**. It has a network of 13,419 branches throughout the country and is a significant provider of financial services, including savings, insurance, and remittances, through 7,276 bank branches. The Pakistan Post Savings Bank (PPSB) serves as an agent of the Ministry of Finance for a range of financial services including savings mobilization, life insurance, postal giro accounts, and money transfers. It is present throughout the country and is the only banking service available in some remote areas. Pakistan Post has been able to upgrade the technology for its operations with help from the Islamic Development Bank. Internet services were launched in the late 1990s and are widely available at post offices, attracting the interest of small entrepreneurs and providing limited financial services. The PPSB offers several savings schemes, and in 2006 it had 3.6 million savings account holders. In addition, Pakistan Post acts as an agent to sell government-backed savings instruments. The Postal Life Insurance offers 10 insurance options and had 252,810 active policies in 2004. Pakistan Post provides several options for national and international remittances in addition to hosting Western Union in some of its branches, and acting as an agent to Western Union for international remittances.

Government policy has been to encourage financial institutions to use the extensive network of post office branches to extend outreach to more people. In recent years two MFBs, Khushhali Bank and First Microfinance Bank, have linked up with the Pakistan Post to offer services at their branch offices. To date, though, the volume of this business has remained small, mainly due to poor management, inability to

---

Box 3.2   **Lessons from Successful Postal Financial Systems**

Brazil presents one of the most interesting cases in postal financial systems. With no histori-cal legacy in postal financial services, *Correios* (Brazil's Post Office) benefited from a strong gov-ernment policy agenda that was seeking to improve access to finance and that used direct and indirect incentives to attract new operators. The government modified the regulatory framework to allow *Correios* to become a "correspondent" of a bank. *Correios* selected, through a transparent bidding process, a strategic partner (*Bradesco,* the most important retail bank in Brazil) and launched Banco Postal in 2002. Its range of services spans from traditional giro and savings accounts to pay-ments and remittances, and, since 2003, microfinance. Building effective and strong partnerships between state-owned postal operators and private financial institutions has proven to be a complex and cumbersome process. In the case of Brazil, it took seven years between the first feasibility study and the actual launch of postal financial services. Today, Banco Postal is a leading player in retail banking in Brazil. Its success arises from a clear strategic vision, a new regulatory framework to reflect the government policy, a balanced contract with the strategic partner, and substantial investments in the network (in particular in information systems) to offer quality services.

China Post offers another success story from which Pakistan can draw valuable lessons. China Post has operated the Postal Savings Bureau since April 1984, a key source of revenue for the postal service. Postal savings are provided at nearly 40,000 post offices—approximately the same size as China's entire bank branch network (37,000 branches). Postal savings have grown rapidly since their operational launch in 1986 and in 2002 accounted for 189 million accounts and more than $65 billion in deposits, representing a market share of 8 percent and the fifth-largest deposit taker in China. The Postal Savings Bureau operates an ATM network and debit card linked accounts ("green cards"). It also provides 90 percent of private remittances in China (postal money orders). The volume of transfer operations has featured fast growth amounting to 210 million transactions in 2002, approximately 15 percent of the total volume of cashless payments transactions in China.

A few lessons can be taken from international experience:

- Sustained political support and policy reform drive are key success factor (Brazil, Romania); when this is lacking, reform is difficult to deliver (Uganda).

- Historical institutional usage of postal savings to fund public sector investment programs can constitute a major roadblock to significant reform aiming at commercializing the Postbank (Vietnam, Sri Lanka).

- Assessing market gaps between supply and demand can be a powerful analytical tool to convince policy makers of the potential role that post offices can play in improving access to finance (Brazil).

- Not splitting postal and financial services slows down the potential performance of the postal financial services (Namibia, Kazakhstan).

- Private sector participation, through commercial partnership (Brazil), capacity-building invest-ments, or equity participation (Romania) can accelerate the reform implementation.

(continued)

Box 3.2   continued

- Including postal operators in payment reforms and encouraging investment in payment cards and systems (Tanzania, Tunisia, South Africa) exploits best the comparative advantages of the postal system network.

- Linking microfinance and postal networks is crucial for a considerable expansion of financial access and outreach. Different schemes can be envisaged: the postal retail network distributes on behalf of a local MFI through a service-level agreement, or the post office acts as a wholesaler to MFIs.

Source: World Bank (2006d).

track funds transparently, limited capacity to deal with complex services, as well as little initiative and vision in broadening the product range in cooperation with private financial outfits. Box 3.2 presents successful experiences from Brazil and China and lessons learned from international case studies on improving the efficiency and viability of postal financial systems.

There is a diverse group of other players in the Pakistan microfinance market, including **remittance firms**, which are the focus of chapter 5.[3] While **commercial and Islamic banks** do not generally focus on serving underserved populations, the SBP does require them to provide some services along these lines, including low-value savings accounts and agriculture credit. Four **leasing companies** have provided microleasing services in the past decade. The volume of services has always remained small but at least one leasing company still has an active program managed under a separate department. Over the past 10 years, there has been a growing interest in providing microinsurance services. Four commercial **insurance companies**, one of which is state owned, provide microinsurance services and the number of clients served is growing. Most of these services are provided in collaboration with microfinance institutions.

Prominent amongst the **financial institutions owned by federal and provincial governments** and serving lower-income clients are First Women's Bank, Bank of Khyber, Bank of Punjab, SME Bank, and the Zarai Taraqiati Bank Ltd. (formerly the agriculture bank). The Central Directorate of National Savings (CNDS, under the Ministry of Finance) borrows from seven National Savings Schemes (NSS). In 2006 the CNDS had more than 4 million savings accounts. It is estimated that more than two-thirds of all small-value savings accounts are held by these institutions, and the percentage might be as high as 80 percent (Duflos, Latortue, Mommartz, Perrett, and Staschen 2007). At the same time, these institutions have received large amounts of government and donor subsidies over the years, and most are still not particularly well managed.

Table 3.3 Distribution of Microclients

	Microcredit		Micro Savings		Micro Insurance	
	Active Borrowers	Value (PKR Millions)	Active Savers	Value (PKR Millions)	Policy Holders	Sum Insured (PKR Millions)
2008-Q2	1,754,118	19,648	1,732,950	4,692	1,576,381	15,183
2008-Q3	1,871,508	21,427	1,857,737	4,961	2,300,289	37,824
Increase (Net)	117,390	1,779	124,787	269	723,908	22,642
Increase (%)	7	9	7	6	46	149

Source: Microwatch, Issue 9 Quarter 3, 2008.

Products

There is little variety in the available choice of financial products for underserved populations (table 3.3), though demand for all types of services is not lacking.

Microfinance policies and activity of banks and other financial institutions have emphasized credit services, though demand for savings instruments is more robust. The vast majority (more than 90 percent) of loans in Pakistan follow the group lending model (figure 3.1). Individual loans, usually larger and often tied to an identified microenterprise, are mostly allotted to men, at loan maturities varying from 3 to 18 months. Increasingly, MFIs are diversifying their credit product offerings, with housing improvement loans and microleases on a hire-purchase basis. Burki and Shah (2007) present a detailed description of common credit products in Pakistan.[4] Much more can be done to expand microsavings, judging from existing demand.[5] Product customization to diverse client needs is much needed, especially for female clients, where a considerable market potential for savings exists. Offering

Figure 3.1 Number of Borrowers and Loan Portfolio by Lending Methodology

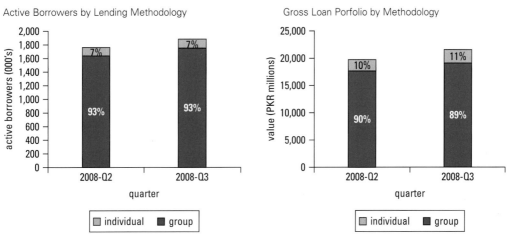

Source: Microwatch, Issue 9 Quarter 3, 2008.

savings products can also lower the cost of funds for MFBs. Other microproducts, such as insurance and payments, are few and far between, though they have great growth potential.[6] Over the past five years, for example, banks in Brazil have used technology to expand outreach of financial services to millions of people that were not previously served by the formal financial sector. More than 95 percent of the volume of these transactions is related to payments.

Microfinance Clients and Credit Growth

Investments in the microfinance industry have resulted in sector outreach (active loan clients) growing by 22 times, from around 60,000 active borrowers in 1999 to 1.7 million active borrowers by mid-2008. This translates into an average annual growth rate of 40 percent, the second highest in the region after Afghanistan. The major share of microfinance lending goes to trade, followed by agriculture and livestock. Rural areas receive the majority of microlending (56 percent), in contrast to 44 percent going to urban areas (SBP Microwatch).

Women represented 47 percent of active borrowers, 33 percent of savers, and 57 percent of policyholders in the third quarter of 2008. In other South Asia countries, even Afghanistan, between two-thirds and 95 percent of all active borrowers are women. Of the MFIs with significant outreach, only Kashf Foundation is designed to target women specifically. There are other MFIs focusing exclusively on female clientele, but given their current capacity, they are less likely to influence the trajectory of financial services access to women. BRAC, which has recently started operations in Pakistan, is also exclusively focused around women.

Sources of Financing

The total lending portfolio of all MFIs could surpass $1 billion by 2010, provided such growth can be funded and continued demand exists. The most promising funding source that could keep up with the rapid growth of the sector is microsavings, estimated at $1.2 billion by 2010.[7] The distribution of noninstitutional deposits held in formal financial institutions shows only 0.04 percent of savings amounts and 0.31 percent of the number of savings deposits held at MFBs, as compared with commercial banks (74.4 percent and 77.4 percent, respectively), Pakistan Post (1.5 percent and 11.3 percent), and NSS (24 percent and 11 percent).[8] Another promising strategy is for MFIs to deploy a larger percentage of their assets into their loan portfolios. At the end of 2007 this stood at 56 percent, much below regional standards (for example, more than 80 percent in Bangladesh, 2006). This also reduces the overall asset yield of the sector since funds that are deployed in things other than loan portfolios (investments, cash) yield lower returns.[9] The microfinance sector received $463 million in donor funding, as well as indirect IFI investments.[10] Generally, nonmarket-based funding aid has not resulted in robust sector development.

Patterns in sources of funds vary by country based largely on what regulations allow, the extent to which government and donor sources of funding exist, and MFI

Figure 3.2 Sources of Financing for MFIs

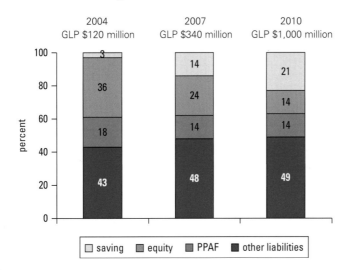

profitability. For example, among NGO MFIs in Bangladesh, 29 percent of funding came from savings and 37 percent from equity.[11] By comparison, Indian MFIs have almost no savings for regulatory reasons, and are highly leveraged with 7 percent equity and 62 percent commercial borrowing.

The sources of financing for the gross loan portfolio of all MFIs in Pakistan show some clear trends (figure 3.2). Savings as a source of funds increased, and equity got increasingly leveraged. The percentage share of donor-funded PPA Floans[12] fell as MFBs became ineligible for concessionary funding. The main challenge in the future will be to increase the amount in other liabilities so as to maintain this at about half of the total. This will require significantly increased use of commercial funding by MFIs, mostly from domestic capital markets. Current efforts by the industry and the SBP to fill the projected funding gap are focused on increasing access by MFIs to commercial sources of funding, partly based on the fact that commercial banks are quite liquid and there is a market appetite for bond issues.[13]

MFI Performance

The microfinance sector in Pakistan is indeed reaching relatively poorer people. The average microfinance loan size in Pakistan is about 15 percent of GDP per capita income (figure 3.3), which compared very well with the much larger loan sizes prevalent in Eastern and Central Europe (95 percent of GDP per capita), Latin America (about 55 percent), and the Middle East and North Africa (about 20 percent). Asia does even better than Pakistan, by lowering the average microloan size to slightly more than 10 percent of GDP per capita. MFI portfolio quality is adequate, and profitability is low but improving.[14]

Figure 3.3 Average Loan Size

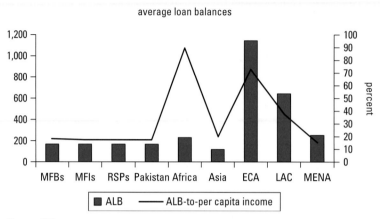

Source: SBP.

Table 3.4 Key Performance Indicators of MFBs (%)

	2004	2005	2006	2007	2008*
Nonperforming loans to advances	7.2	4.4	1.8	4.2%	3.3%
Operating expenditure to gross income	91.66	87.6	100.2	126.7%	135.5%
ROA	−0.49	−0.2	−0.36	−1.8%	−5.3%
Operating sufficiency**	71.9	84.06	76.27	75.8%	65.1%
Financial self-sustainability***	42.27	51.49	61.89	53.4%	50.6%

Source: SBP, September 2008.

*Data for March 2008.

**Operating sufficiency = (total income less income from donations, etc.)/(total operating expense plus actual cost of funds).

***Financial self-sustainability = (total income less income from donations, etc.)/(total operating expenses plus actual cost of funds plus implicit cost of subsidized funds plus implicit cost of equity; computed at SBP discount rate).

The financial health of the MFIs sector in Pakistan has been a concern (table 3.4). While asset quality has been improving (as evidenced by declining nonperforming loans), return on assets (ROA) has seen a decline, as have operating sufficiency and financial sustainability. SBP has encouraged the better institutions to obtain a banking license, to improve funding efforts, and to subject them to tighter prudential regulation. Overall, however, MFI financial health and management practices require urgent attention to improve sustainability, outreach, and efficiency of the sector.

Microfinance and Mobile Telephone Technology in Pakistan

Recently, there has been a rapid increase in the use of new technologies to increase access to financial services in many countries. This has included the widespread use of smart cards and of mobile telephone networks. In Pakistan, mobile phone

Table 3.5 Mobile Telephone Subscribers

	June 2005	June 2006	June 2007	March 2008
Total Subscribers	**12,771,203**	**34,506,557**	**63,159,857**	**82,514,536**
Market coverage*				
• Punjab	3.4%	8.5%	23.9%	35.1%
• Sindh	4.5%	11.7%	27.3%	39.8%
• NWFP	1.7%	3.6%	8.1%	23.0%
• Balochistan	1.5%	3.6%	8.1%	16.6%

Source: Pakistan Telecommunication Authority (2007).

*These figures are provided by the mobile telephone companies. Market coverage is the percentage of the estimated total number of subscribers who have an active SIM card.

penetration has increased at a rapid pace recently (see table 3.5). Half or more of all Pakistanis have access to a cell phone, including among women and rural areas (two-thirds in urban areas). While more than 86 percent of men have their own cell phone, 40 percent of women do. These figures suggest a much higher access to cell phones (available in the household or within the extended family) than the figure for regular usage. Both access to and usage of cell phones increase with income. Baluchistan is the least served (still, a third of the population have access to mobile phones). Per the survey, cell phone usage is 35.4 percent in Sindh, about 44 percent in North West Frontier Province (NWFP) and Azad Jammu and Kashmir (AJK), and highest in Punjab, at 51.5 percent (the figures in table 3.5, as estimated by mobile phone providers, are somewhat more conservative). However, access to a cell phone is much higher: over half of the population in all provinces except Baluchistan have access. The pervasive use of mobile telephony creates a ready market for financial service delivery over mobile phones. This effect is somewhat limited by the finding that face-to-face interactions are highly valued, equally by men and women (76 percent).

Use of cell phones is still mostly confined to voice services (for 78.5 percent of cell phone users). Basic data services, such as Short Message Service (SMS), are used by 40.2 percent cell phone users, with higher usage in urban areas (45 percent) than in rural (36.7 percent). SMS usage is also more frequent among men and in AJK and increases as income rises. Internet usage remains low and is concentrated in urban areas and among men. Internet and e-mail are more accessed/used at home. Close to two-thirds of Pakistanis (60.8 percent) have their own prepaid mobile phones. Mobilink is the most used network, across rural and urban areas, except in AJK and NWFP, where Telenor is most often cited. There is a large gender divide on cell phone payments. While a majority of men pay for themselves, the majority (84.5 percent) of women's cell phone expenses are paid by their spouse or family. This limits somewhat the usefulness of cell phone credit records as a source of credit information. Nevertheless, World Bank (2008a) concludes, on the basis of cross-country analysis, that mobile technology does expand financial access.

Figure 3.4 Cellular Penetration and Projected Mobile Telephone Trends by Province

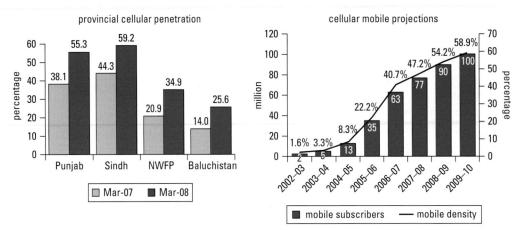

Source: Quarterly Report of PTA (Jan–Mar 2008); Pakistan Telecommunication Authority, Annual Report 2007.

The potential for using mobile phone technologies to reach many more people is evident from figure 3.4. By July 2008, there were 89.3 million mobile telephone connections and the networks coverage potentially extends over 90 percent of the population. Teledensity in the country stands at 56 percent as of January 2009. Growth has been very rapid over the past few years and will continue to be in the future. It is also clear that even poor people are using mobile telephones, since it is easy and inexpensive to get a prepaid account. By comparison, during the past 60 years, the banks have only been able to accumulate 25 million deposit accounts, and barriers to entry (documentation, minimum balance requirements, and so forth) have kept most of the poor out of the banking system.

With five mobile operators backed by strong international shareholders, Pakistan's active and competitive mobile phone market, combined with the presence of regulatory guidelines for branchless banking, provides an enabling environment for partnerships between MFIs and telecommunications operators. Such partnerships have already materialized in Pakistan, with the acquisition in November 2008 of Tameer Microfinance Bank, pioneering new commercial ways to increase outreach to the underserved.

Informal Finance

Informal finance markets have a long history predating formal markets and a strong presence in most of rural and urban Pakistan.[15] These markets cannot be strictly classified. They are generally stand-alone, operating without the links that characterize well-integrated financial markets. The multiplicity of informal finance markets is reflected in the observed diversity of transactions in these markets, such as committees or rotating saving and credit association (ROSCAs), moneylending, interlinked financing, and suppliers' credit, among others. However, informal finance markets face constraints in getting access to institutional credit. This lack of well-functioning financial markets has an additional adverse effect on poverty, as the poor who have credit requirements but few assets that can serve as collateral cannot resort to formal finance markets, but are left instead at the mercy of current conditions in informal markets.

Qadir (2005) quotes a 1996 estimate of informal borrowing in Pakistan at 78 percent of total borrowing in the country. A comparison of the share of informal rural credit in Asian countries shows that this share is high in all countries, especially Pakistan. The share along with the reporting year is: Bangladesh, 63 percent (1974); India, 70 percent (1972); Indonesia, 52 percent (1985); Malaysia, 62 percent (1986); Pakistan, 73 percent (1985); Philippines, 71 percent (1978); South Korea, 50 percent (1981); Thailand, 52 percent (1985) (World Bank, 1996).

Informal Borrowing. It is very common for poor people in particular to borrow from relatives, friends, and other people with whom they have close relationships, especially for consumption smoothing. Recognized moneylenders operate all over the country and are often a source of larger amounts of finance or are approached as a last resort. A popular source of financial services for all income levels, especially women, are ROSCAs, commonly known as "committees." These take different forms, but all involve participation in a group where everyone saves money by contributing to a pool and each one in turn is able to access and use the pool amount.

Urban financial markets are different from rural ones in certain important respects. Many urban markets cater to traders, especially wholesalers, and are quite well developed in terms of the amounts of funds intermediated, the speed and efficiency of the intermediation, and the sophistication of participants and of the market as a whole. Suppliers' credit is a common feature: in old markets with established players, as much as 90 percent of transactions are carried out on suppliers' credit resting on good faith. A *chit* (*parchi*, or informal receipt) is the norm for making business transactions and is not dishonored; it represents a convenient and flexible method that allows business to be conducted at arms-length and does not require documentation or entail tax liabilities.

Credit in the rural areas is mostly supplied by *aartis* (commission agents) and other middlemen at high interest rates through interlinked transactions. The acute shortage of capital at affordable rates severely constrains the growth of the rural economy and prevents efficient resource mobilization and risk management.

Informal savings. Poor people save in both financial and nonfinancial forms but often lack the ability to make use of small savings flows when larger lump sums are needed. Even the committee system does not always meet this need. Given the dearth of institutional channels to tap into rural savings, people in rural areas save through traditional channels. Saving in livestock, which can be bought and sold when needed, is a good livelihood diversification strategy for low-income households. Livestock is also kept through share leasing, which is a saving arrangement between landlords and professional strata (*kammis*). Other traditional saving arrangements in Punjab are called *vartan bhanji and wanghar*, meaning asking others for help on a voluntary and reciprocal basis. Hoarding gold and silver is also common in rural and semi-urban areas.

Traditionally, such jewelry is supposed to be kept for a lifetime and transferred to the children of the family, to be utilized only as a last resort through sale or mortgage.

Informal transfers involve transfers or exchanges between households of cash, food, clothing, informal loans, and other informal assistance. While informal transfers help the poor in risk management, they are not adequate substitutes for public action in social protection. A popular informal system of transferring money around the world is the *hawala* system, marked by low commissions, fast transactions, little documentation, and round-the-clock operations. The system works through individual brokers or operators collecting funds at one end of the payment chain and others distributing the funds at the other end. This is an especially popular means for migrant workers to send money home.

Informal markets are generally characterized by high interest rates, widespread rationing, segmentation, and a sizeable gap between lending and deposit rates. There is extreme variability in the interest rate charged by lenders for similar loan transactions. Informal finance markets are generally marked by low levels of default due to social sanction, group sincerity, past history, and repeat transactions. Informal credit markets are marked by widespread rationing; that is, there are upper limits on how much a borrower receives from a lender. Segmentation is another feature of informal credit markets. Typically, a moneylender serves a fixed clientele, whose members he lends to on a repeated basis, and is extremely reluctant to lend to outsiders. Qadir (2005) estimates a cost of informal borrowing of 23 percent on average, as opposed to an average of 19 percent in the formal market. The total transaction cost of informal lenders on average constitutes only 5 percent of the total volume of lending. Interestingly, cash credit is considerably more expensive at 85 percent per year (table 3.6).

Social sanction and market limitations are the most common instruments for enforcement of contracts as well as for recovery of loans. Resorting to the legal

Table 3.6 Interest Rates Charged in the Informal Market in Pakistan, 2005

	Effective Annual Interest Rate
Auto-rickshaw informal credit market (Lytton Road, Lahore)	26.4%
Faisalabad yarn market	17.31% to 46.15%, average 28.39%
Moneylenders in rural areas, for household and consumption	120 to 150%
Moneylenders in rural areas, for businessmen and agriculturists	12 to 50%
Moneylenders average, all loans	55.2%
Commission agents, for farm inputs	12.57 to 15.38%
Farm input dealers	2.2% to 74.2%, average 25.81%
Self-reported by farmers, for lending in kind	29.81%
Self-reported by farmers, for lending of cash	85%

Source: Qadir (2005).

system of the country is fairly uncommon. Moneylenders usually take various precautionary measures before taking on a new client. These include the practice of dealing with the potential client in other markets, extensive scrutiny of new clients, and small "testing loans." In an environment of weak contractual enforcement, those engaged in business, especially arms-length transactions, have to be very discreet and often rely on individual goodwill and social pressure in the absence of security (collateral). In cases of default, market players normally mediate and decide about receivables and payables and, in extreme circumstances, dispose of assets.

It is often said that informal finance markets exist because formal markets are poorly developed and many people, especially the poor, do not have access to formal sources. But informal financial markets still thrive even after all the efforts of the past few decades to expand formal institutional markets. This suggests that informal sources might have some advantages over formal sources. In general, informal sources of credit are more expensive than formal sources and there is much evidence to suggest that they exploit poor people, but they have the advantages of being available all the time, not requiring documentation, operating outside the purview of formal authorities, and not requiring collateral. Moreover, many upper-income groups use the informal market as a substitute for or complement to formal ones, which indicates that informal markets can be competitive. One response to recognition of the informational advantages of informal financial markets can be to try to encourage them rather than replace them by expanding formal finance to economic agents who are likely to use these funds in informal markets. Another response is to actually design and help expand MFIs that will take advantage of local-level information. The modern microfinance movement has made use of some of the characteristics to build up its business, not least substituting social contracts for other forms of collateral that are often not available to the poor. But the persistent use of informal finance in the face of concerted efforts to improve access to formal sources suggests that much more could be done to learn from informal financial systems as well as to develop linkages between these systems, or even find ways to incorporate informal institutions such as the *hawala* system into the formal sector.

Regulation

In 2000, microfinance was elevated to a core aspect of the government's poverty reduction program. The introduction of the Microfinance Institutions Ordinance 2001, under which MFBs are licensed, was driven by a poverty reduction agenda. The ordinance is not concerned with NGO microfinance programs and relates only to MFIs that wish to mobilize deposits. The MFBs are licensed and regulated by the SBP under specially designed prudential regulations. There are four categories of license, each with a different paid-up capital requirement: national, province, region, and district. At first, the regulation did not lead to rapid expansion of services, but the regulator adopted an open approach to the sector, including the creation of a microfinance consultative group chaired by the SBP and composed of representatives from the sector, and changes in the ordinance and regulations gradually made this a more attractive option.

By 2008, there were six MFBs, including the largest such bank, Khushhali Bank, that was initially established in 2000 under a special ordinance but relicensed under the MFI Ordinance in early 2008. To date, First Microfinance Bank is the only case in which an NGO program was "transformed" into a MFB, but the two largest NGO programs both intend to apply for MFB licenses in 2008. It is expected that by the end of 2008 the share of total active clients served by MFBs will be more than the NGO total for the first time. Considering that demand still far outstrips supply and that it will take huge amounts of funding to satisfy that demand over the next decade or more, MFBs that mobilize deposits and can more easily access commercial funding have the potential to take a large share of the market if they have good business models. An important change in microfinance investor mindset will aid the commercialization process for MFBs. When the government encouraged the commercial banks to invest Rs 1.7 billion ($285 million) to capitalize Khushhali Bank, some commercial bank executives invested out of a sense of corporate social responsibility. This is changing as more commercially minded investors enter the market.

The Pakistan regulation is now considered to be the most conducive regulation in the region with respect to promoting financial inclusion for poor people. Amendments to the MFI Ordinance and its regulations made in 2007[16] have improved the situation even further, and the SBP is open to making further adjustments in future. The ordinance has the potential to significantly improve the delivery of formal financial services to excluded populations. In fact, the SBP has taken on a leadership role to promote and facilitate the development of the microfinance sector. In addition to making the MFI Ordinance and its regulations increasingly friendly, the SBP has issued a series of guidelines for commercial and Islamic banks to engage in the microfinance sector.

Growing the Microfinance Sector

The main focus of government policy aiming to increase access to finance to larger groups of poor and underserved people is the development of the microfinance sector. Recent policy interventions include SBP regulations on branchless banking, a newly created class of MFBs, basic banking, literacy and awareness efforts, and various programs to support microfinance. These programs have spurred fast growth in the microfinance sector, but have had mixed results on improving the sector's sustainability and rapidly expanding its outreach. More encouragingly, electronic transfers already represent 10 percent of payments for government workers and 3 percent of payments for pensions (SBP figures). Basic banking is currently used by 2.5 percent on average, especially among men and in rural areas (SBP figures). Much more remains to be done, and some promising strategies are outlined below.

Private Sector Actions

Improving MFI sustainability and ability to muster commercial funding/savings deposits, and their further integration into the financial system: The main requirement for microfinance outreach growth is the presence of strong, profitable

MFIs. More could be done to improve efficiency and increase profitability. One of the main conditions for sustainability is increased reliance on commercial funding and the ability to attract deposits, in order to fund an expansion of outreach to more clients. Efficiency improvements will also be required, in order to deliver financial services in a cheaper manner and manage risks better. The ultimate goal for MFIs should be to firmly integrate into the financial system. While the microfinance sector in Pakistan is currently too underdeveloped to be adequately interlinked with the rest of the financial sector, integration would guarantee that MFIs are subject to market signals and are sustainable because they would respond to the need to raise resources from the market and thus improve their financial performance.

The sector can refocus from microcredit to microsavings, given the large untapped demand for such products. Besides being the service that poor people want more than any other, savings mobilization by MFBs will also provide a longer-term stable source of funds to grow credit outreach. MFBs need to pay more attention to developing their savings services, especially through strengthening their systems and developing appropriate products. The commercial banks and other financial institutions that provide savings services can also do more to refocus further on poor people.

World Bank (2008a) also notes that many rich countries and some developing countries are also experimenting with new ways to promote savings, such as matching schemes and tax advantaged schemes. Savings methods that have worked for microfinance—doorstep collection schemes and periodic contribution or "commitment" programs—are also being offered by some banks in developing countries.

Enlarging the product range and client segmentation: Client segmentation allows financial institutions to better tailor products to tastes and client needs, as well as reduce costs and manage risks more efficiently. A particularly relevant example is gender segregation. Understanding women's needs more precisely, and reflecting those in the financial products and the provider policies and procedures, would ensure an increase in women's access to finance in spite of cultural norms, gender segregation, and low literacy and incomes, as detailed in box 2.1 and the recommendations section in chapter 2. Products (savings, insurance, and credit) for old age, children's education, pregnancy and medical expenses, and livestock are a few examples of those that take account of women's needs for life-cycle events. Saving products, which are expected to be especially popular, can be built upon traditional saving arrangements and ROSCAs that women use.

Lower loan size and deposit size would permit better matching to women's needs, given their lower incomes. Repayments should be frequent so that installments are smaller and correspond to women's income cycles. More simplified procedures, as well as documentation that does not depend on the men in the household, will address women's reluctance to avail themselves of financial products. Global experience suggests offering women credit that is not tied to specific use, instead allowing the borrower to suggest the activity. Access would also improve with the use of alternative forms of collateral, such as social collateral, compulsory savings, personal guarantees, crops or machinery to be purchased, or household assets. Access to financial services should be broadened beyond the head of household to include more women from the same household, especially through saving programs. Home-based businesses should be given consideration. Literacy should not be a requirement to access financial service. Simple policies and procedures that speed the transaction, lower transaction cost for women, and do not preclude uneducated women tend to maximize outreach to women clients. Decentralized operations, operating units located near women clients, use of mobile units, and transactions at clients' doorsteps tend to make banking convenient for women. Female staff will improve approachability for clients and alleviate cultural concerns. Some successful examples of home-grown solutions to women's banking are Bank Al-Falah women's credit card and Meezan bank's Ladies Banking.

Public Sector Actions

Expanding financial awareness: Further gains in financial literacy are critical, though even more critical is the population's awareness and better understanding of financial services and products, which will promote trust in the sector. A national awareness campaign is needed to support financial inclusion, especially for women, as well as to encourage people to open savings accounts. A large number of people still do not have any account at all. While financial literacy arguments are quite compelling, empirical evidence from Indonesia (Cole and Zia 2008) suggests that financial literacy has very little if any impact on the use/uptake of financial services among households. To the contrary, it is financial incentives (which remove/reduce affordability barriers of opening a bank account) that have an impact.

Strengthening institutions: Access to finance growth will be accelerated by an integrated financial system, and a strong regulatory framework. SBP is working toward creating an enabling framework for access, and is set upon an ambitious Financial Inclusion Program to make further inroads into the matter. Other regulators and institutions would need to rise to the occasion as well, including the SECP. Among the important features of a complete financial system is a well-functioning national-level credit bureau for credit referencing. All commercial banks, development financial institutions, leasing companies, and MFBs are currently reporting to CIB on all borrowers irrespective of the size of loan. A private sector initiative along these lines is being prepared by the PMN members with Datacheck, a consumer finance credit bureau, to create a microfinance credit bureau in the competitive Lahore market, which is expected to bear initial fruit in 2009. By establishing a credit history and thus a potential collateral substitute, a credit bureau can be instrumental in access to finance for groups that may not have cash or asset collateral required to access a loan but have a stellar credit history to present to the bank. Upgrading the existing credit bureau managed by SBP to more than just a black list and increasing its coverage to the whole finance service sector, including NGO-MFIs, can place many more potential borrowers within reach of some access to finance.

Public-Private Partnerships

Technology can help address efficiency challenges within the microfinance value chain, while opening the way for innovative applications designed to increase outreach. Enhancing outreach via technology solutions can involve banks adopting a combination of devices as well as "branchless banking" through cell phone and mobile devices. These are different directions, and each has shortcomings and difficulties. In Pakistan, the banking access infrastructure is particularly weak, as noted in chapter 1—there are few bank branches and ATMs relative to the population size and geographic expanse of the country. In addition, as demonstrated by the Brazil correspondent banking experience, obstacles to expanding outreach can also arise from contractual as well as regulatory and prudential factors regarding agency arrangements (Kumar et al. 2006). In contrast, while mobile banking presents regulatory challenges (as in the case of the Philippines G-Cash and Kenya M-Pesa models), it can be a promising channel to help shift some of the financial flows from informal to formal channels, in particular if combined with other correspondent banking channels. Demand-side results do show us a very high mobile penetration, and our economic analysis highlights significant positive linkages between financial inclusion and regular mobile use, as well as informal inclusion and access to a cell phone.

Expanding outreach via mobile telephony, smart cards, and POS devices: Given the wide, relatively equitable, and rapidly growing access in Pakistan to mobile phones, technology has a major potential to become a conduit for access to finance in the country. In addition to access expansion, mobile phones, smart cards, POS devices, and other technology improvements can lower transaction costs, as well as help enhance credit information on a much wider population segment. The simplicity and low cost of these services have enabled poor people to use them easily and successfully in spite of their novelty and recent penetration. This stands in sharp contrast to the complexity and lack of user-friendliness of traditional bank products, and their relative failure to penetrate a wider population range. Box 3.3 illustrates some of the global good practices leveraging technology to improve back-end processing and expand delivery channels, increasingly through partnerships between banks and nonbank institutions.

These technologies have been very successful in promoting payments services worldwide. In Pakistan, given population preferences and needs, it is important to find ways to extend access to savings services as well, via technology gains. International experience points to (1) regulatory methods of promoting savings, such as matching schemes and tax advantaged schemes, as well as (2) savings methods which have worked for microfinance—doorstep collection schemes and periodic contribution or commitment programs. But if the full potential of this new approach is to be realized, it will need to go well beyond the microfinance sector, where there is already a strong interest in using technology to reach more people and lower costs, and include the banks. So far, commercial banks have not shown much interest, though this might change as time goes on.

Box 3.3 **Case Study: Technology Innovations Have Improved Back-End Processing and Expanded Delivery Channels in the Microfinance Value Chain**

Shared Microfinance Services Hubs Make Technology-led Efficiency Gains Accessible

While the benefits of automating core banking systems to cut operating costs, streamline lending processes, and scale up and integrate with the rest of the financial sector are widely recognized, these solutions often remain out of reach for individual microfinance institutions. Challenges include high upfront costs, connectivity requirements, unavailability of technical support, and high maintenance costs. Outsourcing management information systems to application service providers (ASPs) who manage centralized microfinance processing hubs has emerged as a solution to address some of these challenges. The automation of MFIs opens the door to new products and services.

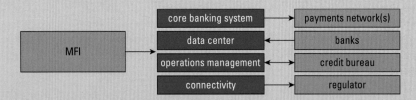

- FINO (Financial Information Network & Operations Ltd), an ASP **in India** incubated within ICICI Bank, now provides a **centralized technology platform** via a biometric smart card to clients of MFIs, banks, insurance providers, and the government. FINO claims to have enrolled 5 million customers who perform balance enquiry, deposit and withdrawal of cash and statement, and receipt printing.

- Similarly, IBM Global Services is in the early stages of planning for a **Latin America–wide strategy for a centralized ICT platform for microfinance,** located in Mexico and serving all MFIs in Spanish-speaking Latin America through a Web-based solution. The platform envisioned includes a model of service delivery, hosting, and tailored functionality.

Innovative Technology Applications, in the Hands of Microfinance Agents or Clients, Increase Outreach

- The Andhra Pradesh Government **in India,** after a successful pilot reaching half a million villagers, is rolling out the **delivery of government pensions and unemployment benefits** under the rural employment guarantee program. A network of bank business correspondents operates with a Near Field Communication–enabled mobile phone, synchronizing with a bank's server over a wireless connection and a fingerprint scanner to enroll the villagers. All deposit/withdrawal transactions get reported to the partner bank on a daily or hourly basis while the bank ensures that the business correspondent has enough funds to take care of daily withdrawals. During the pilot, the government gave banks 2 percent of the amounts being transferred as commission, to be shared with their business correspondents.

(continued)

Box 3.3   **continued**

- In Pakistan, Tameer Bank has partnered with local retail outlets, including pharmacies, telecom outlets, and post offices, to install point of sale devices closer to the customers. Bank customers (individual and small businesses) can visit these registered outlets to withdraw and make deposits, repay loans, pay utility bills, and remit money. Costs of using correspondent agents as alternatives to setting up bank branches are reportedly 30 times lower set-up costs and 100 times lower running costs.

- Similarly, in Kenya, Equity Bank is using the Nakumatt chain of retail stores as branchless banking agents, while WIZZIT, a South African cell-phone banking facility with 16 million registered clients, has partnered with Dunn, a chain of 400 clothing stores acting as WIZZIT account-opening locations.

- The Rural Bankers Association of the Philippines, with support from USAID, has partnered with Globe Telecom's G-Cash to allow its retail clients in 375 branches to send sales receipts and bank deposits via their mobile phones, without being subject to minimum balance and fees charged by the commercial banks. Microfinance institutions under this program become "cash in" and "cash out" outlets that are accredited to convert actual money into electronic money and vice versa.

- Mexico's Banamex Bank offers two products, a prepaid MasterCard credit card and a savings card, to an average of 25 million clients in 240 Soriana stores, the second largest Mexican retailer. The two companies plan to co-invest to set up 150 retailer-run bank units in 2009.

Source: CGAP, World Bank (2008a).

Experimentation with using mobile telephone networks is just beginning. On the other hand, cards have been in use for many years, though not generally by poor and underserved populations. "As of December 2007 the total number of active cards in the Pakistan banking system stood at 6.7 million, as compared to a total of 16 million personal bank accounts. Of these, 1.7 million were credit cards (25.4 percent) and 4.8 million were debit cards (71.6 per cent). ATM-only cards were 0.191 million or 2.8 per cent. Ninety-nine percent of the time, these cards were used for withdrawals while only 1 percent of the transactions were deposits (envelope based). Each ATM had an average of 70 transactions per day, of an average size of Rs 6,127. Until December 2007, there were 2,618 ATM machines (as compared with over 8,000 bank branches), and 52,474 POS terminals across the country. Almost two-thirds (61 percent) of the bank branch network consisted of Real Time Online Branches. One-quarter of the total transactions in the system were electronic-based. Although the electronic banking system is growing, it is still in its infancy and its expansion in coming years is a basic premise for the inclusion of the majority of the population" (Lindh de Montoya and Haq 2008).

Expanding outreach via basic banking—a mixed experience: Another avenue for harnessing technology to enhance access to finance is basic banking (see box 3.4 for international experience).[17] Basic banking implies the provision of some package of free or low-cost services to clients, with some restrictions on the menu of services and on the amounts held in the accounts. For example, such accounts may have free transactions up to some limit provided they are undertaken by ATM cards and do not use teller services. Fees and charges for some transactions may be waived—up to a free limit in terms of numbers of transactions. The World Bank (2008a) concludes that regulation in this area, on its own, is inadequate, and there is a positive but weak association between basic banking and share of the banked. However, in many places where banks have voluntarily offered commercial products of a basic banking character, there is a positive association with access. The experience of Pakistan has been mixed, whereby a "basic account" regulation was introduced in November 2005,[18] without much uptake from either banks or clients.

Box 3.4 **Basic Banking in India, Mexico, and South Africa**

In December 2005, India introduced a new type of bank account designed for the poor. The Zero Balance account provided for a zero minimum balance; simplified application forms, low maintenance charges, transparency in disclosure of free transactions limits, and simplified identification documents. It also included a small overdraft facility. Banks were urged to give wide publicity to the new "no-frills" accounts.

More recent is Mexico's basic banking regulation of July 2007. For accounts with less than a minimum balance, it provides a list of minimal services that banks should offer free of fees to all persons who comply with normal application requirements. There is no minimum opening amount, though banks can set ongoing minimum balance levels. There is also an ongoing maximum balance of 165 times the daily minimum wage. After it is exceeded, banks can charge commissions for client transactions. The minimum services to be provided include: opening and maintaining an account, providing a debit card, and allowing free deposits as well as free withdrawals and account inquiries from the ATMs of the providing bank. Mexican regulations have also provided for employer-sponsored basic accounts. If employers have an arrangement with a bank for opening payroll deposits for their employees, there is no ongoing minimum balance. If the employee leaves, commissions may be charged on his or her account.

South Africa offers an example of a country where there is a "voluntary" commitment to provide basic banking, with the launching of its Mzansi Accounts in October 2004. The government encouraged banks to provide such accounts, following the adoption of its Financial Charter of 2003, which called for access to banking for all clients. The account, offered by four major South African banks, has no minimum balance, no monthly maintenance fee, and a limited number of free monthly deposits and withdrawals. Mini-statements by cell phone are available.

(continued)

Box 3.4   **continued**

What has the impact of basic banking been?

While basic banking has grown in popularity, information about its impact is still limited. One such assessment is done in India's Gulbarga district, where 400,000 new "no-frills" accounts opened between August 2006 and June 2007, under a government-supported drive (Ramji 2007). The study found that most respondents (75 percent) had opened accounts for receiving government funds under the National Rural Employment Guarantee Program. Very few persons opened accounts for savings (4 percent), or transactions purposes. It concluded that there was no large-scale impact on bank access.

The evidence from South Africa is more positive. The "voluntary" code led to the opening of a number of new accounts—a million in the first year alone, amounting to an additional 8.5 percent of total accounts and 4 percent of the population. Over 91 percent of new account holders were previously unbanked. Recent estimates of the use of the Mzansi account suggest 3.5 to 4 million users, of whom 60 percent are new to the banking system (Teschler and Schneider 2008). But graduation from the Mzansi account to regular banking is difficult. Banks complain that the account is unprofitable, with relatively low use and high dormancy and abandonment rates.

Source: World Bank (2008a).

In sum, the Pakistan microfinance market has much potential and faces considerable unsatisfied demand, creating potential for a rapid outreach expansion. The financial sector has not yet taken up SBP encouragement to that effect, and will unlikely change course given the recent financial crisis fallout. Yet, it is important to persevere in this agenda, which directly links into poverty reduction. Promising strategies include financial awareness campaigns, strengthening of MFI viability and commercial sustainability, inclusion of women and client segmentation, and focus on savings products development. Smaller size of products, and bulk service (for example, microinsurance, microleasing, micro-home improvement loans, micropayment services, agriculture credit, remittances services, and microsavings), might better attract lower-income groups. The increasing use of technology (ATMs, POS, mobile banking, basic banking, branchless banking, smart cards) will make this approach a viable business proposition for banks as well as affordable for clients. With close to 90 percent coverage and 59 percent reach (and no gender divide), mobile banking is an up-and-coming opportunity to deliver remittances. Increasing penetration will have to rely on such outfits as the Pakistan Post Office, whose more than 13,000 branches nationwide present an attractive point of launch for wider access to finance, but whose capacity and efficiency would benefit from an overhaul, so as to permit effective cooperation with the private sector in broadening service provision.

Notes

1. Includes indigenous self-help groups. Formal MFI estimates for India amount to 3 percent.

2. These estimates are based on country reports by local authoritative organizations: Microinvestment Support Facility for Afghanistan, Credit and Development Forum for Bangladesh, Access and MCril for India, Center for Microfinance for Nepal, Pakistan Microfinance Network (PMN) for Pakistan, and National Development Trust Fund for Sri Lanka. Microfinance reaches people living below the poverty line as well as the vulnerable poor with slightly higher incomes. All of these people have generally been excluded from the formal financial system.

3. There are as many as 53,000 primary cooperative societies, and until the late 1990s there was a Federal Bank for Cooperatives as well as provincial cooperative banks that provided financing to the cooperative societies. But because of some cooperative scandals in which many poor shareholders lost their money, the generally poor quality of financial management within cooperatives, and lax oversight by the authorities, the cooperative movement went into decline. While there are still many cooperatives all over the country, little is known about the extent of their active membership or their financial performance.

4. The MFI Ordinance defines microfinance as very small loans, presently of less than Rs 150,000.

5. The largest microsavings providers are NSS and PPSB, with $12 and $0.85 billion in savings deposits, respectively.

6. In addition to group life insurance, which enjoys the highest popularity amount microinsurance products, MFIs have started experimenting with micro health insurance. RSPs is the largest health insurance scheme, covering about 200,000 of their group members for hospitalization benefits.

7. Burki and Mohammed (2008) describes demand for savings services among the urban poor.

8. June 2007 data (PMN 2008).

9. Average yield on investments is 4–10 percent depending upon the tenor and risk of investments, whereas yield on portfolio averaged 21.5 percent for the sector as a whole in 2006.

10. This includes the Asian Development Bank project under which Khushhali Bank was established ($150 million), grants from bilateral donors ($31 million), and two PPAF projects funded by the World Bank ($215 million). The International Fund for Economic Development began a $32 million microfinance project with PPAF in 2007 and another project with PPAF ($35 million) began in early 2008. The largest of the indirect investments is the Asian Development Bank (ADB) project ($322 million), as well as the UK Department for International Development (DFID) support ($100 million) toward strengthening SBP's Financial Inclusion Program to increase financial access to the poor and small enterprises.

11. Figures from 2006. This analysis excludes Grameen Bank, the only MFB in Bangladesh. All the other MFIs are NGOs.

12. PPAF consists of a mix of loans and grants to MFIs.

13. The discussion, like the entire report, does not take into account the oncoming financial crisis. Given the crisis, the process of increasing MFI commercial funding becomes more difficult, and more urgent. Likely consequences of the macroeconomic crisis include (1) rising delinquency and slowing of growth as poor clients (or potential clients) suffer severe hardship, (2) savings flight from MFIs into safer options, and (3) less funding being available for MFIs.

14. Portfolio at risk at 30 days is below 5 percent. The effects of the crisis are yet to be assessed at the time of printing of this report.

15. The summary in this section is largely drawn from Qadir (2005).

16. For more details about these amendments and their implications for MFBs, see Ahmed and Shah (2007).

17. Countries introducing basic banking include Malaysia, Mexico, Vietnam, and Brazil, among many more.

18. It includes a minimum initial deposit of Rs 1,000 (around $17) for a transactions account. There is no maintenance fee and no minimum ongoing balance. It permits two free deposits and two free check withdrawals per month; and unlimited free ATM withdrawals from the banks' own ATMs. It includes an annual statement of account. Should the ongoing balance of the account be zero for six months, the account will be closed.

Chapter 4

Improving Financial Access for Small and Medium Enterprises (SMEs)

There are 3 million SMEs in Pakistan; they constitute more than 90 percent of all private enterprises in the industrial sector, employ nearly 78 percent of the nonagriculture labor force, and contribute more than 30 percent to GDP. Small and microenterprises have seen a worsening of access to finance; they internally finance 90 percent of working capital and 81 percent of new investment. In contrast, medium-size enterprises and those with a credit history have seen improved access to finance. Studies estimate an SME credit demand gap of Rs 277 billion (compared with current SME credit of Rs 400 billion). However, enterprises do not seem to be excluded from financial markets because of poor performance. Instead, an incomplete legal and regulatory framework and non-SME-friendly products and procedures hamper increased SME lending. Indirect costs—legal fees, collateral registration, and documentation—make bank lending expensive for SMEs. A typical small business loan requires up to 27 steps for the bank and 9 meetings with clients.

An enabling role has been played by the expansion of Credit Investment Bureau's (CIB) scope in 2006; the SME Policy 2007, which emphasizes SME access to finance; and, above all, the new SBP Prudential Regulations for SMEs. However, banks continue to find it difficult to serve SMEs profitably for several reasons. First, the legal framework (namely, the secured transactions regions and, to a lesser extent, the credit information infrastructure) limits the pool of potential applicants. Second, bank products are not tailored to SMEs, resembling instead corporate lending practices. Finally, banks do not have organizational structures and monitoring tools conducive to achieving high efficiency. SME demand-side factors, including limited SME accounting, budgeting, and planning capacity further constrain the market. Continued promotion of an enabling environment for SME lending and a large-scale downscaling effort involving both the public and private sectors can forge rapid growth in SME lending. Increasing access to finance for SMEs could also be facilitated by attracting an institutional investor with a track record in SME lending and assisting other banks to go downmarket.

Access to Finance for SMEs: Supply-side Evidence

SMEs account for a substantial part of the economy, yet small enterprise lending remains limited. There are about 3.2 million enterprises in Pakistan, of which about 3 million (93 percent) are SMEs. SMEs spread across the economy with varying density: Most are in wholesale and retail trade and restaurants and hotels (53 percent), followed by other services (27 percent) and the manufacturing sector (20 percent).[1] The SMEs census shows that SMEs contribute more than 30 percent to the GDP and 25 percent to the country's total export earnings, and they employ close to 70 percent of the labor force in the manufacturing industry, services, and trade. Their share in the manufacturing value addition is estimated to be around 35 percent. Despite the importance of SMEs in the economy, as of December 2007 fewer than 200,000 borrow from the banking sector and SME lending volumes (that is, loans of up to Rs 75 million) account only for 16 percent of total credit. Although no disaggregated supply-side data are available, demand-side data and interviews with banks have shown that there is a particularly acute financing gap for loan sizes between Rs 100,000, the maximum loan size that microfinance institutions (MFIs) can offer, and Rs 5 million, the loan size range required mainly by small businesses.

Private banks are the leading lenders in the SME finance market. Four of the five banks with the highest number of individual shares in SME finance portfolios are private commercial banks. Among the public sector banks, National Bank of Pakistan (NBP) has slightly more than 8 percent of the total SME financing extended by the banking sector. The public sector banks (Bank of Punjab, Bank of Khyber, and First Women's Bank Limited) have the third-largest share of SME financing, after the big-five banks and private banks. Islamic banks are also making significant improvements in capturing the SME finance market. Among these, Meezan Bank has the highest outstanding portfolio, approximately Rs 3.7 billion, followed by Dubai Islamic and Dawood Islamic Banks. Specialized banks' share in SME financing extended by the banking sector is low, 2.19 percent; SME Bank has the largest portfolio, Rs 8 billion. Foreign banks play a negligible role in SME finance (table 4.1).

Most loans to SMEs go to finance working capital. SBP data show that a major portion (71 percent) of SME borrowing is spent on working capital, followed by trade financing and long-term/fixed investment (December 2007). The breakdown of lending to SMEs, by type of facility, is presented in table 4.2.

Government Policies to Improve Financial Access to SMEs

The government of Pakistan (GOP) and State Bank Pakistan (SBP) have introduced policies to improve the legal framework and create a demonstration effect. The GOP and SBP have launched a number of initiatives to support the growth of SME lending. These can be broadly grouped in two areas: initiatives aiming at facilitating SMEs provision of collateral and credit history and activities aimed at creating a

Table 4.1 Distribution of SME Finance among Banks

Banks	% Share in SME Finance Portfolio
Big-five banks	43.40
Habib Bank Limited	15.55
National Bank of Pakistan	7.86
Allied Bank Limited	7.46
Muslim Commercial Bank Limited	6.72
United Bank Limited	5.81
Private banks (excluding big-five)	44.36
Public sector banks (excluding NBP)	4.82
Foreign banks	0.42
Islamic banks (excluding Al-Baraka Bank)	4.82
Specialized banks	2.19

Source: SBP.

Note: SBP figures for 1st quarter 2008, rescaled to add up to 100.

demonstration effect for other financial institutions, that is, financing technical assistance for selected financial institutions to increase SME lending, thus showing to other market participants that the SME segment is indeed a profitable one and ultimately creating competition in the segment. Finally, to monitor SME lending, the SBP has introduced a more detailed SME definition on a pilot basis and requires banks to report on their SME portfolio on a quarterly basis.

SBP has made two unsuccessful attempts to increase lending to SMEs, first, through the creation of an effective secured transactions system and, second, through the relaxation of collateral requirements. The traditional corporate lending products of Pakistani banks emphasize security, especially immovable collateral, audited financial statements, and business plans, rather than doing first-hand research on cash flows and business performance. This makes it more difficult for financial institutions to extend loans to SMEs, the collateral of which is limited and movable, and

Table 4.2 Breakdown of Lending to SME by Type of Facility (Rs billion)

Type of Facility	Dec 04	Dec 05	Dec 06	Dec 07	Mar 08
Fixed investment	23.9	34.1	41.8	60.3	47.9
Working capital	204.2	267.7	308.4	309.1	293.3
Trade finance	55.9	59.6	58.1	67.9	61.6
Total	284	361.4	408.3	437.4	403.4*

Source: SBP.

*Provisional figure.

which do not find financial statements and business plans easy to produce. The general resistance of banks to accept movable collateral is compounded in Pakistan by a secured transactions system that makes it unsafe to lend to a sole proprietor by collateralizing the loan with a movable asset. Currently, only limited liability companies can register, and hence notify to the public at large, a lien over movable assets. They do so in the company registry, which is not available for unlimited liability companies, as these are not registered (more details on this are provided later in this chapter). To remove this barrier for sole proprietor SMEs, the SBP has attempted to introduce a registry for liens over movable assets. However, encountering delays in setting the new system in place, the SBP introduced a regulation in 2004 allowing uncollateralized lending for loans up to Rs 3 million and without financial statements for loans up to Rs 10 million. Despite the new legality of this lending, the lending practice is proving too risky for conservative Pakistani banks.

To facilitate the creation of a credit history for SMEs, SBP has promoted the establishment of credit bureaus, both public and private. However, despite their improved performance, their coverage is limited, especially for smaller borrowers. As in other countries, Pakistani SMEs have no or little formal credit history; this makes formal financial institutions more hesitant to lend to the segment. To promote the creation of formal credit histories by small businesses, SBP founded a public CIB in 1992. The CIB records both positive and negative information about companies, as well as all the assets they use as collateral for the loans. CIB performance was enhanced in 2006 with the introduction of an e CIB system, which improved speed, reliability, and security of data. In that same year, CIB coverage was expanded to all loan sizes. In addition to the state-owned CIB, two privately owned credit bureaus now operate in the country. Despite their improved performance, credit bureaus cover only 10–20 percent of the borrowers and very few SMEs requiring loans smaller than Rs 6 million. This is partly because the banks lend to this segment and partly because the bureaus do not collect information from the telecom and utility companies, which could substantially contribute to building a credit history for SMEs.

To create a demonstration effect for other market participants, the GOP has supported the creation of a specialized SME Bank, which, in three years since its inception, has served a mere 1 percent of the market. To challenge the market and demonstrate that the SME segment is not only viable but very profitable, the GOP created a bank dedicated to serving only SMEs (table 4.3 and box 4.1). SME Bank was created by merging two failed state-owned banks. In 2007, two years after starting operations, SME Bank had only 2,200 clients (1.2 percent of total SME borrowers) and offered less than 2 percent of total SME finance extended by the banking sector.

Lack of shareholders with the required know-how is the primary reason for the failure of SME Bank to catalyze the market. A number of factors, but most notably two, have contributed to the failure of the SME Bank experiment. First, because the

Table 4.3 Results for Selected Small Business Banks (December 2007)

	Pro Credit Ukraine	BancoSol Bolivia	BRAC Bank Bangladesh	SME Bank Pakistan
Total assets (million $)	454	269.9	676.1	107.4
Year of establishment	2001	1992	1999	2002
Number of outlets or branches	71	49	Branches: 36 SME unit offices: 392	27
Number of loan officers	246*	297*	1,369	18
Average time to disburse a loan (days)	5	5	15	40
Gross loan portfolio (million in $)	389.2	209	473.2	126.6
Average loan size outstanding (in $)	7,358	2,360	4,067	13,703**
Portfolio at risk (PAR) >30 days	0.98%	1%	18%	72%***
Total assets for holding/fund (in $)	6 billion	140.3 million	2.4 billion	Not Applicable

Source: Pro Credit Ukraine; BancoSol, Bolivia; BRAC Bank, Bangladesh; SME Bank, Pakistan.

*Data for 2005.

**Average loan size disbursed ($).

***Percentage of the portfolio classified as loss as per SBP regulations.

Box 4.1 SME Bank

To act as a catalyst for the SME market, in 2002 the GOP created SME Bank Ltd. through the merger of two failed Development Financial Institutions, the Regional Development Finance Corporation (RDFC) and Small Business Finance Corporation (SBFC). SME Bank received a commercial banking license in 2004 and started operations in mid-2005. Its current shareholders are the federal government (92.68 percent) and six banks (7.32 percent). The bank was poised to be privatized shortly after becoming operational. However, the Supreme Court decision to reverse the Pakistan Still Mills privatization, the fact that the SME bank was a small-ticket item in the privatization list, and the increasingly deteriorating security situation in the country have put the privatization on hold.

SME Bank operates a total of 27 branches: 13 commercial banking branches and 14 recovery branches. In December 2007, its total assets were Rs 6.6 billion, and its net outstanding loans amounted to Rs 2.1 billion. As of 2007, the bank had only 2,200 clients, or 1.2 percent of total SME borrowers in the country, for an average loan size of Rs 840,000 over the three years. In theory, the bank provides loans of terms up to seven years. In practice, however, working capital loans of up to Rs 500,000 are given up to a term of three years, and asset finance up to four years; in exceptional cases, the term can be up to five years.

(continued)

Box 4.1 **continued**

Despite this growth, SME Bank has not been able to meet the credit needs of the SME sector; this stems from its use of traditional lending technology that does not distinguish between large corporations and small businesses, inappropriate product design, and lengthy application procedures (it takes on average 40 days to receive a loan). Unlike at other SME banks, SME Bank loan officers do not have a bonus system based on the performance and size of the loan portfolio that they generate and manage.

A comparison with successful SME banks in the region and beyond is presented in the table below. Pakistan's SME Bank has by far the worst portfolio performance, with 72 percent of the gross loan portfolio in volume classified as loss. The limited attention paid to lending is also reflected in the bank human resource policy of employing only a small number of loan officers, fewer than one per branch.

Source: Author's interview with SME Bank management.

intended privatization of the bank never took place, the bank does not have institutional investors with the know-how required to support the bank (for example, the board did not give clear and ambitious quantitative targets to bank management). Second, being created from what remained of two failed institutions meant that SME Bank management had to expend energy on restructuring rather than expanding and modifying its operating model to serve a new market segment.

The GOP has funded technical assistance for NBP to enter the SME segment, with some success. Starting in 2005, the GOP facilitated the delivery of technical assistance to the NBP to substantially expand SME lending. Lending on a cash-flow, not collateral, basis was introduced, and loan officers were put on performance-based contracts. NBP has achieved some promising results after three years (box 4.2). Nevertheless, while the program has certainly increased NBP's lending to SMEs, the size of the SME loan portfolio remains quite small. By comparison, similar programs in China over the same time period expanded to loans for an average of $10,000 with a portfolio at risk (PAR) >30 days of 1 percent, totaling $380 million in 15 regions in the country (see box 4.4). The Pakistan program's limited success is most likely attributable to the lack of competition. While downscaling programs with state-owned banks can work, usually they are combined with downscaling programs for faster-moving private banks, which implement the required changes at a faster pace.

In addition, SBP has introduced a more detailed SME definition on a pilot basis and requested banks to report quarterly; although this is a step in the right direction, the brackets are too many, which makes banks reporting too complex. To monitor SME lending, SBP created an SME department and now requires banks to report all loans smaller than Rs 75 million on a quarterly basis. Thus, implicitly, SBP

Box 4.2   National Bank of Pakistan's SME Lending

NBP is a state-owned bank with the largest branch network (1,243 branches) in the country. Its total assets exceeded $12 billion in 2007. In 2005, NBP signed a technical assistance agreement with ShoreBank International under a U.S. Agency of International Development (USAID)–financial sector project to substantially increase small business lending (loans typically under Rs 2 million). As part of the agreement, ShoreBank International introduced a bonus system for its loan officers based on the number of loans issued and quality of the performance of the loan they managed. Loan officers were trained in the new lending methodology and onsite support was provided to active branches. NBP and ShoreBank International are continuing to work together on a new bilateral agreement paid for by NBP that runs through 2009.

Initially, the task of convincing loan officers and managers to focus on small enterprise loans proved to be difficult. The branches lacked a performance-based culture, and there were many management layers. Most credit decisions were based on the basis of immovable collateral. The challenge for the ShoreBank International team was to shift the focus from collateral to underwriting on cash flows and business performance. After extensive fieldwork, forms and formats were designed to assess repayment capacities based on projected cash flows and financial ratio analysis. In addition, a tool was developed to assist loan officers in converting informal cash book receipts into standard financial documents. But more important than the underwriting approach was the need to effectively motivate loan officers to leave their branch offices to market and underwrite new loans at the business premises.

The start was slow, but the key step in the process was introducing a regular monitoring report that was shared at all levels of NBP, providing a transparent measure of progress. This report, circulated at least monthly, served to stimulate interest and keep senior management and branch-level teams focused on measureable objectives. NBP's loans to SMEs increased starting in June 2006. Over the first 18 months of the agreement, 658 loans were issued for a total loan portfolio of Rs 1.4 billion. Data on performance of outstanding loan portfolio are presented in the table below.

Portfolio Quality of the SME Lending Program (November 30, 2007)

Number of loans	510
Amount of outstanding loan portfolio (Rs)	Rs 813,089,934
Amount of outstanding loan portfolio (USD)	$13,439,503
Average loan size	$26,352
Number of overdue loans >90 days	8
% of overdue loans (volume) >90 days	2%

Source: ShoreBank International staff.

Table 4.4 Credit to the Private Sector: A Profile (Rs billion)

Sector of the Economy	December 2004		December 2005		December 2006		December 2007	
	Amount	Share (%)	Amount	Share (%)	Amount	Share (%)	Amount	Share (%)
Corporate	873	53.9	1,076.20	52.7	1279.1	53.3	1520.1	56.3
SMEs	284	17.5	361.4	17.7	408.3	17	437.4	16.2
Agriculture	119.3	7.4	138	6.8	141.9	5.9	150.8	5.6
Consumer finance	152.6	9.4	252.8	12.4	325.2	13.5	371.4	13.8
Commodity operations	122.1	7.5	140.6	6.9	171.9	7.2	148.4	5.5
Staff loans	40.8	2.5	42.4	2.1	48	2	52.2	1.9
Other	28.6	1.8	31.6	1.5	26.4	1.1	20.6	0.8
Total	1,620.40	100	2,043.00	100	2,400.80	100	2700.9	100.0

Source: SBP.

has defined SME loans as those smaller than Rs 75 million; this definition is intended to facilitate bank reporting. While this could allow tracking of lending to the segment to begin, the breakdowns are too many and might actually discourage banks from reporting accurate information.

Government efforts to increase SME access to financing have had modest results, with loans to SMEs declining as a percentage of total lending. Against the backdrop of a growing banking sector, SME lending has witnessed a slight downward trend over the period 2004–7. SMEs accounted for 16.2 percent of total credit to the private sector in 2007, down from 17.5 percent in 2004. In contrast, both corporate and consumer finance grew, from 54 percent to 56 percent and from 9 percent to 14 percent, respectively, in the same period (table 4.3). The average SME loan has also slightly increased in size, reaching Rs 2.4 million.

Access to Finance for SMEs: Demand-Side Evidence

To complement the broad picture of SME financial access presented from supply indicators, this section measures access from the demand side. The analysis presented here is mainly based on the 2005 urban demand survey, conducted by KfW. The survey covered 510 SME businesses operating in manufacturing, trade, and other service sectors in the Punjabi cities of Faisalabad, Gujranwala, Lahore, Sargodha, and Sialkot. The survey defined SMEs as those businesses employing no more than 100 permanent employees (see Annex 4.1 for detailed description of the survey building blocks, methodology, and sampling).

The analysis here also draws on the 2005 European Commission Survey and the 2002 and 2007 Investment Climate Assessment (ICA) surveys (World Bank 2003 and 2009). The European Commission Survey covered 100 manufacturing SMEs in the golden triangle,[3] while the 2002 and 2007 ICA surveyed 965 and 1,184 enterprises, respectively, in manufacturing and services in urban Pakistan.[3] It should be stressed that, although the definitions of SMEs used by the European Commission and ICA surveys vary slightly from those used in the KfW survey, the difference is negligible and their key findings on financial access (access, sources, obstacles) coincide. All the data presented here, unless specifically mentioned otherwise, refer to the 2005 KfW dataset.

Although a considerable number of Pakistani SMEs have a bank account, few borrow from banks. The SMEs have also more limited access to finance than their counterparts in India and Bangladesh (figure 4.1). Thirty-six percent of **Pakistani** SMEs have a bank account, while only 7 percent had at least one loan outstanding in the previous three years (2002–5). In comparison, in 2006, 43 percent of SMEs in Bangladesh, and 95 percent in India, had a bank account,[4] and 32 percent and 33 percent, respectively, had a loan from a bank. Moreover, it should be highlighted that Bangladeshi and Indian SMEs also have access to finance from other financial institutions, mainly MFIs in Bangladesh and finance companies in India.

Over the 2002–6 period, SME access to finance increased, though this is attributable to increased access for medium enterprises rather than for the whole segment. The number of enterprises that reported having at least one outstanding loan or overdraft facility increased substantially from 2002 to 2005 (ICA 2002 and 2007). However, when disaggregating the data, access to financial services has increased only marginally for small enterprises (from 10 percent to 11 percent) and has increased substantially for medium-size enterprises (from 27 percent to 43 percent). This finding is in line with the result of interviews with banks that identified a financing gap at the bottom of the market (Rs 100,000–5 million).

During the same period, enterprises that had a credit history found it easier to access finance. Firms covered in the KfW survey that had applied for loans in the 2002–4 period were asked whether access to bank loans had become easier over the period, and 53 percent claimed that is was very/fairly easy in 2004 versus 33 percent in 2002.

Figure 4.1 Access to Finance for SMEs in Pakistan, India, and Bangladesh

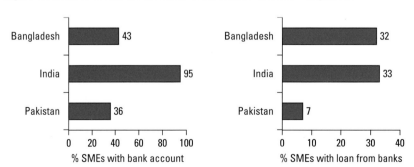

Source: India ICA 2006 Manufacturing Enterprise Survey, Bangladesh 2006 Rural MSME Finance Services Survey, Pakistan KfW Demand Survey 2005.

Improvement in access to financial services mainly for medium-size enterprises and for enterprises that already have a credit history is probably a short-term outcome of the privatization. Immediately post privatization, as banks reduce non-performing loans, reorganize, and start expanding their portfolios, they tend to apply stricter risk management rules and to focus on more established clients. This, combined with a reduction of mandated lending to smaller clients and government-financed products, often causes a short-term reduction in lending to the lower end of the market. Only after competition in the more established segment has intensified do banks start focusing on a lower segment.

The SME total demand is at least Rs 277 billion, pinning estimates of the market gap at above Rs 250 billion. The KfW survey asked respondents to estimate the amount of external financing required to finance working capital and fixed investments in 2005. Based on these estimates, the potential market size for serving small businesses is approximately Rs 300 billion (see box 4.3). More than 90 percent of this demand is still unserved, making small business finance a highly attractive

---

Box 4.3   How Big Is the Potential Market for Providing Credit to SMEs?

Although it is impossible to precisely quantify the overall demand for credit by small businesses in Pakistan, an approximation can be attempted by extrapolating from the results of the 2005 KfW urban demand survey. According to Small and Medium Enterprise Development Authority (SMEDA) estimates, there are close to 3.2 million micro, small, and medium-size enterprises in Pakistan.

Close to half of all businesses surveyed required external financing of Rs 100,000–5 million. (Eighty-two percent of respondents needed loans for working capital and 61 percent of this demand fell into the Rs 100,000–5 million range; 40 percent of the respondents needed loans for fixed capital, of which 74 percent fell into the Rs 100,000–5 million range.) Fifty percent (61 percent of 82 percent) of SMEs require financing in the Rs 100,000–5 million range, and there are around 1.6 million such enterprises. However, not all of these will qualify for bank loans.

Assuming that 70 percent of firms that want to borrow are creditworthy and that 70 percent of these are borrowing at the same time, there are around 800,000 eligible SMEs in Pakistan. All of these clients want to borrow working capital, and around 500,000 want to borrow to finance fixed investments. For the sake of simplicity, it is assumed that fixed investment borrowers are a subset of the larger group needing working capital and only 20 percent of all potential borrowers will get a parallel loan.

Survey results indicated that, in the case of working capital, 85 percent of clients require loans in the Rs 100,000–1 million range, while 15 percent require loans of up to Rs 5 million. In the case of fixed investments, loan requirements are nearly evenly split. Forty-nine percent of clients wish to borrow in the lower range, while 51 percent want to take out a loan of between Rs 1 million and 5 million.

(continued)

Box 4.3 **continued**

Amounts and Purposes of Loans Required by Small Businesses

Loan Purpose	Lower Range (Rs 100,000–1 million)	Upper Range (Rs 1–5 million)	Total Borrowers
Working capital	680,000	120,000	800,000
Fixed investments	78,400	81,600	160,000

The absolute minimum total loan volume required by small businesses can be derived by multiplying the number of borrowers in each category by the minimum loan amount. In other words, all lower-range borrowers are assumed to require only Rs 100,000. Upper-range clients are assumed to require exactly one loan of Rs 1,000,000 each.

Minimum Credit Needs of Small Businesses in Pakistan

Loan Purpose	Lower Range (Rs 100,000–1 million)	Upper Range (Rs 1–5 million)	Total Credit Needs
Working capital	68,000,000,000	120,000,000,000	188,000,000,000
Fixed investments	7,840,000,000	81,600,000,000	89,000,000,000
All loans			**277,000,000,000**

While calculating the total credit demand, only minimal loan amounts were taken into account for working and fixed capital needs. Hence, the total credit demand can be safely rounded up to close to Rs 300 billion and perhaps even higher.

Source: Authors' calculations based on the 2005 KfW demand survey.

venture for profit- and growth-oriented banks in Pakistan. Huge credit demand coupled with minimal supply promises high profit margins and strong growth for banks going downmarket. Thanks to the large market size, banks will be able to sustain growth rates in SME loan portfolios for years to come if they can understand well this particular market segment and change their banking practices to effectively cater to the needs of small businesses.

SMEs use limited bank funding for both working capital and fixed investments; formal funding is even more limited for small than for medium enterprises. Approximately 89 percent of working capital and 75 percent of fixed investments were financed from retained earnings in 2003–5 and the percentages are even larger for micro- and small enterprises: 90 percent for working capital and 81 percent for new investment (figures 4.2 and 4.3). Microenterprises also do not substitute banks with MFIs, but rather borrow more from family and friends. This is explainable by the more acute gap that there is in the market for loan sizes between Rs 100,000 and Rs 5 million (equivalent to between $1,280 and $64,000). This segment is also not

Figure 4.2 External Sources of Working Capital

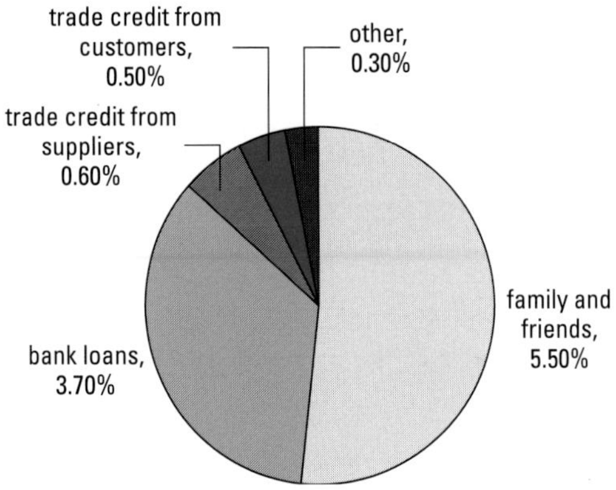

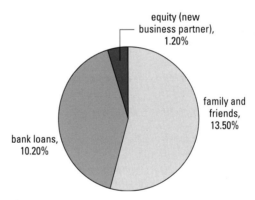

trade credit from customers, 0.50%

other, 0.30%

trade credit from suppliers, 0.60%

family and friends, 5.50%

bank loans, 3.70%

Source: KfW Demand Survey 2005.

Figure 4.3 External Sources of Fixed Capital

equity (new business partner), 1.20%

family and friends, 13.50%

bank loans, 10.20%

Source: KfW Demand Survey 2005.

served by banks for the reasons mentioned above, or by the microfinance sector, which is legally bound to lend up to Rs 100,000 and traditionally focused on the lower end of the market.

Not only do microenterprises apply less frequently for loans, when they do, they are much more likely to be rejected than medium-size ones. Access to credit becomes progressively more constrained as the size of the enterprise becomes smaller: only 10.7 percent of microenterprises applied for credit compared with 25 percent of medium enterprises, and nearly 75 percent of them were refused a loan, whereas more than two-thirds of medium enterprises managed to secure the loan for which they applied (figure 4.4, table 4.5).

Enterprises do not seem to be excluded from financial markets because of poor performance. The European Commission survey reports that 60 percent of the

Figure 4.4 Loan Application and Disbursement by Firm

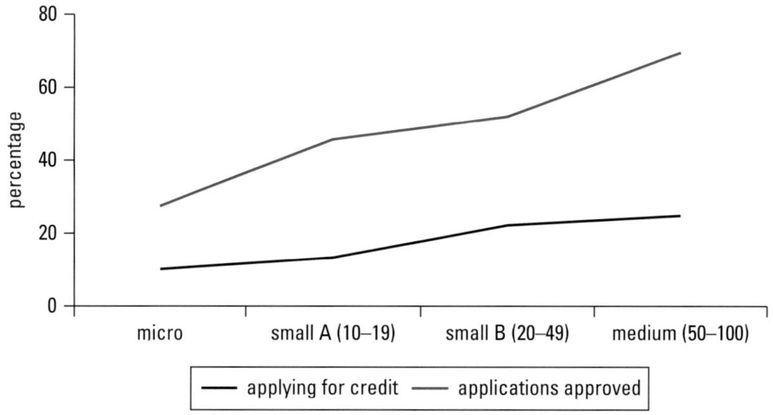

Source: KfW Demand Survey 2005.

SMEs have profit margins in the range of 5–10 percent, while 12 percent have higher profit margins of 15–20 percent. This is corroborated by SME owners' favorable perceptions of their own business performance in the preceding two years (2003–5). More than 60 percent think that business has improved, while only 12 percent think that business has declined (table 4.5). It would seem that many

Table 4.5 Ease of Obtaining Credit 2002–4

	2002 (%)	2004 (%)
Very easy	0.0	27.8
Fairly easy	33.3	25.0
Fairly difficult	27.3	16.7
Very difficult	39.4	30.6
Total	**100.0**	**100.0**

Source: KfW Demand Survey 2005.

Table 4.6 Business Development in the Past 24 Months, by Firm Size (Number of Employees)

	Micro	Small (10–19)	Small (20–49)	Medium (50–100)	Total
Declined significantly	3.7	4.2	2.2	1.9	3.3
Declined somewhat	8.9	8.4	10.8	7.7	9
Remained the same	30.7	13.7	23.7	30.8	26.3
Improved somewhat	39.6	38.9	33.3	26.9	37.1
Improved significantly	17	34.7	30.1	32.7	24.3
Total	**100**	**100**	**100**	**100**	**100**

Source: KfW Demand Survey 2005.

SMEs are excluded from financial markets not because of bad performance but because of a gap in the market.

When asked, SMEs state that banks are only the third preferred source of borrowing, mainly because of high direct and indirect costs and complex products. Of the 85 percent of the sample that did not apply for credit in 2002–5, the majority (54 percent) cited availability of other sources of financing as the reason.

When asked to rank their preferred sources, SMEs rank banks only third, after nongovernmental organization MFIs and family/friends. Other sources are preferred because of lower direct and indirect costs (50 percent), because banks do not offer Islamic banking products (24), and because banks require a lot of collateral (10 percent). Direct costs include interest and fees; indirect costs include the cost of producing the required documents, time the owner needs to spend with bank officials, and length of the process, which translates into missing earning opportunities.

Banks require immovable collateral almost exclusively. Firms interviewed in the 2007 ICA survey reported that banks accept almost exclusively immovable assets and personal assets of the owner (also mainly immovable assets) as collateral; 92 percent of the interviewed SMEs had to provide immovable assets only or immovable and movable assets, with the latter in a secondary amount.

These findings are corroborated by the features that SMEs look for in loan products: low direct and indirect costs, convenient repayment periods, and no requirements for immovable collateral, in very close order. Respondents assessed the importance of each aspect of borrowing on a scale of 1 to 5, 1 being "least important" and 5 being "very important" (table 4.7). For the respondents, low direct and indirect cost and convenient repayment period are the most important features of a loan product and must be emphasized in the design of a loan product. The constraints to improving SME access to finance are noted in the next section.

Table 4.7 Demanded Loan Product Features

	Mean
Low direct and indirect cost	4.37
Convenient repayment period	4.39
Absence of requirement for immovable property as collateral	3.94
Convenient location of financial institution	3.81
Quality of service of financial institution's staff	3.75
Availability of other financial services from same provider	3.63

Source: KfW Demand Survey 2005.

Constraints to Improving SME Access to Finance

Pakistani banks treat SMEs as large corporate enterprises, when, in fact, SME lending has more similarities with consumer finance. In recent years, SME lending in relative terms has decreased, while lending to corporate and consumer finance has grown. This is mainly because banks make little or no distinction between larger corporations and SMEs in terms of product and procedures. Similarities between consumer and SME finance include low-value transactions and sensitivity to loan delivery time. However, unlike consumer finance, SME lending requires a more individualized assessment of cash flows, because SMEs often have limited and sometimes inaccurate written statements.

SMEs are characterized by limited formality and are sensitive to loan delivery time and complex procedures. SMEs are usually small, family-owned businesses, run and managed by one or two people taking full responsibility for all aspects of the business. These individuals typically know their business well but lack the skills to produce written business and financial plans and are discouraged by the extensive documentation requirements of banks. Moreover, when such enterprises require financing, they usually need it immediately because their management rarely plans operations far in advance. It also is common that these enterprises have limited or no formal credit history, lack formal financial statements, and possess few immovable assets. Business and household finances are strongly intertwined, and are mainly cash. It should be noted that the banking needs of SMEs are very different from those of large corporations, and even among the SMEs, product preferences differ significantly.

Large volumes, efficiency, and quality are key to profitable small business lending. To profitably serve SMEs, banks need to minimize transaction costs and generate a large number of high-quality loans. As in similar activities with small profit margins, banks need to increase revenue by making many loans while lowering expenses—for example, by making loan officers more productive and avoiding bad loans.

An incomplete legal and regulatory framework and lack of SME-friendly products and procedures hamper increased SME lending. Banks in Pakistan find it difficult to serve SMEs profitably for several reasons. First, the legal and regulatory framework (namely, the secured transactions regions and, to a lesser extent, the credit information infrastructure) limits the pool of potential applicants. Second, lending products and bank procedures are more suited to large corporations than smaller enterprises. Finally, banks do not have organizational structures and monitoring tools conducive to achieving high efficiency.

In spite of substantial improvements in the legal and regulatory framework, work remains to be done in the area of secured transactions.[5] Progress has also been substantial on creating credit bureaus, though more could be done to facilitate the creation of credit histories by SMEs. In spite of the reform that the GOP and SBP initiated five years ago, there is still no coherent secured transactions regime and no registry where unlimited liability companies can register a lien on movable assets. SBP has tried to compensate for this by waiving collateral requirements for very small loans (SME prudential regulation). However, banks have proven to be too risk averse to take full advantage of the regulation and still prefer loans collateralized with immovable assets. Both a well-functioning secured transactions regime and a more complete credit information system could help gap the bridge between demand and supply of SME lending.

An effective secured transactions regime plays a vital role in a country's financial system.[6] By expanding the pool of assets that can be offered as collateral, a secured transactions system can help expand financial access for those who were previously excluded or had only limited financial access. Furthermore, a reformed secured transaction regime can promote access to credit and allow credit to be extended on better terms, by improving transparency in determining the debtor's creditworthiness and by increasing security in establishing claimants to collateral. Empirical evidence from a number of developing countries suggests that an increase in the index of acceptable collateral is associated with better financial access to bank loans for firms, including for SMEs (figure 4.5).

The existing secured transactions system has major deficiencies that limit, in particular, SME use of movable collateral. Key components of an effective secured transactions regime are:

1. Creation: establishing a claim to property to secure payment of credit;

2. Priority: determining ranking of claims over collateral;

3. Publicity: making priority interests publicly known; and

4. Enforcement: repossessing collateral and selling it for satisfying claims.

Figure 4.5 Bank Access Increases with a Wider Range of Acceptable Assets to Secure a Loan

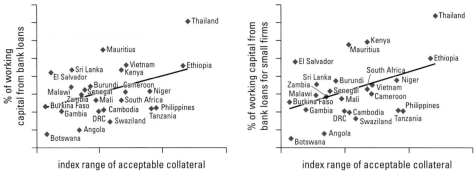

Source: World Bank (2008a).

Note a: A cross-country regression of the % of firms with working capital funded by bank loans on the index of acceptable collateral shows that a 10% increase in the index is associated with a 3.3% increase in firms using bank loans to fund working capital (t-stat: 1.78).

Note b: A cross-country regression of the % of small firms with working capital funded by bank loans on the index of acceptable collateral shows that a 10% increase in the index is associated with a 2.8% increase in small firms using bank loans to fund working capital (t-stat: 1.78).

Annex 4.2 presents a detailed analysis of the secured transactions regime in Pakistan, and underscores several shortcomings of the system, including certain legal provisions that slow down enforcement, the lack of specialized courts, and the absence of a comprehensive, single registry for all moveable charges in respect of all types of debtors (corporate or otherwise). The system's main limitations are described below.

Multiple laws and systems: In Pakistan, there is no simple, unified statute pertaining to the creation of security over movable property. The multiple laws and systems create uncertainty and difficulties in using movable property as collateral. Another important limitation is that the debtor must possess any collateral being pledged. In addition, the legal framework for enforcement against not-yet-existent collateral is weak. This affects the use of agricultural products (such as future crops), inventory, or after-acquired property as collateral and would make it difficult for many small businesses that do not have a significant amount of other classes of assets beyond after-acquired property to obtain secured credit.

Availability of secured transactions over movable property only to registered companies: Another important limitation is that the system of secured transactions over movable property is available primarily to registered companies only. This is because the registration of security interests is generally only available for registered companies (unless the assets being used are themselves subject to registration) and not for any other organizations or business entities falling outside of the Companies Ordinance, 1984. This strongly discriminates against small businesses, which are not registered companies.

High transaction costs: There is no unified registry for all types of security interests granted by all types of entities on all types of movable property. Pakistan has a mixed system of asset-based registries and an entity-based registry. Not all registries operate on a notice filing basis and entire agreements need to be filled. In addition, presently, only the companies' registry is available online and is networked across the country. With a paper-based system, verification of collateral becomes a time-consuming process that does not allow potential lenders real-time searches of existing liens. This substantially increases the transaction costs of filing security interests.

Slow enforcement process: Enforcement of debt recovery is slow in Pakistan. A security holder has to file a suit in court to recover his claim. However, for financial institutions, expedited procedures are available under the Financial Institutions (Recovery of Finances) Ordinance, 2001. But even in these cases, should the debtor dispute the enforcement by the creditor (which is usually the case), a fairly lengthy court procedure will ensue. In practice, if a financial institution is enforcing its security right under the special summary procedures, it would take one and a half to two years for the enforcement to be completed. In other cases, it may take 10–15 years or more. By this time, most movable property would have lost its value, thus discouraging financial institutions to accept such collateral.

Having a formal credit history is particularly important for SMEs, which are often less known entities to the banking community. Credit registry, through which lenders share information about their clients' repayment records, is an established way of enhancing the ability of borrowers to signal a good credit record. Credit

Table 4.8 SME Application Process for Bank Loans

Indicator	Average Number
Steps	27
Meetings with borrower	9
Staff involved	8
Borrower time (hours)	10

Source: Authors' calculations.

registry is even more important for SMEs, many of which have had limited contact with the banking community (64 percent of the Pakistani SMEs do not have a bank account), less formal accounts, and a more limited ability to produce a written business plan. While progress on the credit infrastructure has been substantial, work remains to be done. In particular, the inclusion of information from utilities and telecom providers in the registry could greatly facilitate the creation of credit history for SMEs. This information could then be used as the platform through which SMEs can in the future show a track record of repayment to banks.

Bank procedures and policies used for SME lending are too complex, making them time consuming and costly for both parties (table 4.8). Banks apply the same rules and policies to small enterprises as they apply to large corporations; as a result, a typical small business loan requires up to 27 steps for the bank (or 20 hours) and 9 meetings with clients (or 10 hours of the potential borrower). Total time taken to obtain a loan can vary from 30 to 45 days on average. Such long and expensive procedures limit the number of loans that can be made a month per loan officer. Furthermore, it translates into missed business opportunities for SMEs, because the manager/employee must spend time away from the business to complete procedures to obtain a loan. In addition to these high transaction costs, indirect costs in terms of legal fees, collateral registration, and documentation make bank lending expensive for SMEs.

Banks have limited specialization in SME lending and no measures of SME business performance. Banks further shy away from SMEs due to lower value per transaction and distinctive features of SMEs, which are considered an additional credit risk. Bank SME lending is thus mainly driven by risk concerns and no attention is really paid to efficiency, which is the key to serving this particular market segment profitably. Risk concerns must carefully be balanced against considerations of customer orientation and efficiency when designing products and procedures for small clients. To achieve higher efficiency, specialization of staff, training, and procedures are essential. In Pakistan, banks do not engage sufficiently in such practices.

Most Pakistani banks do not have specialized loan officers, training, or procedures for SME lending. Additional efficiency gains could be achieved by measuring this type of lending and aligning staff rewards to the quality of the portfolio they manage. Even though Pakistani banks have sophisticated management information systems, they do not currently use them for monitoring the efficiency of individual staff members and lending departments, and staff rewards are usually unrelated to their performance. An example of a successful downscaling program for banks is presented in box 4.4.

Box 4.4   China SME Lending Project

Since 2005, China Development Bank has sponsored technical assistance programs with lines of credit to encourage banks to increase SME lending. The program, which is funded by KfW and the World Bank, includes both privately owned and state-owned banks. The key components of the program are represented graphically below. As illustrated, each participating bank signs a binding performance agreement (indicating, for example, how many loan officers will be devoted to the new product, how many loans will be disbursed per month, and the PAR to which the banks commit).

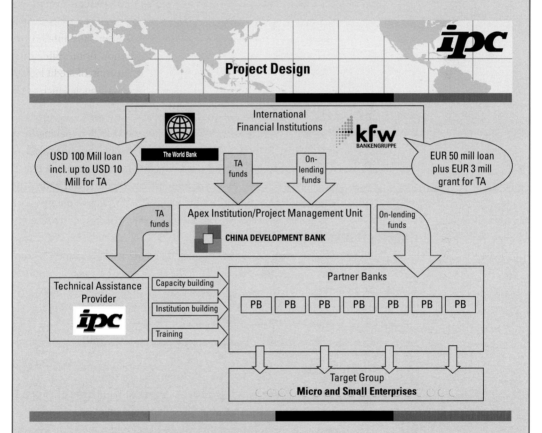

About 12 banks in China have participated in the program, and 6 of them have already successfully graduated. All banks have some sort of local government or government enterprise ownership, except for one bank, which is fully privately owned.

The program has achieved very impressive results: As of June 2008, three years since the start of its operation, $380 million had been disbursed, with an average loan size of less than $10,000 and PAR for less than 30 days at less than 1 percent. The program had expanded to

(continued)

Box 4.4   continued

15 regions and 42 percent of the loans had been disbursed in rural areas. Product profitability assessments show that most participating banks broke even within two years of starting the micro, small, and medium enterprise (MSME) loan business. The most profitable bank had a return on assets of more than 4 percent after three years of operation.

There are various incentives for banks to join the program. First, MSME lending is profitable, and the consultant working with the bank helps the bank to build a model that can track that lending. Second, lending to MSMEs allows the participating banks to diversify their portfolio and hence their risk. Third, the technical assistance provided under the program forces bank management to think of their risk management practices for all lending products (although changes are introduced only for MSMEs). Last, participating banks mitigate financial risks by diversifying their sources of funds with subloans from the China Development Bank.

Key features behind the success of the products include: (1) an efficient decision-making process, thanks to which a customer usually gets a small loan within three days; (2) equal loan repayments required to be made by customers every month, allowing the bank to closely monitor the risk especially in the early days; and (3) flexible collateral requirements make micro loans more accessible to smaller clients. In some cases, collateral requirements are waived altogether.

Source: Discussion with *Internationale Projekt Consult (IPC) GmbH*, World Bank staff, and China Development Bank.

Helping Banks Serve SMEs

To bridge the gap between supply and demand, the GOP and SBP could continue to promote an enabling environment that facilitates SME lending. This includes, first and foremost, creating a complete and well-functioning secured transactions regime. Security interests over movable assets should be easy and allowed on most assets and by every entity (both physical and juridical persons). Priority rankings should also be clearly defined among those who might have claims on property offered as collateral. The new secured transactions regime should also include a place (such as a registry) for making priority interests publicly known, and enforcement of security interests for all assets should be fast and cheap. Second, to facilitate the creation of a credit history for SMEs, SBP should also ensure that the credit bureau collects information from utility and telecom companies. Third, to facilitate SME lending monitoring, SBP should mainstream the piloted reporting requirements and simplify bank reporting for SME portfolios to include volumes and number of loans only in four sub-brackets (Rs <2M, Rs 2–6M, Rs 6–25M, and Rs 25–75M).

The GOP should also continue to promote initiatives aimed at proving a demonstration effect because an enabling environment is a necessary but not sufficient condition for SME lending expansion. These include attraction to the market of an institutional investor that has a track record in SME lending. This should ideally be achieved by selling the SME bank or giving controlling rights on its board to an institutional investor. To stimulate competition in the market from the very beginning, the GOP could also support long-term technical assistance programs for selected banks. As illustrated by the China MSME lending program (see box 4.4), for this program to be successful, the GOP needs to ensure correct market incentives are in place. Key features of programs that have worked are outlined below.

1. *Long-term technical assistance is required to ensure that the necessary substantial changes take place.* Lending to small businesses requires profound changes in the way commercial banks operate. With its high transaction costs, small business lending is only profitable if done in high numbers with excellent portfolio quality. It is therefore important to provide banks long-term support in this challenging process. Technical assistance to improve lending technology should focus on reducing transaction costs for both the bank and the client, increasing loan officer productivity (in terms of number of loans disbursed), and maintaining high portfolio quality.

2. *Selection of bank advisers and content of the technical assistance are key to success.* The technical assistance package should be comprehensive because the changes that are required are substantial. In addition to its scope, the success of the technical assistance program will depend upon three elements: selection of committed banks, selection of consultancy firms with a strong record in banking, and close monitoring by a fully dedicated and experienced staff. The technical assistance should include redesigning bank products to meet client needs, a robust management information system, and use of staff incentives linked to their performance.

3. *A mix of committed banks should participate in the program to create competition among them.* Technical assistance should be provided only to those banks that are fully committed to SME lending. Serving such enterprises requires a change in the entire corporate culture and in the way banks operate. Thus, only banks whose investors are willing to engage in such substantive transformations should be offered technical assistance. Often, banks with a large banking network and a focus on retail lending have a comparative advantage in entering this market segment. Smaller banks could also be targeted, however, to act as catalysts. Many countries have developed specialized SME programs in state-owned banks with large networks. However, success usually takes a few years because, as was just noted, the changes required are substantial and banks take time in implementing them. It is therefore essential that technical assistance be also given to small, faster-moving private banks, which transform at a faster speed but may reach stagnation due to their smaller networks.

4. *Performance agreements for banks participating in the program are key.* Furthermore, performance agreements should also incorporate terms on the number and volume of loans disbursed and outstanding by a given date, as well as portfolio quality indicators, such as keeping PAR over 30 days to less than 3 percent.

The technical assistance should last at least two years and performance agreements should be monitored on a monthly basis so that timely remedial measures could be undertaken when targets are not met.

In sum, while policy efforts have had some success, more work is needed, especially on bank downscaling products. Few SMEs in Pakistan borrow from banks, as compared with SMEs in other countries in the South Asia region including India and Bangladesh. In spite of substantial improvements of the legal and regulatory framework, work remains to be done in the area of secured transactions. Progress has also been substantial on credit bureaus, though more could be done to facilitate the creation of credit histories by SMEs. Access to finance for small and microenterprise is particularly stalled. Yet those are the entities most likely to contribute to employment and poverty reduction. Together with microclients, discussed in the previous chapter, and remittance clients, the object of the following chapter, the underserved micro- and small enterprises require urgent policy making to expand access to finance.

Notes

1. Economic Survey 2008.
2. An SME study was conducted by the European Commission in 2005 under its Pakistan Financial Services Sector Reform Program. The SME definition used was: small (medium) enterprises that employ up to 50 persons (51–250 persons), assets excluding land and building not more than Rs 30 million (Rs 30–100 million), and sales up to Rs 100 million (up to Rs 300 million).
3. The 2002 ICA survey defines small enterprises as those employing 1–19 employees and medium enterprises as those employing 20–99 employees. The same definition of firm size is used for the analysis of the 2007 ICA in this current study.
4. Data for Bangladesh are based on the 2006 Rural MSME Finance Services Survey, which includes 226 SMEs in cities outside of Dhaka and Chittagong. Data for India refer to ICA 2006 manufacturing enterprise survey, which includes 2460 firms in 16 states across India; only data for SMEs (enterprises with less than 100 employees) were used in this analysis.
5. SBP, in cooperation with ADB, have recently completed a detailed study on improving the secured transactions regime and the public registry office, incorporating issues of the creation of interest over movable assets and charge for SMEs and rural finance.
6. Secured transaction is defined as any transaction, regardless of its form, that is intended to create a security interest in personal property or fixtures, including goods, documents, and other intangibles. A security interest is a right given to one party in the asset of another party to secure payment or performance of an obligation. Collateral constitutes the assets over which security is granted.

Annex 4.1 Sample Description of KfW SME Survey

Urban Demand Survey

In March–April 2005, KfW undertook a survey of 510 SMEs in Pakistan in towns/cities (Lahore, Faisalabad, Gujranwala, Sargodha, Sialkot) of Punjab district to understand their financial access and demand for financial services.

Survey Instrument

The survey instrument covered the following areas:

- Financial performance (profits, sales, exports, investments)

- Relations between enterprises and financial providers (ease of obtaining external finance in 2002–4)

- Structure of demand for external financing (intent to borrow, amounts, conditions demanded, creditworthiness)

- Perception of obstacles to doing business.

Choice of Locations

The survey was conducted in five cities/towns of Punjab. The cities/towns were selected based on the size of their population, to allow verification of the difference between demand and access to finance based on this criterion.

Definition of Population

Owners of micro, small, and medium businesses operating in the economic sectors of trade, production, and services in one of five selected urban areas is considered as the population of urban demand survey.

Selection Method

First a segmentation criterion was developed based on (town/city, size of enterprise, economic sector). Then sampling areas were enumerated with a concentration of target enterprises within each urban location, and specific areas were allocated to the interviewers. At least five interviews were conducted in each area to have representation of the whole city/town. Selected respondents were owners/chief managers, had employees up to 100, and were at least 18 years of age. Total sample size for the urban demand survey was 510.

Basic Sample Data

The overwhelming majority of the respondents were male (98 percent) with average age of 35 years. The tables below report the sample composition by sector, size, legal status, location of business, and average years of schooling of owners/managers.

Table A4.1 Principal Sector of Respondent's Business

Sector	Frequency	Percentage
Trade (wholesale and retail)	202	39.6
Manufacturing	194	38.0
Services	114	22.4
Total	**510**	**100**

Source: KfW Demand Survey, 2005.

Table A4.2 Definition of Firm Size

Firm Size	Number of Permanent Employees	Sample Size (%)	Average Number of Employees
Micro	0–9	270 (52.9)	4
Small	10–49	188 (36.9)	20
Medium	50–100	52 (10.2)	75
Total	**0–100**	**510 (100.0)**	**17**

Source: KfW Demand, 2005.

Table A4.3 Legal Status of Sampled Enterprises

Status	Number of Enterprises	Share of Total (%)
Not registered with authorities	47	9.22
Publicly listed company	16	3.14
Privately held limited company	26	5.10
Sole proprietorship	394	77.25
Partnership	27	5.29
Total	**510**	**100**

Source: KfW Demand Survey, 2005.

Table A4.4 Location of Business of Sampled Enterprises

Location	Number of Enterprises	Share of Total (%)
Business office	67	13.14
My house	5	0.98
Marketplace/shop	306	60.0
Factory/industrial building	125	24.51
Other	7	1.48
Total	**510**	**100**

Source: KfW Demand Survey, 2005.

Table A4.5 Average Years of Schooling of Owners of Sampled Enterprises

Location	Number of Enterprises	Share of Total (%)
Illiterate	9	1.76
Read/write only	3	0.59
Primary (Class 5)	18	3.53
Middle school (Class 8)	57	11.18
Matriculate (Class 10)	151	29.61
Intermediate (Class 12)	110	21.57
Graduate	110	21.57
Postgraduate	52	10.20
Total	**510**	**100**

Source: KfW Demand Survey, 2005.

Annex 4.2 Framework for Movable Collateral in Pakistan

Three critical shortcomings exist with respect to the framework for moveable collateral in Pakistan:

1. The requirement for court orders to be obtained before proceeding to enforcement, even for most types of secured creditors, significantly erodes the utility of charges over moveable collateral.

2. The lack of specialized courts to deal with enforcement and insolvency matters considerably slows enforcement.

3. The absence of a comprehensive, single registry for all moveable charges in regard to all types of debtors (corporate or otherwise) limits the scope of moveable security.

For these and other reasons, although the legal mechanisms for creating security over moveable collateral exist and are widely used, they pale in comparison to the use of real property, particularly for long-term business debts.

A. Creation of Security Interests over Movable Property

Process of Creation. To the extent possible, the process of creating a security interest should be easy and cost-effective. One of the most effective ways to do this is through a simple, unified statute dealing with security interests. A simpler and cheaper system of creation could translate into lower transaction costs, and, subsequently, lower interest rates for potential debtors. In Pakistan, however, there is no simple, unified statute pertaining to the creation of security over movable property. According to some users of the system, the multiple laws and systems create uncertainty and difficulties in using movable property as collateral. In general, these laws include the Contract Act, 1872; Transfer of Property Act, 1882; Companies Ordinance, 1984; Civil Procedure Code, 1908; Banking Companies Ordinance, 1962; Financial Institutions (Recovery of Finance) Ordinance, 2001; the Prudential Regulations issued by the State Bank of Pakistan; Non-Banking Finance Companies (Establishment and Regulation) Rules 2003; Sale of Goods Act, Partnership Act 1932; The Cape Town Convention and Aircraft Protocol (Implementation) Rules, 2003; and all other banking regulations issued from time to time.

Types of Security Interests over Movable Property

Hypothecation. A hypothecation agreement or letter of hypothecation operates as a charge over movable property, including book debts and receivables. The essential security conferred upon a lender is the right to seize and sell the hypothecated property in realization of the security. Stamp duty on an instrument creating a hypothecation is—unless exempted or remitted—very high. Registration is required for companies creating such security under the Companies Ordinance, 1984, but not for other forms of business organizations or individuals.

Floating charge. In addition to hypothecation, and to ensure that the borrower is free to deal with the property in the ordinary course of business, and to ensure that all the borrower's assets and undertaking are covered by the terms of the charge, the lenders usually require the borrower to create a floating charge by a separate deed. The charge only crystallizes upon the happening of one or more stipulated events of default where upon the lender is entitled to seize the property and sell it to recover his dues. No interest in the property accrues to the lender until crystallization, and the description of the property is given only in the most general terms. This charge is stamped at a nominal rate. Registration is required for companies creating such security under the Companies Ordinance, 1984, but not for individuals or other entities. Generally speaking, such a charge can be created through a two-step process, requiring two documents: execution of the underlying agreement between borrower and debtor and registration of that agreement in the Companies Registry.

Leases. Leases may be operating leases or finance leases. Nonbanking financial institutions that provide leasing facilities are regulated by law and controlled by the Securities and Exchange Commission of Pakistan (SECP). At times, the Islamic mode of leasing, which is structured as an *Ijara*, is used. Here, ownership does not pass to the user. The main features of this form of leasing are that a written contract is mandatory; the asset should exist at the time of the contract; the asset must have a real and lawful use and should not be used for an activity prohibited by Islamic law. Total loss is the owner's responsibility, however; the user is responsible for damage through misuse or negligence. If one party dies, the contract becomes void. The purest form of Ijara is almost the same as an operating lease. An Ijara contract may also be structured as a finance lease with certain refinements and alterations.

Restrictions on Who Can Become a Party to a Security Agreement. To the extent possible, and taking into account the country's specific legal culture, the law should not limit the types of creditors and debtors that can become party to a security agreement. Expanding the classes of entities that can serve as creditors could translate into more available credit in the market. On the other hand, allowing more types of entities as debtors could mean easier access to credit for many non incorporated entities, particularly those that are small or medium-size.

Creditor. Under the Banking Companies Ordinance, 1962, "creditors" have been defined as "persons from whom deposits have been received on the basis of participation in profit and loss and a banking company or financial institution from which financial accommodation or facility has been received on the basis of participation in profit and loss, mark-up in price, hire-purchase, lease, or otherwise." There are no serious restrictions on who may become a secured creditor under Pakistani law. The Financial Institutions (Recovery of Finances) Ordinance, 2001 defines a "financial institution" as "any company whether incorporated within or outside Pakistan which transacts the business of banking or associated or ancillary business in the country through its branches within or outside Pakistan and includes a government savings bank, but excludes the State Bank of Pakistan." The definition also includes other entities, such as a *modaraba*,[1] venture capital, a financing or leasing company, an investment bank, a unit trust or mutual fund of any kind, a credit or investment institution, corporation, or company, or any other company authorized by the federal government to carry on similar business.

---

1. For a definition of modarabas, please see www.irtipms.org/OpenSave.asp?pub=40.pdf (p. 15).

Debtor. While there is no restriction on who may grant a security right, there is a restriction on the types of debtors over whose assets security interests can and must be registered so they are enforceable against third parties. A charge may be registered under the Companies Ordinance, 1984 with the Registrar of Companies by a company formed and registered under the Companies Ordinance.

Problems Associated with the Creation of a Security Interest over Movable Property. It appears that one of the most important limitations on the use of movable property as collateral in Pakistan is that the debtor must possess any collateral being pledged. In addition, the legal framework for enforcement against not-yet-existent collateral is weak. This affects the use of agricultural products (such as future crops), inventory, or after-acquired property as collateral, and would make it very difficult for many small businesses that do not have a significant amount of other classes of assets beyond after-acquired property to obtain secured credit. Another important limitation is that the system of secured transactions over movable property is available primarily to registered companies only. This is because an efficient system of registration of security interests is generally only available for registered companies (unless the assets being used are themselves subject to registration), and not for any other organizations or business entities falling outside of the Companies Ordinance, 1984.

Best Practice	Pakistani Practice	Recommendation
1. The manner of the creation of a security interest* should be simple, fast, and cheap.	As explained above, the system of creation of a security interest in Pakistan is ambiguous because of the fact that there are multiple laws that govern secured transactions in the country and multiple types of security interests each with their own system.	A single law should be created that would govern secured transactions over movable property in Pakistan regardless of the type of asset or the type of security interest being created.
2. Any legal entity should be able to grant and take a security interest.	Although any entity is able to become party to a security agreement, practically, nonincorporated entities find it difficult to grant security interests over their movable assets because there are no efficient registration systems in place for security interests over the movable assets of such entities.	The country's legal system should facilitate the creation of a security agreement by making an effective secured transactions system available to all types of legal entities.
3. There should be no limit on the type of obligation that can be secured.	It appears that there are no limits on the types of obligations that can be secured. Future obligations,	No additional recommendations made.

(continued)

Best Practice	Pakistani Practice	Recommendation
	foreign currency obligations, and changing pools of debt can all be secured, although foreign currency obligations are subject to additional legislation. However, these additional regulations do not significantly affect the ability to secure foreign currency obligations.	
4. A security interest should be granted over all types of movable property to maximize the debtor's potential to obtain credit.	In the text of the law, it appears that there are no limits on the types of movable assets that can be used as collateral. In practice, however, there may be some difficulties. For example, for the purposes of an assignment of a book debt, if the stamp duties are too high, there will be a disincentive to use this type of asset as collateral.	Practical obstacles that hinder the efficient application of the law should be removed.
5. Assets used as collateral should be allowed to be defined generally in the security agreement so that revolving classes of assets (including accounts ireceivables, inventory, etc.) can be used as collateral.	At least in the context of a floating charge, the assets do not need to be defined specifically. For the purposes of registration of security interests over the assets of nonincorporated entities, however, the assets need to be defined specifically.	The system of security interests over movable property that allows for a general description of assets should be made available to all types of business entities, including nonincorporated entities.
6. Future assets should be allowed to be used as collateral.	As was explained earlier, one of the major limitations in Pakistan is that the debtor must own the collateral at the moment of granting a security interest over the asset. This will limit the use of many future assets as collateral.	The limitation on the use of future assets as collateral should be removed.
7. Multiple security interests should be allowed to be made on the same collateral, to maximize the potential of the debtor to obtain credit based on the value of a particular asset.	In practice, banks, when taking a floating charge over the assets of a company, include in the agreement a clause that prohibits the debtor from using the assets as collateral for any subsequent loans from other creditors without the consent of the first creditor. This is done because, under the Pakistani system, fixed charges often take priority over floating charges. So, if a debtor grants a fixed charge over its assets to	The law of Pakistan could be reformed to accommodate a "first-registered first-priority" system," which would generally not distinguish between the types of interests, and which would dictate priority based on the time of registration (with some reasonable exceptions) and not the type of interest. This would be a system similar to what has or is being advanced in common law countries, such as the United

(continued)

Best Practice	Pakistani Practice	Recommendation
	any subsequent creditors, that subsequent creditor will have priority over a previous creditor with a floating charge.	States, Canada, New Zealand, and Australia. This system could discourage the use of prohibitive clauses by banks, which would effectively disallow a debtor to use its assets as collateral with subsequent creditors. However, it should be kept in mind that, despite the benefits, this would constitute a complete overhaul of the system, which may not necessarily be desirable at this time.

*Security interest/charge in this section refers to a nonpossessory security interest over movable property.

B. Priority of Security Interests

The rules concerning priority should be clearly laid out in the law. In the absence of clear rules, creditors, not being able to evaluate their chances of recovery upon default and assess their risk, will offer credit at a higher price to compensate for this unknown variable.

Separate from the question of clarity is the question of ranking of creditors. This is an issue that encompasses a broad set of legal and cultural values. For example, what type of priority should be given to employee wage claims? What rights should the state have to recover tax arrears from the debtor? In general, however, as traditional commercial lenders in many economies tend to lend based on the value that the underlying security offers them (affected by such factors as the ranking of the secured creditor), according relatively high priority to secured creditors is generally viewed as having a positive impact on both the availability and cost of credit. The issue of "absolute priority" of secured creditors is often framed as a binary one (absolute priority is good and absence of it is bad). This distinction, however, is a false one as virtually no advanced economy has true "absolute priority" for secured creditors. Rather, policy makers must be made aware of the need to balance competing interests and the consequences of preferring one group of stakeholders over another.

There is a basic statutory priority order set out in law. For nonpossessory security interests granted by companies, clearly the "first to file" system (with respect to filings in the Companies Registry) applies. With regard to unsecured claims, the following scheme of priorities generally applies in liquidation:

- Government revenue and taxes;

- Wages to a maximum of Rs 2,000 or 12 months, whichever is less;

- Holiday payments;

- Employer contributions to pensions; and

- Workmen's compensation.

In practice, however, secured creditors enforce outside of this liquidation, leaving very little if anything for these "priority" claims.

Moreover, given the multiplicity of laws dealing with secured transactions, it is difficult to concretely determine priority because of the prevalence of more esoteric forms of security that might take precedence (construction liens, mechanical liens, and so forth). This underscores the need for bringing all types of secured transactions over movables under one law.

Best Practice	Pakistani Practice	Recommendation
8. To ensure reasonable access to credit, secured creditors should have a *relatively* high ranking in priority compared with other interests once their interest is registered.	The laws governing priorities are spread throughout the various laws that govern secured transactions. As such, further investigation is required to ensure the validity of any observations made in this area. However, it appears that a number of interests rank above a registered security interest. These include creditors adding value to the collateral (equipment repairer's/mechanic's lien) and creditors storing the collateral. Furthermore, it appears that creditors secured by means of title financing have priority over all other secured creditors regardless of the order of registration. What is interesting, however, is that it appears that other interests, such as purchase money security interests, bona fide purchasers without notice, or those who provide financing for rehabilitation after the commencement of insolvency proceedings, which in many advanced systems do have priority over secured creditors, do not enjoy such priority over secured creditors in Pakistan.	Further research may prove to be beneficial to confirm the findings in this section, and to develop a priority system that would best suit Pakistan.

(continued)

Best Practice	Pakistani Practice	Recommendation
	Finally, it appears that, in the course of a bankruptcy procedure, the collateral of the secured creditor is exempt, and, as such, the secured creditor enjoys priority. However, should the secured creditor wish to participate in the procedures, taxes and wages will gain priority over the secured creditor.	
9. The law should set out clearly the priorities of the different interests.	Although a basic legislative scheme for priorities exists, it appears that the fact that many security interests, such as state claims, title finance agreements, judgments, purchase money security interests, and financial leasing agreements, are not registered creates a lot of confusion at the moment of enforcement of rights because determining priority becomes very difficult.	A system of registration that would meet Pakistan's needs and that would increase predictability for secured creditors by requiring the registration of various types of interests should be explored and promoted.

C. Publicity of Security Interests

A registration system that is not simple and cheap or a registry that is not effective could diminish the confidence of secured creditors in the system. One side effect of this could be the availability of credit at higher interest rates. In the alternative, secured creditors may become more reluctant to make credit available at all.

In Pakistan, the system of registration of security interests over movable property is as follows:

Registration of Security Interests

a. Registrar of Companies under the Companies Ordinance, 1984:

- Registration applies only to companies, that is, bodies corporate incorporated under the Companies Ordinance, 1984 of Pakistan, and not to statutory corporations, or partnerships or firms or other unincorporated forms of business organization.

- Registration in the case of companies has to be done at the Registrar of Companies where the registered office is situated, and in the case of branches of companies, at the Companies Registry where the principal office in Pakistan is situated.

- The Companies Ordinance, 1984 requires a creditor to create and register a charge within 21 days from the date of execution of the security agreement. The entire process from the submission of the Registration Form to the issuance of a certificate of registration must be completed within the said time.

b. Vehicles Registry

c. Pakistan Aircrafts Register under the Rules, 1994:

- In the case of mortgage over an aircraft (excluding military aircraft), a notation must be made in the Remarks Column of the Aircraft Register maintained by the Civil Aviation Authority of Pakistan (we have been advised that, despite this practice, there is no specific provision providing for the registration of a charge over an aircraft; this issue could be investigated further).

d. International Registry under the Aircraft Rules. We do not have further information regarding the scope of this registry.

It is important to highlight that, while the Pakistan Aircrafts Register and the International Registry cover security interests pertaining to aircrafts alone, the Registrar under the Companies Ordinance registers a charge over all types of moveable assets as long as the creditor is a company incorporated under the Companies Ordinance.

The cost for registering a floating charge is Rs 5,000 and the cost for conducting a search is Rs 200. The list for prescribed fees is contained in the Sixth Schedule of the Companies Ordinance 1984. Searches cannot be conducted online.

The process for the search is fairly straightforward. Any person can file an application for inspection of files along with the prescribed fee of Rs 200. This involves physically visiting the SECP and inspecting the relevant register. It is theoretically possible to do this in one day, provided the fee is deposited early in the day. However, this may well stretch to two days.

As regarding the process for registration of the floating charge, the application in the prescribed form (Form 10) along with relevant documents, namely, the document creating the charge and the prescribed fee are submitted physically at the office of the SECP. Normally, if all the documents are in order and the SECP makes no objection to the documents, it takes a few days to register the charge.

Best Practice	Pakistani Practice	Recommendation
10. All types of legal entities (creditors/debtors) should be able to register security interests.	As mentioned earlier, the registration of security interests can only be made in an efficient manner over the movable assets of incorporated entities. Other types of entities do not have access to such an efficient system unless they use assets that themselves are registrable as collateral. In that case, security interests over those assets could be registered in such asset-based registries. As for security interests over other assets of unincorporated entities, the registration system is paper and regionally based.	It would be beneficial to extend an efficient system of registration of security interests to other types of entities so that priorities of security interests created on the assets of those entities can also be more easily determined, there by making it more attractive for creditors to take the movable assets of these entities as collateral.
11. Registration should be mandatory for the purposes of making the security interest enforceable against third parties, in order to facilitate the ease of determining priority by creditors.	It appears that the registration of security interests over movable assets of nonincorporated entities is not mandatory for the purposes of perfection.	Registration should not only be made available but should be made mandatory for security interests over the movable assets of all entities for the purposes of perfection.
12. With very limited exceptions, the first to file should have first priority.	Although not necessarily an issue, as mentioned in the previous section, some security interests have priority over the secured creditor, regardless of the time of registration by the secured creditor.	The country's social, economic, and cultural values need to be taken into account to develop a comprehensive system of priority that works for Pakistan while, at the same time, granting the necessary protection and clarity to secured creditors.
13. The security interest should extend to replacements and proceeds of the underlying asset in order to make the use of revolving pools of assets as collateral practical.	It appears that security interests extend to replacements and proceeds of the underlying asset in Pakistan.	No further recommendations made.
14. There should be a notice-filing registry to reduce the burden on the registering party and the registration system.	It appears that registries do not function on a notice-filing system. Rather, the entire agreement is what needs to be filed.	An efficient system of notice-filing should be implemented for all registries.

(continued)

Best Practice	Pakistani Practice	Recommendation
15. The registry should be geographically linked across the country so that a potential secured creditor can ascertain its priority over the asset more accurately.	The Companies Registry is online and networked across the country. However, this is not the case for the registries for security interests over movable assets of nonincorporated entities.	An online and regionally networked system of registration should be made available for all entities.
16. The registry should be computerized so that records can be registered and accessed faster.	Please see the previous response.	Please refer to the previous recommendation.
17. There should be a unified registry for all types of security interests, granted by all types of entities on the most important types of movable property so that potential creditors can refer to one central location to ascertain whether there are other security interests on a particular asset.	There is no unified registry for all types of security interests granted by all types of entities on all types of movable property. Pakistan has a mixed system of Asset-Based Registries (Aircraft Registry) and Entity-Based Registry (Companies Registry).	Preferably, a unified registry that would apply to all types of security interests over all types of movable property by all types of entities should be created.
18. Registration (or amendments to the registration) should be inputted into the registration system in a timely and cheap manner in order to make the system more reliable and accessible.	Some lawyers have complained about the fact that registrations and amendments are not inputted in a timely and accurate manner, especially in registries other than the Companies Registry.	The system of registration should be timely and cheap in all registries and for all types of security interests, entities, and assets.

D. Enforcement of Security Interests

Without an effective enforcement system, secured creditors will have a diminished ability to recover their interest. Creditors will naturally include this business risk in their loan pricing. Although it is technically possible to obtain a prejudgment lien over disputed assets, in practice this is rarely granted in cases other than those dealing with real property. This could mean higher interest rates for debtors trying to use moveable collateral as security.

Pakistan's enforcement system is as follows:

Enforcement Mechanisms
Enforcement (by financial institutions) without the involvement of the court. The laws relating to banks and financial institutions provide for special summary procedures for determining the judgment and enforcing the security.

Under section 15 of the Financial Institutions (Recovery of Finance) Ordinance of 2001, a secured creditor may sell the pledged property (under a possessory pledge) with minimal involvement of the court. The secured creditor is required to send two notices successively to the defaulting debtor company demanding payment of the outstanding sum within 14 days from service of each notice. Thereafter, a final notice may be served. If payment is not made within 30 days after that notice, the financial institution may, without the intervention of the court, sell the mortgaged property or any part thereof by public auction and appropriate the proceeds thereof toward total or partial satisfaction of the outstanding mortgage money. As a prerequisite, before exercising its powers, the secured creditor is required to publish a notice giving at least 30 days for the submission of offers with respect to the mortgaged property by advertising it in one reputable English and Urdu daily newspaper with wide circulation in the province in which the mortgaged property is situated. The financial institution shall also send such notices to all persons who, to the knowledge of the financial institution, have an interest in the mortgaged property as mortgagees. However, according to some of the users of the system, even though the agreement between the parties may provide for the secured creditor to enforce its right over the security directly, in practice, a debtor company is likely to obtain a stay order from the court and initiate legal proceedings against the secured creditor on any point of law or fact to restrain the alienation of the secured asset for as long as possible.

Enforcement with the involvement of the court, where out-of-court enforcement is not available. The secured creditor may file a suit for the recovery of the sum due from the debtor company. The debtor company is required to file an application for leave to defend within 30 days from the date of notice. Leave is only granted if substantial questions of law or fact are raised and may be accompanied by a requirement for the deposit of cash or furnishing of security. Upon pronouncement of judgment and decree, the suit automatically converts into execution proceedings without the need for the secured creditor to file a separate application for the execution of the judgment.

Enforcement under the Civil Procedure Code. A suit for the recovery of the sum secured or repossession of the secured property may be filed under the Civil Procedure Code. Again, the court is extensively involved and the procedure is lengthy because of (a) the possibility of several appeals from interlocutory orders in such proceedings; (b) the need to commence separate execution proceedings after obtaining a final decree that is no longer capable of appeal; and (c) the consumption of additional time in filing execution proceedings. In practice, we have been advised by local lawyers that if it is a financial institution enforcing its security right under the special summary procedures, it would take about 1.5 to 2 years for the enforcement to be completed. In other cases, it may take approximately 10 to 15 years or more.

Best Practice	Pakistani Practice	Recommendation
19. Parties should be able to agree to out-of-court enforcement at the time of the creation of their security agreement (subject to some judicial protections, secured creditors should be able to seize and sell the collateral upon default without judicial involvement). Alternatively, there should be a fast-track enforcement procedure available to secured creditors.	As explained, a security holder will have to file a suit in court to recover his claim. However, for financial institutions, expedited procedures are available under the Financial Institutions (Recovery of Finances) Ordinance, 2001. But even in these cases, should the debtor dispute the enforcement by the creditor (which, as it appears, is usually the case), a fairly lengthy court procedure will ensue.	The country's economic needs and legal structure must be studied to determine whether making a system of out-of-court enforcement available to all types of entities as secured creditors would suit Pakistan or not. At present, some mechanisms for out-of-court enforcement exist for certain types of security granted to financial institutions. These mechanisms are being challenged before the Supreme Court for constitutional validity and, in any event, do not appear to apply to nonposessory security interests.
20. The debtor should have limited defensive measures to stop the seizure and sale of the asset by the secured creditor.	The debtor, as it appears, has broad powers to challenge the enforcement by secured creditor (even a financial institution that has a right to enforce out of court). Based on a question of fact or law, the debtor can stop the seizure and sale procedures, at least temporarily.	The classes of appeal available to debtors need to be studied further to determine whether the imposition of any limitations on the right to appeal is worth considering or not. For example, the right of the debtor to appeal can be limited to very specific circumstances (for example, proving that a payment has already been made). Outside of these restrictive courses of appeal, the debtor should have the right to challenge the creditor in court after enforcement by the secured creditor has taken place. At present, most such matters fall under the general jurisdiction of the High Court. It may be worthwhile to explore the idea of having a specialized court of well-trained judges to deal with commercial disputes on an expedited basis. The concept of out-of-court enforcement for secured creditors, while generally laudable, needs to be approached with some caution in the absence of the necessary regulatory framework to prevent widespread malfeasance by receivers, liquidators, and trustees. This regulatory framework does not yet exist in Pakistan.

Chapter 5

Harnessing Remittances for Access to Finance

Remittances to Pakistan are estimated at around $16 billion and have experienced considerable growth in recent years. International flows (through both formal and informal channels) total $9 billion, with domestic flows at approximately $6.95 billion. These remittance flows play a valuable role in supporting the economy by providing foreign exchange and improving the balance of payments and external debt position. They also offer significant potential to support incomes of poor and vulnerable groups. The lion's share of remittances is transferred by banks (80 percent), with a further 17 percent accounted for by exchange companies (ECs) and a small share by the Pakistan Post Office. Banks operate a fully automated system that runs seven days a week, has excellent urban and some good rural coverage, and usually can deliver within 24 hours. The majority of remittances are received in less than one week, although service tends to be slower in rural areas. Pakistan Post has a large rural network and is the most common channel for domestic remittances, but services remain relatively inefficient. Home consumption constitutes the largest use of remittances.

State Bank of Pakistan (SBP) has taken various measures that have significantly increased remittances through formal channels, though a large share of domestic remittances continues to be transferred informally. SBP has been encouraging the private sector to provide mobile banking solutions. The mobile coverage (about 90 percent of the population of Pakistan), and the success of mobile money transfer solutions in other countries, suggests that mobile phone banking offers significant potential to scale up access to financial services in Pakistan. There is already a lot of activity in this sector and both banks and mobile phone companies are working to structure viable models.

Overview of the Remittance Markets

Recorded remittances have increased fivefold since 2001.[1] This impressive growth has been driven to some extent by the increasing efforts of SBP to bring remittance flows into the formal net. Ten years ago, about 15 percent of international remittance flows came through formal channels, compared with more than 70 percent currently. This achievement is impressive. Yet a considerable share of remittances remains in the informal markets. There are no official data of the overall size of the market. Various estimates of international informal remittances put *hawala* flows at around the $2.5 billion mark, in an overall international flow of $9 billion. In addition, household consumption survey results indicate evidence that the domestic remittance market is, if anything, of comparable size to the international one, but might involve many more transactions of smaller value. Unofficial estimates put the overall remittance market at more than $16 million. To gain a comparative perspective of the size of remittances relative to the economy, consider foreign exchange reserves, which stood at $5.7 billion as of September 2008, total credit to the private sector at $34.8 billion, and stock market capitalization at $44.7 billion.

Remittance flows are a potent lever for the Pakistan economy, and a significant source of foreign exchange, as well as a considerable help in improving Pakistan's external debt situation, building the foreign exchange reserves, strengthening the balance of payments, and preserving the value of the rupee. Moreover, remittances can potentially form a large part of income for poor and vulnerable groups (not yet the case in Pakistan), helping lift this population out of poverty. This chapter attempts to understand the structure, players, and clients of the remittance market, including domestically and within the informal sector, in order to help co-opt more of the flows into the formal net, make them accessible to the poor and underserved, and achieve the above-noted desirable goals.

In absolute terms, recorded international remittances surpassed $6.45 billion during fiscal 2008, an average annual growth of 29 percent from 2001 (figure 5.1). Worldwide, international formal remittance flows to developing countries were $265 billion in 2007, and unrecorded flows were estimated at another $80 to $185 billion (World Bank 2008a). Compared with other countries in the region, Pakistan is at par with Indonesia and Bangladesh in absolute terms, while India is far ahead, with more than $25 billion received in 2006, although the figures are comparable given the size of the economies (figure 5.2). Remittances in other South Asian countries are even larger in relative terms. In Nepal, remittances exceed export receipts and tourism, while in Sri Lanka, remittances of $2.7 billion are greater than tea exports. In Bangladesh, remittances are five times the level of foreign aid.[2]

Market Players

The main players in the formal remittance market are banks, ECs, and Pakistan Post, while informal channels consist of *hawala* or money carried by hand. Except for ECs,

Figure 5.1 International Formal Remittances

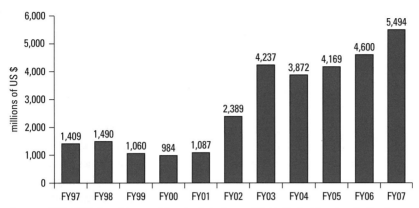

Sources: SBP 2007 http://sbp.org.pk/ecodata/index2.asp; *World Bank Migration & Remittances Factbook 2008.*

Figure 5.2 Remittances—International Comparison

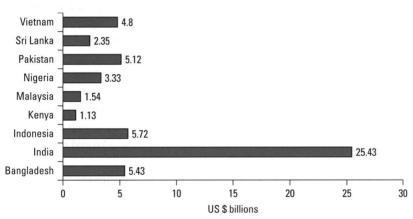

Sources: SBP 2007 http://sbp.org.pk/ecodata/index2.asp; *World Bank Migration & Remittances Factbook 2008.*

which by law cannot operate domestic money transfers, all players provide domestic and international remittance services.

The banks account for 80 percent of international remittances coming through formal channels into Pakistan, given their long history in the sector (table 5.1). The formation of exchange companies in 2002 has significantly increased flows as hundreds of small moneychangers have been brought into the regulated sector and now account for 17 percent of international formal remittances. Both banks and ECs have multiple correspondents and relationships abroad. The breakdown of international formal remittances by sector (detailed time-series) is available in Annex table A5.1. Pakistan Post accounts for almost 2.5 percent of the international remittances received, exclusively via an agreement with Western Union. Money transfer organizations (MTOs)

Table 5.1 Snapshot of the Main Channels of International Formal Money Transfer

	Remittances (Billion $)	Market Share (%)	Branches	Cost	Other Services Provided	Partnership agreements
Banks (Overall)	4.4	80.2	7755			
Habib Bank	1.2	22	1400	Free	Various Banking Products	Al-Rajhi Bank, Travelex
United Bank	0.55	10	1000	Free	Various Banking Products	Western Union, several others
ECs (Overall)	0.95	17.3	>1000			
Zarco Exchange	0.26	27	660	$5–$20	Foreign Exchange	Western Union, Ria, Vigo, and others
Wall Street Exchange	0.22	23	90	$5–$20	Foreign Exchange	Moneygram, Instant Cash, and others
Pakistan Post	0.14	2.5	13419	$5–$20	Mail, Savings, Insurance, and others	Western Union

Source: SBP 2007.

(mainly Western Union), have an estimated share of about 15–20 percent in intermediating international transfers. Transfer service providers in the formal international sector are discussed later in this chapter.

Domestic remittances are dominated to a larger extent by informal flows, relative to international transfers. We estimate domestic remittance flows at $6.95 billion, based on household survey estimates of the share of foreign and domestic remittances in monthly household income as per the latest Household Income Integrated Survey (2005–6). The main formal channels for domestic remittances are the Post Office and interbank transfers. Pakistan Post is the main player in transferring domestic remittances to rural areas, though the five big banks also have a presence in rural areas. Microfinance entities still play only a minor role in remittances. The sections that follow on banks, exchange companies, Pakistan Post, and money transfer organizations overview the limited data available on (mostly formal) domestic transfer services.

Discussions with various stakeholders suggest that the estimated size of the *hawala* market is $2 billion to $4 billion. The informal market is discussed in more detail later in this chapter.

Banks

The main players in the banking sector are the five big banks of Pakistan: Habib Bank Limited (HBL), United Bank Limited (UBL), National Bank of Pakistan (NBP),

Muslim Commercial Bank, and Allied Bank Limited, which also have an international presence. They have been given special incentives by the SBP for fast and secure delivery of home remittances to recipients in Pakistan. These banks have specialized home remittance cells at their respective head offices and collaborate to speed up remittance transfers among their branches. Furthermore, they *do not charge* international customers for remitting money through their network, as SBP reimburses them.[3] This step by SBP helped to significantly boost remittances coming through banks. Initially, in 2002, when reforms were being taken to regulate the remittance market, these banks were given the incentive of getting R 1 for each dollar that was remitted through their network. However, this policy was dropped and replaced with fee reimbursement. Over the past year, international formal remittances coming through banks increased by 13.4 percent.

An analysis of national household survey responses shows a positive perception of bank remittance services by domestic and international remittance users. Bank branches using one's own account are found the most accessible remittance channel nationwide (by 29.5 percent of the population), among formal and informal channels alike. Bank remittance services using one's own account are also considered the least risky channel (by 38.7 percent of the population), while bank remittances via another person's bank account, are perceived as the riskiest money transfer method (by 47.9 percent of the population). Interestingly, rural areas consider banks, but not the Pakistan Post, risky, and urban areas exhibit exactly the opposite perceptions.

Habib Bank Limited. The largest player in the banking sector is HBL. It accounts for $1.2 billion in international formal remittances for fiscal 2007 or a market share of 22 percent overall. It has 40 international branches with operations in 25 countries and is also the largest private sector bank in Pakistan with more than 1,400 domestic branches (box 5.1). HBL also has a large network in rural areas, with almost 50 percent of its branches located there. Hence, HBL's outreach in the rural areas is impressive and allows it to reach recipients in far-flung areas quickly. About 30 percent of foreign remittances coming through HBL go to rural areas. The median transaction amounts for remittances received through HBL are $500 to $700.

United Bank Limited. The second-largest player in the market is UBL, which brought in approximately $550 million in international formal remittances for the year 2006, giving them an overall market share of 10 percent. They have a network of more than 1,000 domestic branches and 15 overseas branches, with a strong presence in the Gulf region. UBL also has many correspondent exchange companies and banks overseas and is continually striving to form relationships with new ones. Until July 2007, UBL had a contract with Moneygram, whereby money sent through Moneygram franchises overseas could be picked up at UBL branches. However, since August 2007, UBL has been operating a deal with Western Union and within the first few months claims to be handling volumes as high as those they handled

---

| Box 5.1 | **A Closer Look at Habib Bank Unlimited** |

HBL has achieved its market leader position through a vigorous marketing campaign in the Middle East. Energetic junior staff stationed in these countries promote HBL services at small exchange companies, banks, and worker camps. HBL has tried to make the process as convenient and simple as possible for Pakistani workers in the UAE so that they will use formal channels instead of *hawala*. Staff in the Middle East visit worker camps on payday and hold special remittance campaigns during the *Eid* (feast) festival. For regular remitters, HBL has created special accounts with options to send money to up to five people in Pakistan. Once the account is set, the address and bank details of each recipient are entered into the system. The customer only has to call and give his account number and the name of the person to whom he or she wants to send money, and the bank processes the transaction.

HBL has associations with banks and ECs in many countries to facilitate remittances. One of its major partners is Al-Rajhi Bank in Saudi Arabia, through which remittances, free of cost, can be channeled to Pakistan. HBL also has an agreement with Travelex, an MTO based in the United Kingdom. Overseas payments are received by HBL Pakistan through SWIFT. Once in Pakistan, HBL has a fully automated system that allows the bank to credit recipient accounts every hour or issue a draft if the recipient has an account in another bank. HBL's unit dealing with remittances operates seven days a week and thus remittances can reach recipients in most places in Pakistan within 24 hours. HBL calls this service *Fast Transfer* and relies on technology bought from Misys International. Other HBL products include fax money orders and express check remittances. On the recipient side, HBL offers special remittance *Munafa Plus Certificates* available in one-, three-, and five-year terms, which have returns ranging from 7 to 11 percent per year.

Source: DFID.

---

with Moneygram at peak times. UBL estimates that about 40 to 50 percent of remittances received in their network are for rural areas (box 5.2).

Exchange Companies

The EC framework was enforced in 2002 to bring exchange and remittance businesses under proper financial discipline. With the transformation of authorized moneychangers into formal ECs, a large number of undocumented and cash international transactions came within the formal net. These transactions are required to have proper documentation, recordkeeping, and adherence to internationally accepted know–your-customer norms. All EC transactions, exclusively international money transfers, are fully automated and have a real-time online network that can be accessed by any branch to track and make payments. Many ECs have set up call centers where the franchisees can call and check a transaction status.

The EC framework also enabled SBP to substantially narrow the gap between interbank and curb market exchange rates, which has played an important role in

---

UBL has several remittance products other than the simple wire transfers from international branches. In 2002, it launched **UBL** *Tezraftaar* (a service similar to HBL's Fast Transfer), which offers free remittance service within the country or from abroad to the doorstep of the recipient. This service trebled UBL's remittance business volume as it ensures free delivery of money within 24 hours for most urban areas. It is open to all, even those who are not UBL account holders, and the remittance is delivered at the doorstep of the recipients by an authorized courier or credited to their accounts. At the same time, in the UAE, UBL launched a scheme, which, along with charging no fee for the money transfer, also gave expatriates a bonus of 10 points redeemable for 10 dirhams on their next transfer, if they remitted at least Rs 7,000 ($114).

UBL also has **online money transfers** from the United States in collaboration with Payquik. With this service remitters can simply send money from a credit card or Internet check to anyone in Pakistan. The money can be credited to an account in any bank in Pakistan or delivered to the recipient at his or her home. The fee for sending money through an Internet check is only $5; with the credit card, a flat fee of $10 is charged, plus 2.89 percent of the transaction amount. The average transaction amount of this online money transfer called "click n remit" is $750. The reason for the high fee on the credit card is that Visa charges UBL this amount to process the transaction.

Source: DFID.

---

improving the inflow of international remittances during the past two to three years. The balance of payments for fiscal 2005 for the first time included the receipts and payments made through the ECs and conveys a more comprehensive and realistic picture of the transactions on the external account of the country. The transformation of authorized moneychangers into formal ECs, however, has posed considerable challenges for SBP in ensuring effective regulatory and supervisory oversight, inculcating corporate culture, good governance, transparency, and proper documentation and recordkeeping structure.

The network of ECs is comprehensive, covering 100 percent of the urban market and slowly making inroads into rural areas.[4] International remittances coming through ECs grew by 53.4 percent from fiscal 2006 to fiscal 2007. According to ECs, 90 percent of remittance transactions they handle are between Rs 10,000 and Rs 100,000.

Zarco Exchange. Zarco Exchange is the top EC in the remittances market and has partnered with Western Union (box 5.3). About $260 million were channeled through it last year. Zarco Exchange has received numerous awards in the last couple of years, such as Role Model EC from SBP and the Federation of Pakistan Chamber of Commerce and Industry, awarded by the Prime Minister of Pakistan, and the Best Computer Sciences Corporation Management award from Western Union.

Zarco Exchange has a large network of more than 660 payment locations. It has an aggressive approach and associations with 15 international MTOs, such as Ria and Vigo, in addition to Western Union. It has also opened its own Zarco Exchange branches overseas in areas densely populated with Pakistanis. In Pakistan, it has partnered with many organizations to ensure prompt delivery of remittances. Its partners include Bank of Punjab, which has approximately 300 branches; Utility Stores, of which 100 are involved in paying out remittances; and Punjab Cooperative Bank. In addition, Zarco Exchange has its own branches and payment booths all over Pakistan. It does not have payment booths in rural areas, like most MTOs, as its systems are automated and online and so the minimum requirement of setting up a branch or payment booth is a phone and Internet connection. However, it has strategically set up branches in towns near villages that require remittance services. For instance, it has seven branches in Jhelum (a small city) as many people from the surrounding villages have migrated to Italy for work.

Other than the money-in-minutes service offered in collaboration with Western Union, Zarco Exchange also offers an online transfer service—"click n send." This service takes two-three days for payment processing, and money can be paid through credit cards or Internet checks. The transaction can be tracked anytime from the Web and can be paid out as cash, bank draft, bank deposit, or home delivery. The fee for paying with an Internet check is $3 per $300, while with credit cards it is a flat charge of $8 plus 2.9 percent of the transaction amount.

Source: DFID.

Wall Street Exchange. The main partner of Moneygram International in Pakistan is Wall Street Exchange, based in Karachi. Wall Street has seven-eight other international correspondents, such as UK–based Instant Cash. Wall Street Exchange has close to 90 branches and franchise offices in 50 cities across Pakistan, and it plans to open 100–150 more payment locations in the coming year. In 2007, international remittances of $217 million came through the Wall Street Exchange network, giving them a market share of 23 percent in the EC segment.

The main product offered by Wall Street Exchange is the "money-in-minutes" service for both inward and outward remittances. It is a fast and convenient service, linked through the Internet and a call center with a toll-free number through which recipients can track their payments. Similar to Zarco Exchange, the basic requirements of Wall Street for opening a payment booth are Internet and phone connection. However, if Internet infrastructure is not available, dial-up connections on wireless phones are used. With the wireless network, Wall Street plans to improve its outreach in small cities and rural areas.

Pakistan Post

Pakistan Post has a network of 13,419 post offices across Pakistan. Recently it started automation of its services and has launched an online Express mail track-and-trace

Table 5.2 Percentage Post Offices by Province and Rural/Urban Areas

	Rural	Urban
Federal Capital & AJK	0.9%	5.0%
Sindh	3.8%	10.6%
Baluchistan	1.3%	1.7%
NWFP	1.4%	15.7%
Punjab	7.5%	52.0%

Source: Pakistan Post Annual Report 2004–5.

system. In the future, Pakistan Post plans to offer an Instant Money Transfer service, collection of utility bills from home, a premier courier service, and Tele Centers up to the tehsil headquarter level.

Apart from being a major channel through which domestic remittances are sent to rural areas, it also has an agreement with Western Union to disburse foreign remittances through 1,700 locations. For fiscal 2007, international remittances through Pakistan Post were $135 million, or a market share of 2.5 percent. Growth in the preceding year was a remarkable 58.9 percent, up from $85 million international remittances for fiscal 2006.

Out of the 1,700 locations used to disburse remittances from Western Union, about a third are fully automated with a real-time online system. About a third have fax facilities, where once the remittance notification is received, a fax is sent to notify disbursal. About one-third of locations telephone into a call center to check the remittance status and carry out the disbursal.

About 85 percent of the post office branches are in rural areas. Table 5.2 shows the distribution of post offices by province and urban/rural status (Pakistan Post 2005). Only the 80 major general post offices have been automated. All the transactions routed to the other 13,000 post offices go through the general post offices, and so their records are computerized even though the post offices themselves are not automated.

The remittance products offered are money orders, postal orders, postal draft, urgent money order, and fax money order. The main product used for domestic remittances to rural areas is the money order, which is issued up to a maximum value of Rs 10,000. For higher denominations, up to Rs 200,000, postal drafts are issued.

Urgent and fax money orders transfer money the same day, but these services are only available in a limited number of cities (204 cities are served by urgent money orders and 49 cities by fax money orders). The charges for these services are nominal. A 5 percent commission is charged for the regular money orders; urgent and fax transfers have an additional flat charge of Rs 30 applied on top of the 5 percent commission.

Post office services are perceived as the least expensive formal method of remitting funds, according to household survey results. Informal methods remain less expensive, with 25.6 percent of the population citing money sent via family or friends as the least costly, 21.5 percent citing check with family or friends, and 15.2 percent citing a check that is hand-carried. This contrasts with perceptions of the high cost of other formal remittance channels. The ECs are considered the most expensive (by 40.7 percent nationwide). Interestingly, more than half of rural respondents complained about the cost of post office transfers.

The paperwork for sending the money orders is straightforward and simply requires the addresses of the sender and the recipient. In cities, the money order is delivered in one-two days; however, in rural areas it takes three-five days officially. In practice the money orders might take longer, and anecdotal evidence suggests that in very small villages, postmen might hold on to the money for personal use and deliver it when they "feel like it." Officially, the sender is supposed to receive a signed receipt from the recipient once the money order is delivered, but in reality it is generally never delivered.

Evidence from the national household survey also points to the relatively slow service of post office money orders compared with other domestic and international remittances services. Informal remittance channels score just as well as formal ones on speed, with 23.6 percent of the population citing money sent with family or friends as the fastest transfer, while 21.4 percent and 20.3 percent point to ECs (Western Union) and electronic bank transfers, respectively. The post office is considered the slowest delivery channel by more than half of respondents (51.8 percent).

Money Transfer Organizations

The worldwide market share of Western Union in the intermediation of remittances is 15 percent, and in Pakistan it probably has a share of 15–20 percent. Its cash-to-cash anywhere in the world model is very convenient, as is a real-time service. It has partnerships with several organizations in Pakistan, including Pakistan Post, UBL, NBP, Faysal Bank, and Zarco Exchange, which in turn has its own partnerships with Bank of Punjab, Utility Stores, and Punjab Cooperative Bank. These associations translate into more than 5,000 payment locations for Western Union across Pakistan. Western Union has an office in Islamabad with a full team that handles operations in both Pakistan and Afghanistan. The company does not offer online remittance services to Pakistan from the United States (USA) like it does to Mexico and Brazil.

The worldwide market share of Moneygram is 7–8 percent, though it does not have a significant presence in Pakistan. It has partnered with few companies, of which only two are well known—Wall Street Exchange and Bank Al-Falah. Moneygram handles business in Pakistan via its Dubai office. This explains the lack of marketing and an aggressive expansion strategy in Pakistan.

Overall, sending money through MTOs is very convenient as they are well located internationally, and pickup of funds within Pakistan is easy. Furthermore, as seen below, the service offered by MTOs is very reasonably priced.

Domestic Remittances

Data on domestic remittances are much less readily available than comparable figures on international transfers. This shortcoming precludes policy action toward encouraging an efficient and accessible sector, in the manner in which international remittance services have developed thanks to SBP efforts. We estimate domestic transfer volume at $6.95 million, roughly 90 percent of international remittance flows in Pakistan. While domestic remittances used to represent a higher share than foreign remittances in monthly household income in Pakistan, national household income and consumption expenditure data for fiscal 2006 showed a reversed trend, most probably due to the faster formalization of foreign remittance flows. Rural areas continue to rely slightly more on domestic remittances than on international transfers (Federal Bureau of Statistics [FBS] 2006, table 11). However, according to the national household survey conducted for this report that corroborates Pakistan Social and Living Standards Measurement Survey (PSLM)[5] 2004–5 data, domestic remittances are more frequently used by Pakistanis. In fact, there are 2.5 times more domestic remittance users among Pakistani households than foreign remittances users. The regional distribution of remittances is discussed further on.

Figure 5.3 presents the most frequently used domestic remittance channels, based on results from the Pakistan Access to Finance (A2F) household survey. The popularity of the post office for domestic remittances is confirmed by national household survey results, which place the post office as the most commonly cited channel for domestic remittances, especially in rural areas, more than money or in kind through friends of family, or bank services (via a branch or electronically).

The main formal channels for domestic remittances are interbank transfers and the post office. Informal channels include hand-carrying the cash, or asking a relative or friend to do so. Pakistan Post transferred $297 million through money orders and another $0.32 million through postal drafts in fiscal 2005. About $56 million was also transferred through urgent and fax money orders but they were purely urban transfers because these services are not offered in rural areas. Annex tables A5.2 and A5.3 present a breakdown of money order and postal draft transfers by province.

The banks with a rural presence in Pakistan are the five big banks: HBL, NBP, UBL, MCB, and Allied Bank Limited. MCB and HBL have the best rural branch

Figure 5.3 Top Domestic Remittance Channels

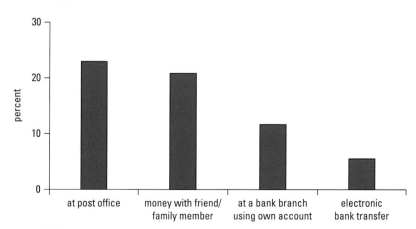

Source: A2F Survey.

Table 5.3 Proportion of Rural vs. Urban Bank Branches

	% Rural Branches	% Urban Branches	Total Branches
Foreign Banks	0	100	49
Five Big Banks	41	59	5448
Private Banks	7	93	1575
Islamic Banks	0	100	93
Specialized Banks	33	67	539

Source: SBP, "Building Inclusive Financial Systems," 2007.

networks. ZTBL is another bank with significant rural presence since its aim is to provide financial services to rural clients and in agricultural development. The proportion of rural versus urban branches, according to SBP, is as given in table 5.3. The provincial rural split of banks is given in Annex table A5.4.

Within the banking industry, the five big banks are primarily responsible for rural-urban transfers. These banks are moving from paper to e-banking, and this trend has considerably shortened the time it takes to transfer money to real-time transfers. The total proportion of branches that are online was 61 percent by the second quarter of fiscal 2008. Some banks offer free online transfers, while others charge up to Rs 200 per transaction.

SBP has allowed Microfinance Banks (MFBs) to engage in remittance services as well; however, First Microfinance Bank Limited is the only MFB currently offering this service. It launched this remittance service in 2003 and, in the 12 months ending May 2005, it increased the monthly volume of transfers from $3.46 million to $7.5 million. The number of transactions increased from around 3,000 in May 2004 to around 6,500 in May 2005. The bank's typical transfer customers are low-income traders, but they get walk-in customers as well. The fee charged is between 0.055 and 0.2 percent, depending on the transfer amount (DFID [UK Department for International Development] and USAID [U.S. Agency for International Development] 2005). The median transaction amount for this service is $1,100.

Informal Channels

In Pakistan, as across the world, money has been transferred through an unofficial system known as *hawala*, which is based on trust. No receipts are given, but the transfer is cheap, fast, and secure. The reason is that *hawaldars* (people who do *hawala*) have very low overhead, they can offer a better exchange rate than that offered by banks, and there is no red tape. The service is generally reliable, convenient, and offers anonymity.

World Bank (2008a) notes that informal remittance costs tend to be much lower than formal charges (about three times lower in Bangladesh, for example). *Hawala* fees are only 0–1.5 percent of the transaction amount, while in formal channels they may be as high as 20 percent (Passas, 2004). Furthermore, the fees are quite flexible and depend on the relations between the *hawaldar* and the client, the ultimate destination, and the frequency and regularity of payments.

Service to remote areas is easier and faster and is commonly delivered to the doorstep, which is very important in Pakistan, where women in rural areas are not very mobile due to cultural and social factors. The main reason *hawala* is popular in Pakistan is because of the lack of banking facilities in rural areas, as well as due to the doorstep delivery, so that the women or older people do not have to travel long distances to receive payments. The market size estimates of the informal remittance sector from our discussions are around $2 billion to $4 billion, including *hawala* and self-carried money.

Besides *hawala*-type systems, informal channels can take a variety of forms: ethnic stores, travel agencies, moneychangers, counter services, or hand delivery. Another informal remittance channel is in-kind remittance, which is the sending or carrying of remittances in the form of goods for personal use or for resale in the informal market. Kazi (1989) notes that this practice is quite widespread—he estimates in-kind remittances at about 16 percent for urban migrants and 11 percent for those returning to rural areas. In-kind remittances have become more significant since introduction of liberal import policies allowing duty-free imports. However, goods brought in under personal baggage are not recorded as remittances or imports. The estimated share of in-kind remittances is around 10–15 percent of overall remittances (Kazi 1989).

Distribution of Remittances by Region and Income Level

International

Figure 5.4 displays the distribution of international remittances by source country. The distribution of remittances from countries abroad is given in figure 5.4. The largest source country for remittances to Pakistan is the USA, with Saudi Arabia in second place, followed by the United Arab Emirates (UAE) and other Gulf countries, and the United Kingdom in fifth place. From the UAE, the largest contributor is Dubai, and from the Gulf countries it is Kuwait. From the European Union the main contributor is Germany. The countries that have experienced the greatest growth in remittances through the Paksitan corridor since 2001 are the USA, Canada, and Italy, probably because of an increased effort by these countries to crack down on the terrorist network, encouraging senders to go through formal channels (see detailed breakdown by country of origin in Annex table A5.5). Historically, the bulk of remittances have come from the Gulf region, as it is closer and easier to migrate to. Only after the events of September 11, 2001, did the USA became a major remittance-sending country. However, if informal flows are taken into account, the remittances coming from Gulf countries would far exceed those coming from the USA.

Figure 5.4 Remittances to Pakistan by Country

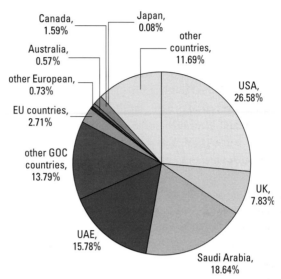

Source: SBP Annual Report 2006–7.

National

The two provinces with a significant share of remittances are North West Frontier Province (NWFP) and Punjab. Together they account for more than 85 percent of both domestic and foreign remittances. Furthermore, the rural areas in these provinces receive the bulk of the flows. Table 5.4 shows the overall distribution in the provinces and gives the split by rural/urban area.

Table 5.4 Regional Distribution of Remittances

Province		Domestic Remittances	Foreign Remittances
Punjab	Urban	17.0%	19.3%
	Rural	39.7%	19.4%
Sindh	Urban	1.9%	2.4%
	Rural	1.3%	1.2%
NWFP	Urban	4.5%	8.5%
	Rural	31.2%	39.1%
Baluchistan	Urban	0.3%	0.7%
	Rural	1.1%	2.8%
AJK	Urban	0.5%	1.7%
	Rural	2.2%	4.5%

Source: P SUM CWK 2004–5.

After Punjab and NWFP, Azad Jammu and Kashmir (AJK) receives 6.2 percent of foreign remittances, with 4.5 percent going to rural areas. With more than 60 percent share of the foreign remittances for rural areas of Punjab and NWFP, it is clear that remittances are not only going to major cities but are also available in villages, where traditionally formal access has been limited. Sindh and Baluchistan receive only a trivial amount of remittances. It is interesting to note that only 17 percent of the population of Pakistan resides in NWFP, but it receives the largest proportion of foreign remittances, 47.5 percent.

Divergent quality and accessibility of services nationally are reflected in differences in provincial perceptions on various channels of remittance transfers. In NWFP, money in person is a risky remittance method (perceived as such by 57.5 percent of the NWFP adult population); in AJK, money transfers via friends is risky (38 percent); in Baluchistan, using bank transfers is perceived as unsafe (38 percent), and in Sindh and Punjab, using someone else's bank account is considered riskiest by 25 percent and 50 percent, respectively.

The pattern of regional remittance distribution follows the migration pattern as noted in Ara (2003). Using the 1998 census data, she writes that Punjab and Sindh were the main destinations for domestic migration. For Punjab, much of the urban immigration was from rural or other urban areas of Punjab. In contrast, urban immigrants in Sindh (predominantly in Karachi) were mostly from other provinces of Pakistan. There was very little emigration from Sindh to other provinces. NWFP, on the other hand, was a major source of migrants to all provinces, particularly to Sindh.

Gazdar (2003) notes that the pattern of migration in Pakistan—from labor-abundant areas of NWFP and Punjab to urban centers of Punjab and Sindh—conforms to a basic poverty-migration linkage. The regions of emigration are, indeed, those parts of the country where agricultural incomes are low and volatile. And the economic gap between areas of emigration and immigration is clear enough. Wages of casual daily laborers can range from around Rs 40 in southern Punjab to around Rs 150 in Karachi.

Poverty and Remittances

It is well recognized that remittances play a beneficial role in reducing poverty. Remittances help families increase spending on basic needs, such as food and clothing, as well as health and education. Certain studies suggest that about 10 to 20 percent is also put in savings and investment (IFAD 2006).[6] Adams and Page (2005) find that a 10 percent increase in remittances leads to a 3.5 percent decline in the share of people living in poverty. Yang and Martinez (2005) determine that remittances not only lead to a decrease in poverty of migrant families, but also have spillover effects on nonmigrant families. Total remittance inflows to Pakistan from fiscal 2002 through fiscal 2006 have amounted to more than $19 billion. About one-third of this significant inflow of money is toward rural areas, helping to relax budget constraints and allowing increased expenditure on health, education, and consumer durables, contributing to poverty alleviation.

Table 5.5 Share of Remittances in Household Income for the Poorest Quintile (%)

By Province	Punjab		Sindh		NWFP		Baluchistan	
	Urban	Rural	Urban	Rural	Urban	Rural	Urban	Rural
Domestic Remittance	1.86	8.01	0.36	1.42	5.36	10.1	0	0.25
Foreign Remittance	0.81	0.7	0.69	0.22	7.27	2.75	0	2.55

Source: Household Integrated Economic Survey 2005, Federal Bureau of Statistics, government of Pakistan.

However, remittances do not appear to make a significant share of household income for the poorest quintile (table 5.5). Only for NWFP do remittances form a significant share of income—more than 12 percent in both rural and urban areas. For Sindh and Baluchistan, the share of remittances in household income is less than 3 percent. In Punjab, for urban poor the share is just 3.6 percent and for rural poor it is 8.8 percent. NWFP received significant remittance flows after the October 2005 earthquake.

Interestingly, we find that remittances form a larger share of household income for the richest two quintiles (Annex table A5.6). For the richest quintile, on average, foreign remittances are 5.5 percent of rural household income while for the poorest quintile, foreign remittances are only 1.9 percent of rural household income. However, across all quintiles, domestic remittances are the same proportion of household income, around 3.5 percent. In conclusion, foreign remittances are much more significant for the well-off households.

In contrast with the four provinces in table 5.5, in AJK, 25 percent of the households are found to receive remittances, which are their primary source of income (Suleri and Savage 2006). *Hawala* is the most common mode of money transfer that is used. The study also found that households whose livelihood included international remittances appeared less vulnerable to the earthquake's effects and also showed more resilience after remittances were reestablished.

A study undertaken by Oda (2007) in the Chakwal district of Punjab finds that external migration helps in poverty alleviation when compared with internal migration, as a high ratio of poor were found in the group of internal migrants, and a low incidence of poverty among external migrants.[7] Furthermore, remittances from external migrants were twice as high as those from internal migrants in absolute terms. The results of this study are corroborated by a study in Ghana by Adams (2006).

Determinants of Remittances and Historical Trends

There are roughly 3.7 million to 4 million Pakistani workers overseas, and more than 90 percent of them are production workers, like laborers, or service workers, such as cooks and operators (figure 5.5). Pakistan has a higher percentage of low-skilled migrant labor when compared with countries like India and Philippines, which have

Figure 5.5 Overseas Workers by Category

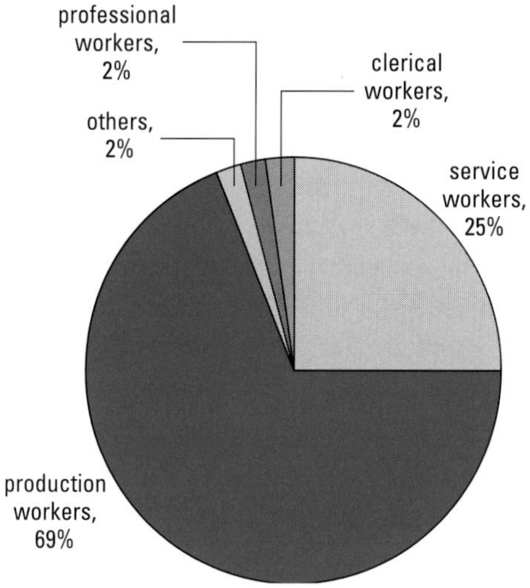

professional workers, 2%

clerical workers, 2%

others, 2%

service workers, 25%

production workers, 69%

Source: Bureau of Emigration and Overseas Employment 2006.

20–25 percent professional migrants, but similar to the levels in Bangladesh or African countries.

The main determining factors of remittances include economic activity in the sender and recipient countries. Swamy (1981) finds that 70–95 percent of variation in remittances is explained by economic activity in the sending country. Until recently, strong growth in Pakistani equity markets, as well as significant economic growth at 7 percent a year, had attracted significant investment from overseas. Remittances are also determined by strong local needs such as natural disasters. Western Union's remittances to AJK increased by 400 percent after the October 2005 earthquake (Shah et al., unpublished).

Table 5.6 displays the annual trend of workers' remittances from 1997 to 2007. Workers' remittances fell to $983 million in fiscal 2000 from much higher levels in the preceding decade. The main reason for the decline in remittances through the banking sector was that people started to prefer the *hawala* channel for its efficiency,

Table 5.6 Remittance Growth

	FY97	FY98	FY99	FY00	FY01	FY02	FY03	FY04	FY05	FY06	FY07
Workers' Remittances (Billion US$)	1.41	1.49	1.06	0.98	1.09	2.39	4.24	3.87	4.17	4.60	5.49
Growth of Remittances		5.7%	−28.8%	−7.2%	10.5%	119.9%	77.3%	−8.6%	7.7%	10.3%	19.4%

Source: SBP (2007); http://sbp.org.pk/ecodata/index2.asp.

low cost, and outreach. Furthermore, following the nuclear testing in May 1998 the foreign currency accounts of residents and expatriates were frozen, which created uncertainty and a severe loss of confidence in the government. Remittances fell by almost 29 percent in fiscal 1999 and further declined 7.2 percent the following year.

In the 2000s, SBP has been trying to curb money laundering and informal means of money transfer, which may have caused a reversion to formal banking channels and MTOs. The main reasons for remittances coming through the formal channels include the conversion of the moneychangers to ECs, which were in the formal net, the reduced exchange rate spread between the bank and curb rates, and incentives given by the government of Pakistan (GOP) and SBP to banks and expatriates. All these efforts supported a 400 percent increase within six years. Remittances continued their significant growth in fiscal 2002 and 2003, by 119.9 and 77.3 percent, respectively. In fiscal 2004, the remittances decreased by 8.6 percent, the decline coming mainly from the UAE for the two following reasons: (1) the Hajj Sponsorship Scheme[8] was canceled, which explained half the decrease, and (2) investment in real estate was opened up to foreigners in Dubai, giving Pakistani expatriates an alternate attractive investment option.

In fiscal 2005–8, remittances increased by 7.7, 10.3, 19.4, and 14.9 percent, respectively, mostly because of increased economic activity in the Gulf countries (a result of higher oil prices) and in the USA. The earthquake disaster prompted many Pakistanis overseas to send increased financial support to relatives back home. The growth is further attributable to increased investment in the Pakistani asset markets, particularly the equity market in fiscal 2007. The increase from the UAE for fiscal 2007 was $146.5 million; this can be attributed to rising construction activity during the real estate boom and increased economic activity as a result of the oil boom (SBP 2007c).

Econometric analysis suggests that education, employed status, and regular cell phone use are individual-level demand determinants for sending and receiving remittances (Annex table A5.8). Interestingly, women, rural areas, agricultural workers, household members other than the head, and participants in the informal sector are not less likely to be remittance clients. Higher income levels also have a higher chance of being associated with access to remittances than the poorest quintile, confirming the poverty impact analysis discussed earlier. This could reflect the fact that the poorest households may have less opportunity to send a family member abroad and receive foreign remittances.

Usage Patterns and Service Fees

The national household survey highlights relatively short delivery times for remittances in Pakistan: it takes a week or less for the majority of respondents to get cash remittances within and outside Pakistan. Only a fifth of recipients of international remittances report delivery delays of more than a week. This is more pronounced in rural areas, where a quarter of respondents note delays of over a week. The typical frequency for receiving domestic or international remittances is monthly or more

Table 5.7 Cost of Sending $300 to Pakistan through Various Channels

	U.S. (New York)	U.K. (London)	U.A.E. (Dubai)	Saudi Arabia (Riyadh)
Western Union	$10	$18.30	$6.80	$6.70
Moneygram	$10	$20.30	$5.50	$5.30
Foreign banks	$35 to $60	$40 to $80	$6.8 to $27	$16 to $24
Pakistani banks	Free	Free	Free	Free

Source: Authors' own research.

frequently. The national survey also reveals that home consumption constitutes the largest use of remittances across for all income groups, rural/urban areas, and gender. Other top uses of remittances after home consumption include health and child care, education, and business/land purchase related-purposes.

The limited presence and outreach of Pakistani banks abroad is the main problem facing Pakistani banks in increasing remittances through their networks. For senders, the most easily accessible banks are their local banks; however, sending money through them takes time and is expensive. Table 5.7 gives an overview of charges from four cities that have a significant share in remittances to Pakistan.[9] The local bank charges vary considerably depending on the speed of transfer (urgent vs. normal), ultimate destination, and the amount sent. These charges are comparable with those for India; however, the fees charged for other countries, such as Brazil and Mexico, are higher from the UAE and Saudi Arabia and lower from the USA and United Kingdom. The rates for Western Union and Moneygram are quite similar but the network of the former in Pakistan is far more extensive. The remittance charges for Internet checks are $3–$10 while for credit cards a flat fee of $8–$20 is charged plus 2.5–3 percent of the amount remitted. A competitive online transfer service in real time at a fee of $2 is offered by Doha Bank in Qatar, which has partnered with HBL and Askari Bank in Pakistan.

For MTOs, fees charged at the sending end are divided between three parties; the sending agent keeps 15–20 percent, the MTO keeps 50–60 percent, and the receiving agent keeps 25–50 percent (Passas 2004). The receiving agent will give a share to the franchise for handling the actual disbursement. The commission paid to franchises in Pakistan by ECs is 5 percent of the amount disbursed.

Outreach and Scope of Remittance Technologies

Roughly 64 percent of the population of Pakistan resides in rural areas; however, only 33 percent of the banking network is in these areas. Limited access to banking in rural areas requires innovative solutions to scale up outreach (box 5.4 presents one such solution for India). Internationally, several new remittance technologies have been in use, such as transferring money on prepaid cards or mobile phones;

| Box 5.4 | **Indian Nongovernmental Organization Helping Domestic Remittances** |

In India, the NGO Adhikar is piloting a domestic money transfer service for the large number of migrants who travel from the eastern state of Orissa to work in the western state of Gujarat. Adhikar's comparative advantages in money transfer services include knowledge of customer needs and preferences, as well as the ability to service clients in remote locations.

When designing its transfer system, Adhikar decided to leave the actual transmission of funds to Corporation Bank, which has branches in both Orissa and Gujarat and the infrastructure to make timely, secure transfers. Although bank transfers take place regularly between Orissa and Gujarat, most migrants do not have bank accounts and find it costly to visit a bank branch. Adhikar centralizes the collection and dissemination of these small transfers and routes them through one account at the bank. This process spreads transaction costs over a larger number of transfers, bringing down the per-transaction fee. Adhikar is now looking to leverage the system by involving NGOs that serve other districts in Orissa as distribution agents, lowering per-transaction fees even further while enabling the NGOs to earn a new source of revenue to support their work.

Source: Consultative Group to Assist the Poor (2005).

however, in Pakistan only online transfers are available. One significant advantage of financial services via mobile phones is their ability to conveniently bring banking to women, who for cultural and social reasons do not go out frequently.

Through the issuance of the "Guidelines for Mobile Banking Operations of MFBs/Institutions," SBP has been encouraging the private sector to provide mobile banking solutions. This shows strong potential as both the banking and telecom sectors are among the most vibrant in the country. In addition, microfinance institutions (MFIs) are growing at a robust rate and can support increased outreach, as 60 percent of their network is in rural areas, although only MFBs are allowed to remit money domestically.

The network of ECs in Pakistan is broad and covers all high-volume areas. The ECs analyze where remittances are flowing to and open franchises/payment booths accordingly, in nearby towns or small cities. However, as the systems of the ECs are automated and the minimum requirement for them to set up a branch is to have a phone connection and Internet, they have technically not opened branches in rural areas, but in cities near villages that receive remittances.

The best strategy for increasing financial access of the poor is to introduce mobile phone platforms. The outreach of the telecom sector is considerable—the mobile network in principle covers about 90 percent of the population of Pakistan. The total consumer base reached 89.3 million by July 2008[10]; the provincial breakdown of the mobile consumer base is given in figure 5.6 (Pakistan Telecommunications Authority 2007).

The penetration of mobile services in each province is around 30 percent (figure 5.7), but this amounts to 80 percent of the total population. However, AJK and

Figure 5.6 Mobile Consumer Base by Province

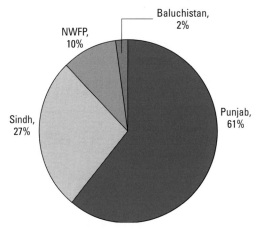

Source: Pakistan Telecommunication Authority (2007).

Figure 5.7 Mobile Penetration by Province

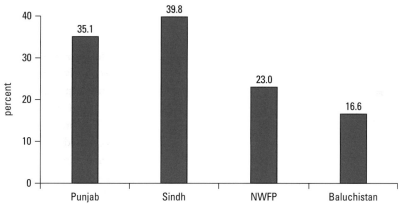

Source: Pakistan Telecommunication Authority (2007).

Northern Areas are still behind and the population covered is 20 percent, or about 1 million people. This mobile coverage, and the success of mobile money transfer solutions in the Philippines and Kenya (box 5.5), suggests that mobile banking offers significant potential to scale up access to financial services. Specifically, in the Philippines, the G-Cash model has achieved excellent outreach and can be used as a model in Pakistan to link mobile phones with financial services. Mobile-enabled business models have low operating costs, and if consumers can become savvy with the banking technology loaded onto mobiles, it offers the best way forward for improving outreach of all financial services, including remittances. According to the Consultative Group to Assist the Poor, using a mobile phone can reduce the cost of a typical bank transaction by 80 percent in the Philippines, while Tameer Bank estimates that, in the Orangi slum of Karachi, the setup cost of a bank branch would be 30 times more than the setup cost of an agent. Mobile money transfers have the

---

| Box 5.5 | **Mobile Banking: G-Cash (Philippines) and M-Pesa (Kenya)** |

The G-Cash product is a facility linking the user's phone to a "cash" account or "wallet." The customer can deposit or withdraw cash from this wallet as needed, while credit can be transferred between mobile users as well. It operates on a credit basis, where the user initially deposits cash at a designated deposit location such as Globe offices or accredited retailers. This service allows mobile users cashless purchasing at a wide range of shops, direct credit from employer payroll, bill payment, and inward remittance from overseas Filipino workers.

Initially, the user registers through sending a short message service (SMS) and deposits money; there are no charges for registration. Each transaction update is sent by Globe in the form of an SMS. Just as easily as cash is deposited at a deposit location, it can easily be withdrawn; however, an acceptable identity document is required. Retail purchases are possible at several thousand participating outlets. This involves a request from the retailer originating the transaction through his own cell phone terminal and a customer authorization from their own phone. Airtime transfers, prepaid top–up, and bill payments can be carried out with similar ease.

For each transaction, the cost is the standard SMS fee ($0.02). For cash deposits and withdrawals, the fee charged is 10 percent of the transaction value with a minimum of $0.19. Globe maintains and operates a clearinghouse facility that records all transactions and arranges settlement between the retailers and the G-Cash customers. This results in Globe having responsibility for the usual banking issues of fraud management and money laundering prevention. However, the cash float from the customer balances is held by the company's usual business bank, although that bank has no knowledge of the individual user activity or account balances. The user has to authorize each transaction by a PIN and the maximum balance that can be maintained by a customer is $189.

The M-PESA mobile money transfer platform in Kenya is very similar to G-Cash and it specifically targets the unbanked population. These people, who do not have access to convenient or cheap cash transfer services or bank branches, simply register with an M-Pesa agent by providing their Safaricom mobile number and identify card. Once they have done this and deposited money with a local agent, they can send money to other mobile phone users through an SMS even if they are not Safaricom users. This cash can easily be withdrawn at an M-Pesa agent. Banks are now beginning to partner with Safaricom to provide further services. For example, two Equity Bank account holders with Safaricom lines can now credit and transfer cash into each other's account using their mobile phones in real time, subject to the availability of funds. Equity bank clients will also be able to pay their utility bills, purchase airtime, request their bank statements and perform other crucial banking enquiries.

Source: DFID.

---

potential to help lower international remittance costs by up to 75 percent and domestic remittance costs by up to 90 percent, providing direct savings to poor households.

SBP has issued guidelines for branchless banking, covering three different models: In the first, banks can work with a particular telecom provider to offer services to the current customer base of that company. In the second, a bank can offer mobile phone banking services to customers using mobile connection of any telecom. The third model is a group of banks and telecoms that can join hands to provide a service.[11]

As telecom providers are not themselves prudentially regulated, they are prevented from taking deposits and so cannot themselves provide savings products (a primary need for many poor consumers). This would also hamper their ability to be able to provide loans. Hence, although "pure" telecom provider models can currently be effective for providing mobile payments, there is a need for a banking relationship, or appropriate regulation, to allow access to other financial services beyond remittances through these models.

To further increase outreach of financial services, SBP has provided more options for branchless banking, such as to the Post Office, fuel distribution companies and other chain stores. However, except for the Post Office, other players are still not involved in providing financial services.

There is a lot of activity in this sector, and both banks and mobile phone companies are working to develop viable models. UBL has launched a product based on the second model called "Orion," accessible only to UBL account holders. The services available through Orion are paying bills, transferring money among other Orion users, and buying phone cards. In time, UBL plans to increase the kind of transactions that can be done with Orion, along with adding remittance transfer facilities. Bank Al-Falah is currently testing a mobile banking product with Warid Telecom.

Another player that will enter the mobile banking market soon is Etisalat of the UAE, the major shareholder of Pakistan Telecommunications Company and Ufone. They have signed a contract with Smart of Philippines in the UAE to offer remittance services. The remittance service will allow subscribers of Etisalat to send funds to Pakistan and other countries anytime, anywhere, using their mobile phones. It will also allow tracking of transactions. The only infrastructure required will be cash in/out merchants and perhaps these can ride on the network of mobile phone card providers, which are all over Pakistan.

In the USA, dual automated teller machine (ATM) cards are very popular with Mexican immigrants. In Pakistan, none of the stakeholders contacted had any knowledge of dual ATM cards. However, various Pakistani banks in the Gulf region do provide for dual ATM cards, and they are quite convenient as recipients back home can withdraw money anytime. It is possible that Pakistani expatriates might be giving their families' ATM and credit/debit cards to use in Pakistan, given the large amounts of money processed through ATMs and point of sale (POS).[12]

Citibank UAE in August 2007 started a Twin Account Facility for expatriate Pakistanis who have a banking relationship in the UAE but also need to send money to Pakistan. Account holders can transfer money round the clock by phone, online, by ATM, or at branches. Customers in both the UAE and Pakistan will be given checkbooks and debit cards to settle payments worldwide.

Ikobo offers prepaid Visa card remittances, which can be used at any ATM provided easy access exists. Although this service is offered for Pakistan, the extent of its current use is unknown.

In Brazil, remittances through Visa Giro are doing well, given the large population that uses credit cards and a good support infrastructure that was already in place.

As these examples show, remittances can be used as a key entry point to bringing the unbanked into the formal sector and increasing financial inclusion. That is, money transferred through financial institutions paves the way for other financial products and services to be provided.

Remittances are often the first, and sometimes the only, financial service that low-income households use. Providing remittance services allows banks to get to know and reach out to unbanked recipients, build up information on the size and stability of their cash flows, and then offer other financial services such as savings or credit.

As remittances are typically lumpy, it makes sense that a remittance receiver may need a secure way to store that money. Increased savings will in turn enable an increase in loanable funds, aggregate credit and wider financial intermediation.

Econometric evidence provides strong support for the notion that remittances promote broader financial development in developing countries, via increases in the aggregate level of deposits and credit intermediated by the local banking sector. This is important considering the extensive literature that has documented the growth-enhancing and poverty-reducing effects of financial development (Aggarwal et al. 2006).

Policy and Regulatory Framework

Since the early 1980s, SBP has been actively working to support a vibrant remittances market. In the 1980s, it encouraged Pakistani banks to establish branches in Middle Eastern countries to where most Pakistanis had migrated. The foreign exchange regime was liberalized, and the option of opening foreign currency accounts in Pakistan was given to expatriates, allowing the free inflow and outflow of foreign currency.

After September 11, 2001, SBP took further actions to formalize remittances, such as setting up centralized home remittance cells. Banks submitted their remittance targets to SBP and an SBP taskforce ensured implementation.

A complaint and monitoring cell was set up to address public complaints. The GOP gave incentives at this time to further boost remittances, such as exemption of custom duties on personal baggage and the use of special immigration clearance counters.

On a governmental level, SBP teams visited and studied several countries to learn from anti–money-laundering (AML) laws and successful remittance practices. MFBs were given permission to offer remittance facilities, and SBP is working with all financial institutions to enhance efficiency and transparency.

Future government plans include adding new products with a better rate of return to the National Savings Scheme for remittance beneficiaries, to discourage consumer spending and channel savings into productive investments.

On the donor side, the World Bank has supported many initiatives, such as establishing a new framework to improve the quality and coverage of data, or formulating General Principles for International Remittance Services to help improve regulation, foster competition and increase transparency. The World Bank has also cooperated with other international financial institutions to work on remittances, and AML/combating the financing of terrorism measures. It has launched a price and cost database on remittances to enhance transparency and is working on improving payment systems so that they are quick, cheap, safe, efficient, contestable, and transparent.

The International Monetary Fund is helping countries implement Financial Action Task Force (FATF) recommendations for remittance systems. It is undertaking a comprehensive assessment of the AML/combating the financing of terrorism measures along with other international financial institutions and is developing an operational guide, as well as offering technical assistance on their implementation. The International Monetary Fund is also working to improve statistics and how they are captured in the balance of payments. Annex table A5.9 gives a snapshot of donor and International Financial Institution activities to improve the remittance system.

Legal/Regulatory Framework

The legal and regulatory framework governing inward remittance transactions is provided for under the Foreign Exchange Regulation Act, 1947. SBP implemented the Act through general or special directives issued as occasional circulars and notifications. The primary instructions regarding foreign exchange transactions are contained in the Foreign Exchange Manual issued and updated by SBP.

The Foreign Exchange Manual provides that there are no restrictions on incoming remittances. However, financial institutions, banks, and other authorized dealers (including ECs) have to obtain licenses to carry on foreign exchange transactions. All transactions have to be reported to SBP, identifying the amount and the source. Both banks and ECs report on a daily, weekly, and monthly basis. Furthermore, the banks have access to a Real Time Gross Settlement System for low-volume, high-value transactions.

SBP has been moving steadily toward automating the system and providing real-time settlements to keep up with international best practices and national and international requirements. To this end, in 2007, the Parliament enacted a Payment and Electronic Fund Transfer Act, which laid down solid foundations for development and further strengthening of payment systems in the country, implemented by SBP. In collaboration with National Interbank Financial Telecommunications (NIFT), SBP has been implementing the real-time gross settlement system called PRISM (Pakistan Real Time Interbank Settlement Mechanism). An automated clearinghouse has been set up, based on MICR Reader and Sorter equipment with code written in house to facilitate local requirements and changing needs. The automated clearinghouse can be directly accessed by each branch and plays a role of a central regulating authority. NIFT collects the outward clearing directly from each bank, arranges all processing, and provides the net position to SBP. It provides services to all 42 commercial banks and their branches. NIFT centers have been established in over 80 cities for 4,000 bank branches to provide NIFT automated clearinghouse services.

SBP is also working on providing all local banks with automated low-cost Society for Worldwide Interbank Financial Telecommunication (SWIFT) connectivity and a local U.S. dollar loop has been set up with NIFT to expedite clearing of dollar transactions. The new system has reduced the clearing time for U.S. dollar checks from three weeks to only four days, along with cost savings to the account holders. At the same time, SBP is also rapidly developing the e-banking infrastructure.

All banks and ECs are subject to both off- and onsite inspections and any violation makes them liable to penalties. Each transaction by the institutions has to be reported on a weekly and monthly basis to SBP and has to be filtered through an in-house AML system. Suspicious transactions—something out of character or inconsistent with the history and pattern of the individual accounts—have to be reported. SBP does the monitoring via supervision units at 16 field offices. A comprehensive inspection manual covering all areas of operations has been developed to help with monitoring. The opening of each new franchise office or payment booth of an EC is carefully scrutinized by SBP, including a background check on the person who is opening the office and a visit to the location to verify the adequacy of the facilities. SBP further conducts mystery shopping by sending undercover staff to ascertain the quality and type of service received.

Know-your-customer regulations are also in force. ECs do not make payments unless the recipient has a national identity card. Furthermore, SBP mandates each bank and exchange company to have a compliance department that monitors accounts and transactions and updates customer information on a regular basis. Proper documentation and record keeping has to be maintained, while correspondent banks have to be carefully chosen after examining their due diligence procedures.

Obstacles

In the rich urban areas of Pakistan, very few obstacles to efficient remittance flows remain. The network of banks and ECs is widespread, the cost is reasonable, and the speed of transfer is prompt. However, similar facilities are not available to low-income and rural areas. SBP has stimulated outreach by its recent branch policy, whereby banks with 100 branches or more are required to have 20 percent of their branches in rural areas. EC expansion in rural areas is severely restricted, because their online systems require phone and Internet connection. However, as mobile and wireless penetration becomes more common, this will improve. A computerized-kiosk system with low-cost ATMs has permitted a considerable expansion of remittance services coverage in rural India (box 5.6).

> **Box 5.6   Kiosks to Help Rural Outreach**
>
> ICICI Bank, a private Indian commercial bank that evolved out of a national development bank, offers a wide range of financial services, including money transfers sent to India by nonresident Indians. In 2004, the bank's "Money2India" service had more than 670 agent locations and recently extended its outreach to remote village centers via computer kiosks.
>
> The computer kiosk system works as follows: A sender remits a money transfer to the recipient's ICICI account, either through an ICICI branch office or a Money2India agent. As soon as the transaction has taken place, the Money2India agent informs the kiosk operator, who in turn informs the recipient. The recipient can then either collect the remittance at ICICI or the kiosk, which is equipped with a low-cost ATM. ICICI estimates that kiosks can be profitably placed in villages as small as 2,000 residents. This option is very attractive for rural recipients because it eliminates transaction costs involved in traveling to a larger town to visit a bank branch.
>
> Kiosks used by ICICI bank offer a combination of telephone, financial, educational, and other services. Kiosk operators are independent business people, remunerated through commissions paid by service providers and user fees paid by customers. They pay for set-up costs themselves, for which they typically obtain a partial loan from ICICI Bank. Since ICICI Bank does not incur any fixed costs, the system has proven a cost-effective way for the bank to extend its outreach to rural areas.
>
> In mid-2004, approximately 150 kiosk operators offered ICICI services and the bank hoped to increase that number to more than 2,000 in about 12 months. From an operator's perspective, the business model is only viable if multiple services are routed through a single kiosk. However, experience indicates that the kiosks can become profitable even without the money transfer service, which can easily be added at a later date.
>
> ICICI Bank was able to offer its Money2India service as the result of a confluence of circumstances: (1) the inventors of the kiosk system were seeking appropriate business applications for it; (2) the technology suited the needs of ICICI; and (3) other nonfinancial service providers, such as companies that offer educational and health information/diagnostic services, also opted to use the kiosks, creating multiservice businesses that ensured operator profits. These circumstances, and therefore the transmission system for Money2India, may be somewhat difficult to replicate in other countries. However, the example of computer kiosks with low-cost ATMs may represent a cost-effective way for financial service providers to expand the outreach of money transfers, as well as other services.
>
> *Source:* Consultative Group to Assist the Poor (2005).

Pakistan Post has the best network in rural areas, though there is space for much efficiency improvement. HBL had an agreement with Pakistan Post to deliver remittances to rural areas where it does not have branches, but delays in the processing and delivery of money orders led HBL to cancel the agreement.

A further issue remains in formalizing informal remittances, especially domestic flows. A large percentage of people do not consider Pakistan Post or formal banking sector as options because they think these are too complicated and inefficient.

An obstacle specific to the Gulf area is that most of the immigrants from Pakistan are illiterate and are shy about going to banks to remit money. These people find it much easier to send money through *hawaldars* whom they know and trust. The convenience and simplicity of *hawala* cannot be matched by banks, as remitting money through banks requires a process of, first, going to the bank and then waiting for the recipient's bank to be credited, and finally the recipient traveling to the bank to withdraw the payment. With *hawala*, the money is delivered to the recipient's doorstep.

An important barrier for mobilizing remittances through formal channels from the USA is that the people who generally send money earn in cash and do not have bank accounts. They are undocumented and unbanked, and it is not possible for them to go to a bank or an MTO. Furthermore, the worker class is also unfamiliar with these organizations and prefers the trust-based mechanism of *hawala*.

The key drivers of the formalization of remittance flows include cost, ease of access, identity requirements, trust, and financial (and technological) literacy. If formal services can be made cheaper, easier to access, user-friendly without prohibitive identity requirements, and with appropriate education to alert people to the benefits of formal systems and how to use them, this will then significantly help bring informal flows into the formal sector. New technologies, such as branchless banking, offer significant potential to reduce transaction costs and so can allow new business models for previously unreached areas to become viable (as noted previously). They also are convenient and can access rural or other hard-to-reach areas where traditional bank branch models are unviable, and so offer great potential toward the key drivers of formalization.

Suggested Avenues for Action

There are vital roles for both the government and the private sector to play in harnessing remittances for access to finance. The private sector should be fundamentally responsible for providing financial services, and the government needs to ensure to the extent possible that the business and regulatory environment is conducive to the private sector provision of safe, efficient, and equitable financial services.

The most comprehensive step to increase access to remittances and potentially to harness access to other financial services would be mobile banking solutions. More than half of the population already regularly uses a mobile phone, and econometric analysis has highlighted that remittance users are likely to be regular mobile phone users. Mobile phones are affordable, and the network has expanded immensely in recent years, and mobile payment platforms offer significant potential for lowering cost and increasing outreach for the rural poor.

One concrete way to make progress in the sector would be to form a public-private working group on remittances. This would enable a dialogue between the government and private companies (banks, ECs, and MTOs, as well as telecoms where relevant) to tackle key challenges in the sector. Discussion could focus on, among other things, legal and regulatory issues, market transparency, competition and cost, as well as research and data issues. The UK has had a successful experience in this regard with a Public-Private Working Group on Remittances, which led to the creation of a private sector–led UK Remittances Task Force. The World Bank has also convened a similar group at the international level bringing together key actors from the public and private sectors. Pakistan can draw on this considerable experience.

Private Sector Actions

Reducing informality: Informality will decrease upon the introduction of efficient, low-cost, easy-access, user-friendly, and trusted remittance services, without prohibitive identification requirements.

Developing new technology-based models for financial services: Several new remittance technologies, such as transferring money on prepaid cards or mobile phones, are already in use in various countries; however, only online transfers are available in Pakistan.

SBP has issued guidelines for three models of branchless banking: first, where banks work with a particular telecom provider to offer services to the current customer base of that provider; second, where banks offers mobile phone banking services to their own customers using the mobile connection of any telecom; and third, where a group of banks and telecoms jointly provide a service.[13]

New technologies such as branchless banking offer significant potential to reduce transactions costs and so can allow new business models for previously unreached areas where traditional bank branch models are unviable. There is a lot of activity in this sector and both banks and mobile phone companies are working to come up with viable models. UBL has launched a product that provides services for paying bills, transferring money between customers, and buying phone cards. Bank Al-Falah is currently testing a mobile banking product with Warid Telecom, and Etisalat of the UAE; it has signed a contract with Smart (of the Philippines) to offer remittance services in the UAE. Banks and telecoms companies should work to develop further money transfer and mobile banking services in Pakistan.

Expanding bank presence and service provision abroad: The limited presence and outreach of Pakistani banks abroad are the main problems they face in increasing remittances through their networks. Foreign banks are more easily accessible to remittance senders abroad, but these may provide a slower or more expensive remittance service to Pakistan, and may not have significant outreach in rural areas. New measures should be taken to increase outreach abroad, particularly in the major remittance source countries. These could be new partnerships, or new innovative ways to reach customers. HBL managed to gain market share by reaching out to the workers in the

Middle East. A similar strategy could be followed in all countries where a sizeable Pakistani worker community exists. Once these workers, who are the main senders, are part of the process and a system is set up to fit their needs, the volume of remittances will grow further. Moreover, if they are given incentives or bonuses based on the amount they remit, they will become more diligent with sending money. One caveat to keep in mind is that the literacy level is low and so paperwork should be kept to a minimum and technology interfaces should not be excessively complex. In addition, the recipients of remittances are generally women or elder groups, for whom convenience is most important. For this group, models that are based on doorstep delivery would be most suitable.

Forming new partnerships within Pakistan: Within the Pakistani financial market, partnerships and linkages between different institutions should be developed to facilitate access to remittances and other financial services by the rural poor. For example, commercial banks should explore working with MFBs to expand their networks in rural areas.

Government Actions

Creating an enabling environment for the private sector: SBP has taken significant steps over recent years to improve the remittance market in Pakistan. It has in some cases provided more options for branchless banking such as to the Post Office, fuel distribution companies, and other chain stores, or issued guidelines for branchless banking, but the private sector has yet to fully respond to these areas. There may be other barriers or lack of adequate incentives preventing the intended response, and hence the government should talk to the private sector to understand these barriers and work to remove them where possible. Telco-based models such as G-cash and M-Pesa have shown some limitations, the most important of which has been the lack of prudential regulation with the attendant security and supervision shortcomings, as well as the narrow range of services that could be provided by such models. Regulatory reforms that may be required include amendments to the Payment and Electronic Fund Transfer Act and Branchless Banking regulations providing for bank–nonbank partnership and use of agents in money transfer services. A data privacy or security law can facilitate e- or m-payments.

Continuing to bring informal remittances into the formal system, particularly on the domestic front: An enabling environment for the private sector, encouragement for opening of bank accounts, as well as improved postal office efficiency will have an additional effect to continue attracting remittance flows to the formal sector. However, until efficient, cheap, easy-to-access, and user-friendly without prohibitive identity requirements and trusted methods permeate the country, including in rural areas, demand for informal remittances, particularly on the domestic front, will be important. Advances in technical and financial literacy will matter as well, with appropriate education to alert people to the benefits of formal systems and how to use them.

Supporting remittance services of Pakistani banks abroad: Further encouragement for Pakistani banks might be required to continue to boost international remittances and forge alliances with international banks. One potential strategy would be to set the reimbursement rate through partner banks higher than those coming solely through Pakistani bank networks. Alternatively, a small fee could be charged to senders when they use partner banks in international countries.

Pakistani missions abroad could do a survey of options available in their respective markets and disseminate the information to immigrants on the cheapest and best sources of money transfer. For example, the Mexican mission in the USA publishes such information. A further successful policy carried out by the Mexican embassy in the USA is issuance of a type of identification card (*Matricula Consular*) for their immigrants, and with this card Mexican immigrants into the USA can open bank accounts. Perhaps the GOP can discuss something similar with the U.S. and other authorities.

Encouraging the opening of bank accounts: Another step that SBP should work toward is encouraging people to open bank accounts, as supported by positive perceptions on accessibility and safety of bank branches as a remittance channel. The high share of banks in the international remittance market in Pakistan also indicates that increasing bank accounts should help increase remittances through formal channels. Currently, the minimum account balance of Rs 10,000 is prohibitive for a large segment of the society.[14] To encourage people to open bank accounts, uncomplicated paperwork and less stringent balance requirements are needed. Banks currently handling remittances can credit accounts within 24 hours; however, delivering money or sending money orders by the Post Office creates unnecessary delays, and the banking sector loses customers to MTOs and informal means of transfer.

Seeking to improve the efficiency of the postal remittance service: Pakistan Post has a significant network and strong outreach in rural areas. However, services can be inefficient. Government should explore ways to improve this service and speed up the automation of postal branches.

Promoting the structuring of international flows into investments: Channeling remittance flows directly into investment in the tradable sectors of the economy has been pursued successfully in the international experience, to counteract loss of international competitiveness associated with elevated remittance flows. International good practices include packaging remittances with payment services (such as Bansefi in Mexico). Successful policies to structure international flows into investments have also focused on organizing and targeting diaspora networks rather than actual remittances flows. At the macro level, diaspora bonds issuances (for example, in Ghana, India, and Israel) or securitization of future remittances flows (in Brazil and El Salvador) have been used, although securitization has proven costly. At the microlevel, governments have facilitated targeted diaspora funds.

Remittances to Pakistan are of considerable economic importance, including domestic flows, and have grown quickly in recent years, providing foreign exchange, improving the balance of payments and external debt position, and supporting incomes of poor and vulnerable groups. Transmission networks work well in urban areas, though outreach to rural and remote locations is difficult, and services are not sufficiently customized to client needs (such as women who might need doorstep delivery). The large network of Pakistan Post offers promise for the future, but considerable gains in efficiency are required. SBP has taken various measures that have significantly increased remittances through formal channels, though a large share of domestic remittances remains informally transferred. To stimulate outreach to remote locations, SBP has been encouraging the private sector to provide mobile banking solutions. Other solutions from international experience include Indian innovations, such as the NGO Adhikar, which developed an efficient domestic customized transfer service, and ICICI Bank, which extended its outreach to remote village centers via computer kiosks. New partnerships among remittance market players and other financial entities both within Pakistan and abroad hold much promise. Further advances in formalizing money transfer flows will bring new clientele and motivation for efficiency gains and customization of services to client needs.

Notes

1. The text does not take into account recent effects of the global financial crisis, instead analyzing the data as of 2007–8. Recent events have caused remittances to drop drastically.
2. *Source:* Dawn Economic and Business Review, March 31, Karachi, Pakistan.
3. SBP has given all banks the incentive to not charge international customers for wiring money, and it reimburses them for each transaction.
4. Information on individual branches can be found on the Web site of each EC.
5. PSLM is a nationally representative household survey carried out by the FBS.
6. World Bank (2008a) quotes estimates in Ghana, where 70 percent of remittances are spent on current expenditures and less than 30 percent on investments, such as land, cattle, or construction. In Mali, 80 to 90 percent is spent on consumption. In the Philippines, 68 percent is spent on debt repayment and current needs, 13 percent on consumer goods, 1 percent on education, 5 percent on business capital, 3 percent on land and buildings, and 1 percent on personal savings.
7. See Annex table A5.7 for the contribution of remittances to household income and poverty ratio in the sample from the study.
8. This scheme was introduced to facilitate the Islamic Pilgrimage (Hajj) to Mecca. In the 1990s, there was a shortage of foreign exchange and people who had relatives abroad could ask them to sponsor the Hajj for them.
9. For Western Union and Moneygram, the charges are based on sending cash.
10. The cellular density as of July 31, 2008, was 55.6 percent.
11. Guidelines available at www.sbp.org.pk.
12. According to the SBP Payment Systems Department, from October 2006 to March 2007, approximately $67 million worth of transactions were processed through ATMs, and similarly $64 million worth of transactions were processed through POS (SBC Payment Systems Department 2007).
13. Guidelines available at www.sbp.org.pk.
14. In an effort to encourage the opening of bank accounts, SBP introduced Basic Banking Accounts (BBA) in 2005 as a new product, with no minimum balance requirements and a minimum opening balance of only Rs 1,000.

Annex

Table A5.1 Workers' Remittances by Sector (Millions US$)

Period	Banks	Exchange Companies	Postal	Encashment & premium of FEBC/FCBC in Pak Rupees	Total
Jan, 2005	284.72	31.44	4.98	0.24	321.38
Feb, 2005	303.61	31.26	4.00	0.42	339.29
Mar, 2005	399.60	38.27	5.36	0.47	443.70
Apr, 2005	348.12	40.15	5.34	7.39	401.00
May, 2005	306.05	43.80	5.04	3.41	358.30
June, 2005	302.26	50.16	5.21	1.35	358.98
July, 2005	262.93	42.08	5.00	3.13	313.14
Aug, 2005	282.99	58.00	5.55	1.87	348.41
Sep, 2005	276.66	57.26	6.01	1.17	341.10
Oct, 2005	300.83	63.28	7.47	0.92	372.50
Nov, 2005	258.94	42.02	7.09	0.76	308.81
Dec, 2005	312.55	49.73	6.82	2.14	371.24
Jan, 2006	338.82	45.64	6.41	0.45	391.32
Feb, 2006	309.40	42.18	6.42	0.13	358.13
Mar, 2006	364.83	49.88	8.73	0.12	423.56
Apr, 2006	346.74	46.44	8.17	0.12	401.47
May, 2006	432.84	64.11	9.33	0.29	506.57
June, 2006	394.86	60.02	8.00	0.99	463.87
July, 2006	305.50	62.78	8.05	0.68	377.01
Aug, 2006	357.86	67.65	9.21	0.12	434.84
Sep, 2006	346.40	66.05	9.11	0.18	421.74
Oct, 2006	323.43	76.96	10.18	0.04	410.61
Nov, 2006	365.50	74.12	8.84	0.15	448.61
Dec, 2006	377.97	86.95	10.12	0.17	475.21
Jan, 2007	315.22	66.25	09.80	0.06	391.33
Feb, 2007	370.12	75.49	11.42	0.15	457.18
Mar, 2007	421.99	84.03	13.86	0.35	520.23
Apr, 2007	413.27	86.26	13.48	0.34	513.35
May, 2007	420.03	101.23	16.39	0.33	537.98
June, 2007	386.51	104.35	14.58	0.11	505.55
July, 2007	370.62	112.89	11.89	0.29	495.69
Aug, 2007	360.77	116.06	12.55	0.13	489.51
Sep, 2007	380.35	121.29	14.20	0.21	516.05

Source: SBP 2007i.

Table A5.2 Inland Money Orders 2004–5 (millions)

	Number	Value (Rs)	Value (%)
Punjab	3.517	12222.7	67.0
Sindh	0.483	1911.2	10.5
NWFP	0.661	2750.5	15.1
Baluchistan	0.04	166.2	1.0
FC, NA & AJK	0.35	1197.7	6.6

Source: Pakistan Post, Annual Report 2005.

Note: FC, NA & AJK: Federal Capital, Northern Areas, and Azad Jammu and Kashmir.

Table A5.3 Postal Orders 2004–5 (millions)

	Number	Value (Rs)	Value (%)
Punjab	0.152	6.7	33.5
Sindh	0.161	6.3	31.5
NWFP	0.367	1.5	7.5
Baluchistan	0.006	0.2	1.0
FC, NA & AJK	0.045	5.3	26.5

Source: Pakistan Post, Annual Report 2005.

Note: FC, NA & AJK: Federal Capital, Northern Areas, and Azad Jammu and Kashmir.

Table A5.4 Rural vs. Urban Split of Bank Branches in Provinces

Province	Urban/Rural	Branches	Percent
Punjab	Urban	2,745	35.4
	Rural	1,484	19.1
Sindh	Urban	1,441	18.6
	Rural	315	4.1
N.W.F.P.	Urban	481	6.2
	Rural	401	5.2
Baluchistan	Urban	219	2.8
	Rural	64	0.8
AJK	Urban	125	1.6
	Rural	204	2.6
FATA	Urban	214	2.8
	Rural	62	0.8
Total Branches		**7,755**	**100**

Source: Pakistan Post, Annual Report 2005.

Table A5.5 Workers' Remittances to Pakistan by Fiscal Year and Country (Millions US$)

Item	1997	1998	1999	2000	2001	2002	2003	2004	2005	2006	2007
I. Cash	*1,078.05*	*1,237.68*	*875.55*	*913.49*	*1,021.59*	*2,340.79*	*4,190.73*	*3,826.16*	*4,152.29*	*4,588.03*	*5,490.97*
1. USA	*146.25*	*166.29*	*81.95*	*79.96*	*134.81*	*778.98*	*1,237.52*	*1,225.09*	*1,294.08*	*1,242.49*	*1,459.64*
2. UK	*97.94*	*98.83*	*73.59*	*73.27*	*81.39*	*151.93*	*273.83*	*333.94*	*371.86*	*438.65*	*430.04*
3. Saudi Arabia	*418.44*	*474.86*	*318.49*	*309.85*	*304.43*	*376.34*	*580.76*	*565.29*	*627.19*	*750.44*	*1,023.56*
4. UAE	*164.39*	*207.70*	*125.09*	*147.79*	*190.04*	*469.49*	*837.87*	*597.48*	*712.61*	*716.30*	*866.49*
Dubai	93.07	101.01	70.57	87.04	129.69	331.47	581.09	447.49	532.93	540.24	635.60
Abu Dhabi	44.91	75.13	38.07	47.30	48.11	103.72	212.37	114.92	152.51	147.89	200.40
Sharjah	22.90	28.54	14.69	12.80	12.21	34.05	42.60	34.61	26.17	26.87	28.86
Other	3.51	3.02	1.76	0.65	0.03	0.25	1.81	0.46	1.00	1.30	1.63
5. Other GCC Countries	*123.33*	*160.85*	*197.28*	*224.32*	*198.75*	*224.29*	*474.02*	*451.54*	*512.14*	*596.46*	*757.33*
Bahrain	29.16	34.31	33.31	29.36	23.87	39.58	71.46	80.55	91.22	100.57	136.28
Kuwait	38.38	52.40	106.36	135.25	123.39	89.66	221.23	177.01	214.78	246.75	288.71
Qatar	9.68	12.17	12.94	13.29	13.38	31.87	87.68	88.69	86.86	118.69	170.65
Oman	46.11	61.97	44.67	46.42	38.11	63.18	93.65	105.29	119.28	130.45	161.69
6. EU Countries	*41.90*	*38.57*	*26.48*	*24.06*	*21.50*	*28.80*	*53.53*	*74.51*	*101.51*	*119.62*	*149.00*
Germany	18.98	16.62	11.93	10.47	9.20	13.44	26.87	46.52	53.84	59.03	76.87
France	6.41	9.00	4.78	3.53	2.22	3.52	3.92	3.64	4.11	8.14	8.94
Netherlands	7.10	5.21	3.03	4.33	3.60	4.63	8.51	5.65	8.80	7.00	7.17
Spain	0.01	0.04	0.02	0.16	0.06	0.18	0.87	0.78	4.59	3.44	7.58
Italy	0.73	0.89	0.58	0.35	0.55	0.47	0.81	2.21	6.74	12.49	12.10
Greece	0.00	0.00	0.00	0.00	0.00	0.07	0.24	0.26	1.24	2.76	2.83
Sweden	0.65	0.58	0.47	0.65	0.74	0.67	2.00	2.06	2.75	3.60	3.69
Denmark	7.05	5.17	4.79	3.75	3.83	4.18	5.87	8.11	10.55	10.87	16.24

(continued)

Table A5.5 Continued

Item	1997	1998	1999	2000	2001	2002	2003	2004	2005	2006	2007
Ireland	0.00	0.21	0.00	0.05	0.20	0.02	0.52	1.26	3.31	6.70	5.59
Belgium	0.97	0.85	0.88	0.77	1.10	1.62	3.92	4.02	5.58	5.59	7.99
7. Norway	7.97	7.16	5.26	5.60	5.74	6.55	8.89	10.22	18.30	16.82	22.04
8. Switzerland	6.32	5.47	3.60	4.23	4.24	16.21	34.67	29.11	22.71	20.50	18.06
9. Australia	5.39	4.78	3.23	3.69	4.15	5.47	8.26	13.66	19.64	25.10	31.24
10. Canada	3.59	4.14	3.46	3.86	4.90	20.52	15.19	22.90	48.49	81.71	87.20
11. Japan	3.05	2.65	3.09	1.58	3.93	5.97	8.14	5.28	6.51	6.63	4.26
12. Other Countries	59.48	66.38	34.03	35.28	67.71	256.24	658.05	497.14	417.25	573.31	642.11
II. Encashment and Profit in Pak. Rs. of Foreign Exchange Bearer Certificates	**331.42** **0.00**	**251.87** **0.00**	**184.64** **0.00**	**70.24** **0.00**	**64.98** **0.00**	**48.26** **0.00**	**46.12** **0.00**	**45.42** **0.00**	**16.50** **0.00**	**12.09** **0.00**	**1.40** **0.00**
(FEBCs) & Foreign Currency Bearer	0.00	0.00	0.00	0.00	0.00	0.00	0.00	0.00	0.00	0.00	0.00
Certificates (FCBCs)	0.00	0.00	0.00	0.00	0.00	0.00	0.00	0.00	0.00	0.00	1.28
TOTAL (I+II)	**1,409.47**	**1,489.55**	**1,060.19**	**983.73**	**1,086.57**	**2,389.05**	**4,236.85**	**3,871.58**	**4,168.79**	**4,600.12**	**5,493.65**

Source: SBP 2007.
Note: GCC: Gulf Cooperation Council, EU: European Union.

Table A5.6 Percentage Share of Remittances in Household Income, 2004–5

Quintile	By Province	Punjab		Sindh		NWFP		Baluchistan	
		Urban	Rural	Urban	Rural	Urban	Rural	Urban	Rural
1	Domestic Remittances	1.86	8.01	0.36	1.42	5.36	10.1	0	0.25
	Foreign Remittances	0.81	0.7	0.69	0.22	7.27	2.75	0	2.55
2	Domestic Remittances	3.47	5.5	0.1	0.54	7.2	12.45	0.9	1.07
	Foreign Remittances	0.51	0.87	0	0.11	1.47	7.42	0	0.33
3	Domestic Remittances	2.61	7.6	1.06	0.54	3.24	10.85	0.97	0.92
	Foreign Remittances	0.98	1.23	0	0.36	2.34	9.15	0.27	2.31
4	Domestic Remittances	3.08	7.28	0.76	0.41	2	10.2	1.48	0.58
	Foreign Remittances	2.28	2.36	0	0.52	6.56	10.79	0.31	1.43
5	Domestic Remittance	3.56	5.64	1.12	1.78	5.67	8.12	0.4	3.51
	Foreign Remittances	7	6.36	2.55	2.3	7.8	11.13	3.32	4

Source: Pakistan Household Integrated Economic Survey (HIES) 2004–5 (The first quintile is composed of the poorest 20 percent, the second quintile of the next better-off 20 percent, and the fifth quintile of the richest 20 percent.)

Table A5.7 Remittances, Contribution to Household Income, and Poverty Ratio

	Nonmigrant households	Internal migrant households	External migrant households
Amount of remittances received (Rs.)	—	44,160.7 (27,185.4)	105,208.7 (83,649.1)
Average annual household income (Rs.)	71,591.9 (67,474.2)	91,901.7 (47,491.0)	199,652.4 (141,628.9)
Ratio of remittances to household income (%)	—	48.1	52.7
Ratio of households below the poverty line (%)	53.7	37.9	15.4

Source: Oda (2007).

Table A5.8 Determinants of Remittances in Pakistan

	Remittance Users vs. Nonusers			Formal Remittance Users vs. Others			Informal Remittance Users vs. Nonusers		
	Model I	Model II	Model III	Model I	Model II	Model III	Model I	Model II	Model III
Female	0.140 (0.142)	0.049 (0.175)	0.047 (0.163)	0.059 (0.150)	0.205 (0.189)	0.203 (0.174)	0.166 (0.243)	-0.171 (0.185)	-0.167 (0.183)
Age	0.003 (0.004)	0.000 (0.003)	0.002 (0.003)	0.001 (0.005)	0.000 (0.004)	0.002 (0.004)	0.003 (0.006)	0.000 (0.004)	0.001 (0.004)
Education	0.104[a] (0.032)	0.079[a] (0.030)	0.067[b] (0.031)	0.104[a] (0.039)	0.084[b] (0.036)	0.070[c] (0.037)	0.080[c] (0.045)	0.055 (0.035)	0.050 (0.036)
Rural	-0.001 (0.110)	0.023 (0.092)	0.008 (0.091)	0.076 (0.117)	0.057 (0.098)	0.030 (0.095)	-0.076 (0.193)	-0.012 (0.130)	-0.013 (0.137)
Employed	0.313[b] (0.144)	0.220 (0.180)	0.315[b] (0.142)	0.265[b] (0.121)	0.312 (0.204)	0.440[a] (0.159)	0.298 (0.211)	0.043 (0.217)	0.088 (0.193)
Household head	0.048 (0.139)	0.135 (0.134)	0.144 (0.139)	0.041 (0.153)	0.196 (0.171)	0.206 (0.177)	0.035 (0.189)	0.027 (0.161)	0.031 (0.161)
Collateral	-0.098 (0.113)	-0.116 (0.137)	-0.117 (0.137)	0.038 (0.137)	0.039 (0.120)	0.036 (0.123)	-0.250[c] (0.152)	-0.283 (0.204)	-0.280 (0.204)
Corporate	0.083 (0.191)	0.310[c] (0.180)	0.329[b] (0.167)	0.028 (0.203)	0.140 (0.210)	0.158 (0.201)	0.109 (0.241)	0.459[b] (0.202)	0.470[a] (0.184)
Government	-0.034 (0.211)	-0.027 (0.190)	0.003 (0.182)	0.180 (0.213)	0.108 (0.204)	0.157 (0.204)	-0.598[c] (0.351)	-0.500 (0.331)	-0.491 (0.310)

Farmer	0.076 (0.153)	0.078 (0.123)	0.121 (0.114)	-0.013 (0.141)	-0.035 (0.161)	0.018 (0.147)	0.177 (0.369)	0.222 (0.291)	0.237 (0.256)
Laborer	-0.209 (0.226)	-0.146 (0.161)	-0.224 (0.200)	-0.453 (0.349)	-0.352 (0.308)	-0.464 (0.327)	0.049 (0.239)	0.112 (0.220)	0.077 (0.219)
Formal sector	0.166 (0.158)			0.218 (0.167)			0.069 (0.226)		
Cell use			0.391[a] (0.091)			0.588[a] (0.132)			0.123 (0.109)
Cell access			0.003 (0.150)			0.068 (0.185)			-0.023 (0.188)
Household income and house/latrine effects	Yes			Yes			Yes		
Personal income and house/latrine effects		Yes	Yes		Yes	Yes		Yes	Yes
Province effects	Yes	Yes	Yes	Yes	Yes	Yes	Yes	Yes	Yes
Number of observations	5,941	10,288	10,288	5,941	10,288	10,288	5,825	10,135	10,135
F(k, d)	140.66	256.3	238.57	176.16	536.08	410.28	331.98	720.21	871.64

Standard errors in parenthesis (a = Significant at 1% level; b = Significant at 5% level; c = Significant at 10% level).

Table A5.9 Organizations That Are Helping and Funding the Global Remittances Market

Area	Primary actors	TA partners	Donors
Indicators	None	None	None
Technology	Firms	CGAP, infoDev	Limited: CGAP-Gates fund
Better business models	Firms	IDB, CGAP	IFAD fund
Increased access	Firms, local authorities	IFIs, CGAP, bilateral agencies, World Bank	IFIs, bilaterals, World Bank, IFAD
Regulation and oversight	Central Banks	World Bank, BIS, some other IFIs. IMF	FIRST, World Bank, IMF
Overall national payment system development	Central Banks	World Bank, BIS, IMF	FIRST, World Bank, IMF, IFIs
Standards and open networks	Some firms	World Bank, BIS	None
Market studies	Consultancies, World Bank AML	World Bank, IFIs, bilateral agencies	World Bank AML, IFIs, bilaterals
Price information	Consultancies, Consumer protection agencies	Consultancies	DFID, bilaterals
Donor coordination	World Bank, currently through the General Principles Coordination Group		
Global price info	None		
Global depository of research and information	Formerly DFID remittances newsletter, now Access Finance newsletter and some on World Bank Web sites (Payment Systems, AML, and DEC)		
Global collection of "what works on the ground"	None, except Gates/CGAP fund on technology		
Convening authorities	World Bank		
Comprehensive assistance in remittances	None, but World Bank has the potential		

Source: Cirasino and Andreassen (2007).

Note: IFAD: International Fund for Economic Development, BIS: Bank for International Settlements, DEC: Development Economic Department (World Bank), IDB: Inter-American Development Bank, FIRST: Financial Sector Reform and Strengthening Initiative.

Chapter 6

Expanding Access to the Underserved: An Action Plan

A major drive to enhance financial inclusion would involve a joint effort of the State Bank of Pakistan (SBP), national government, the private sector, the community, and donors. The best bet of a rapid scaling up of access is to rely on technology, financial awareness improvements, financial reengineering of processes and products, and an enabling legal and institutional framework.

The Role of the Private Sector

Access to All Financial Services

Diversifying the product range to increase outreach, lower costs, and manage risks: The road ahead certainly lies in product diversification, with more services and fewer requirements catering to the mass population of lower-income capacity. Products (savings, insurance, and credit) for old age, children's education, pregnancy and medical expenses, and livestock are a few examples of those that take account of women's needs for life-cycle events. Home-based businesses should be given consideration. Access would also improve with the use of alternative forms of collateral, such as social collateral, compulsory savings, personal guarantees, crops, or machinery to be purchased or household assets. Saving products, which are expected to be especially popular, can be built upon traditional saving arrangements and rotating saving and credit associations that women use. Smaller size of products, and bulk service, might better attract lower-income groups. Literacy should not be a requirement to access financial service. Simple policies and procedures that speed the transaction, lower transaction costs for women, and do not preclude uneducated women tend to maximize outreach to female clients. Innovative ways to reach customers, such as decentralized operations, operating units located near female clients, use of mobile units, and transactions at clients' doorsteps, tend to make banking convenient for women. Female staff will improve approachability for clients and alleviate cultural concerns. Policy makers and banks would note the importance of the market for financial products targeting heads of households, given the finding that being a household head has a significant impact on financial access. This potential is particularly of interest in rural areas as well as clusters of urbanized rural migrants into bigger cities.

Reaching out to the female client, client segmentation: Women's abilities to better manage debt, their stronger savings patterns, and client loyalty present an untapped profitable client base for the financial and microfinance sectors in Pakistan. Understanding women's needs more precisely, and reflecting those needs in the financial products and the provider's policies and procedures, would ensure an increase in women's access to finance in spite of cultural norms, gender segregation, and low literacy and incomes. Lower loan size and deposit size would permit better matching to women's needs, given their lower incomes. Repayments should be frequent so that installments are smaller and should correspond to women's income cycles. Global experience suggests offering women credit that is untied to specific use, instead of allowing the borrower to elect the activity.

Learning from the informal financial sector's success: The gap between the popularity of informal finance and limited formal financial sector outreach, combined with the perception gap between a heavy procedure-driven formal sector and informal sector with minimum requirements, calls for learning from informal financial systems and developing linkages with the informal sector. Strengthening financial infrastructure, by expanding credit information bureaus and other payment systems, would allow banks to lower binding requirements, such as guarantors and immovable collateral, therefore attracting new customers among women, the poor, and rural areas.

Reaching out to the rural client, leveraging technology and partnerships: Within the Pakistani financial market, partnerships and linkages between different institutions should be developed to facilitate access to remittances and other financial services by the rural poor. For example, commercial banks should explore working with microfinance banks (MFBs) to expand their networks in rural areas. Enhancing outreach via technology solutions can involve a combination of devices to be adopted by banks to enhance outreach as well as "branchless banking" through cell phone and mobile devices. These are very different directions, and each has shortcomings and difficulties. In Pakistan, the banking access infrastructure is particularly weak, as noted in Chapter 1—bank branches and ATMs are low as measured against both the population and area of the country. As demonstrated by the Brazil correspondent banking experience, difficulties in expansion of outreach can also arise as a result of contractual as well as regulatory and prudential factors regarding agency arrangements (Chidzero et al. 2006). Mobile banking, on the other hand, presents regulatory challenges (as in the case of the Philippines G-Cash and Kenya

M-Pesa models) but can be a promising channel to help shift some of the financial flows from informal to formal channels, in particular if combined with other correspondent banking channels. Demand-side results do show us a very high mobile penetration and our economic analysis highlights significant positive linkages between financial inclusion and regular mobile use, as well as informal inclusion and access to a cell phone.

Expanding outreach via mobile telephony, smart cards, and point of sale (POS) devices: Given the wide, relatively equitable, and rapidly growing access in Pakistan to mobile phones, technology has a major potential to become a conduit for access to finance in the country. In addition to access expansion, mobile phones, smart cards, POS devices, and other technology improvements can lower transaction costs, as well as help enhance credit information on a much wider population segment. The simplicity and low cost of these services have enabled poor people to use them easily and successfully in spite of their novelty and recent penetration. This stands in sharp contrast to the complexity and lack of user-friendliness of traditional bank products, and their relative failure to penetrate a wider population range.

These technologies have been very successful in promoting payments services worldwide. In Pakistan, given population preferences and needs, it is important to find ways to extend access to savings services as well, via technology gains. International experience points to (1) regulatory methods of promoting savings, such as matching schemes and tax-advantaged schemes, as well as (2) savings methods that have worked for microfinance—doorstep collection schemes and periodic contribution or commitment programs. But if the full potential of this new approach is to be realized, it will need to go well beyond the microfinance sector, where there is already a strong interest in using technology to reach more people and lower costs, and include the banks. So far, commercial banks have not shown much interest.

Experimentation with using mobile telephone networks is just beginning. On the other hand, cards have been in use for many years, though not generally by poor and underserved populations. "As of December 2007 the total number of active cards in the Pakistan banking system stood at 6.7 million, as compared to a total of 16 million personal bank accounts. Of these, 1.7 million were credit cards (25.4 percent) and 4.8 million were debit cards (71.6 percent). ATM-only cards were 0.191 million or 2.8 percent. Ninety-nine percent of the time these cards were used for withdrawals, while only 1 percent of the transactions were deposits (envelope based). Each ATM had an average of 70 transactions per day, of an average size of Rs 6,127. Until December 2007, there were 2,618 ATM machines (as compared to more than 8,000 bank branches), and 52,474 POS terminals across the country. Almost two-thirds (61 percent) of the bank branch network consisted of Real Time Online Branches. One-quarter of the total transactions in the system were electronic-based. Although the electronic banking system is growing, it is still in its infancy and its expansion in coming years is a basic premise for the inclusion of the majority of the population" (Lindh de Montoya and Haq 2008).

Access to Microfinance

Improving microfinance institutions' (MFIs) sustainability and ability to muster commercial funding/savings deposits, and their further integration into the financial system: To create strong, profitable MFIs, the sector needs to improve efficiency, risk management, and profitability, as well as increase reliance on commercial funding and attract deposits. The ultimate goal for MFIs should be to firmly integrate into the financial system. Limiting noncommercial funding for MFBs would create competition for funds and a drive for improvements.

A further strategy for the sector would be to refocus from microcredit to microsavings, given the large untapped demand for such products. Besides being the service that poor people want more than any other, savings mobilization by MFBs will also provide a longer-term stable source of funds to grow credit outreach. MFBs need to pay more attention to developing their savings services, especially through strengthening their systems and developing appropriate products.

Access to Small and Medium Enterprise Lending

Carrying out a thorough bank downscaling program and modernizing SME banking: Key features of the downscaling programs that have worked are described below.

1. *Long-term technical assistance is required to ensure that the necessary substantial changes take place.* Lending to small businesses requires profound changes in the way commercial banks operate. Because of its high transaction costs, small business lending is only profitable if done in high numbers with excellent portfolio quality. Banks could benefit from long-term support in this challenging process. Technical assistance to improve lending technology should focus on: reducing transaction costs for both the bank and the client; increasing loan officer productivity (in terms of number of loans disbursed); and maintaining high portfolio quality.

2. *Selection of bank advisers and content of the technical assistance are key to success.* The technical assistance package should be comprehensive because the changes that are required are quite substantial. In addition to its scope, the success of the technical assistance program will depend upon three elements: selection of committed banks, selection of consultancy firms with a strong track record, and close monitoring by a fully dedicated and experienced staff. The technical assistance should include redesigning bank products to meet client needs, a robust management information system, and use of staff incentives linked to their performance.

3. *A mix of committed banks should participate in the program to create competition among them.* Technical assistance should be provided only to those banks that are fully committed to SME lending. Serving such enterprises requires a change in the entire corporate culture and in the way banks operate. Thus, only banks whose investors are willing to engage in such substantive transformations should be offered technical assistance. Often, banks with a large banking network and a

focus on retail lending have a comparative advantage in entering this market segment. Smaller banks could also be targeted, however, to act as catalysts. Many countries have developed specialized SME programs in state-owned banks with large networks. However, success usually takes a few years because the changes required are quite substantial and banks take time in implementing them. It is therefore essential that technical assistance be also given to small, faster-moving private banks that transform at a faster speed but may reach stagnation due to their smaller networks.

4. *Performance agreements for banks participating in the program are key.* Furthermore, performance agreements should also incorporate terms on the number and volume of loans disbursed and outstanding by a given date, as well as portfolio quality indicators, such as keeping portfolio at risk more than 30 days to less than 3 percent. The technical assistance should last at least two years and performance agreements should be monitored on a monthly basis so that timely remedial measures can be undertaken when targets are not met.

Access to Remittances

Reducing informality: Informality will decrease upon the introduction of efficient, low-cost, easy-access, user-friendly, and trusted remittance services, without prohibitive identification requirements.

Developing new technology-based remittance models: New technologies, such as branchless banking, offer significant potential to reduce transactions costs and therefore allow new business models for previously unreached areas where traditional bank branch models are unviable. Banks and mobile phone companies should continue working to implement viable models, following on existing efforts, such as United Bank Limited's services for paying bills, transferring money between customers, and buying phone cards; Bank Al-Falah's mobile banking product with Warid Telecom; and the remittance venture of Etisalat's (UAE)-Smart (Philippines).

Expanding Pakistani bank presence and remittance service provision abroad: The limited presence and outreach of Pakistani banks abroad is the main problem they face in increasing remittances through their networks. Foreign banks are more easily accessible to remittance senders abroad, but these may provide a slower or more expensive remittance service to Pakistan and may not have significant outreach in rural areas. New measures should be taken to increase outreach abroad, particularly in the major remittance source countries. These could be new partnerships, or new innovative ways to reach customers. Habib Bank Limited managed to gain market share by reaching out to the workers in the Middle East. A similar strategy could be followed in all countries where a sizeable Pakistani worker community exists. Once these workers, who are the main senders, are part of the process and a system is set up to fit their needs, the volume of remittances will grow further. Moreover, if they are given incentives or bonuses based on the amount they remit, they will become more diligent with sending money. One caveat to keep in mind is that the literacy level is low and so paperwork should be kept to a minimum and technology interfaces should not be excessively complex. In addition, the recipients of remittances are generally women or older groups, for whom convenience is most important. For this group, models that are based on doorstep delivery would be most suitable.

The Role of the Public Sector

Access to All Financial Services

Creating awareness of the benefits of access to financial services: Further gains in financial literacy are critical, through more critical is the presence of awareness of financial services to promote trust in the sector, as well as information about services and products available. A national awareness campaign can support financial inclusion, especially for women, as well as encourage people to open savings accounts. There is still a large number of people who do not have any account at all. Awareness creation and trust building could be forged through social mobilization and mass media.

Strengthening institutions (SECP, Credit Investment Bureau [CIB], Pakistan Post): Access to finance growth will be accelerated by an integrated financial system, and a strong regulatory framework. Stronger institutions (including SECP and CIB) are a major part of a rapid increase in financial inclusion.

Among the important features of a complete financial system is a well-functioning national-level credit bureau for credit referencing. By establishing a credit history and thus a potential collateral substitute, a credit bureau can be instrumental in providing access to finance for groups that may not have cash or asset collateral required to access a loan but have a stellar credit history to present to the bank. All commercial banks, development financial institutions, leasing companies and MFBs are currently reporting to CIB on all borrowers irrespective of the size of loan. For the NGO-MFIs, a special CIB has recently been developed and SBP allows MFBs to share credit history of their borrowers to MF-CIB. Consolidating these achievements and ensuring the full usage and functional availability of the accumulated data can place many more potential borrowers within reach of some access to finance. To facilitate the creation of a credit history for small and medium enterprises (SMEs), SBP should also ensure that the credit bureau collects information from utility and telecom companies. Finally, to facilitate SME lending monitoring, SBP should amend reporting requirements for SME portfolios to include volumes and number of loans in four sub-brackets (Rs $<$ 2M, Rs 2–6M, Rs 6–25M and Rs 25–75M).

A more efficient Pakistan Post is a must (following the successful examples of Brazil and China) to capitalize on its significant network and strong outreach in rural areas. The government of Pakistan (GOP) should explore ways to improve remittance and other services and speed up the automation of postal branches. Given the significant developmental potential of Pakistan Post to enhance financial access, it needs modernization in operations and regulations. Following most success cases in East Asia, as well as many other continents, PPSB should be placed under the supervision of SBP.

Creating an enabling environment for expanding access to the underserved: Regulations should keep up with the needs of the sector and technological developments, to enable expansion. Simultaneously, an enabling environment should go hand in hand with a carefully chosen government presence. Indiscriminate subsidies, especially focused on interest rates, can be detrimental to the expansion of the sector, as they not only distort prices but crowd out efficient institutions and products. The GOP should resist populist perceptions that low interest-rate funding can serve a developmental purpose. Even more detrimental are state-owned institutions created to promote financial access. In addition to weak evidence in the case of Pakistan that such institutions actually improve access (for example, SME Bank), these efforts waste valuable public resources that could more usefully be deployed elsewhere, and eliminate the level playing field for market participants.

Access to Microfinance

Refocusing on microsavings: International experience shows that government savings promotion models can be considered, including awareness raising, matching schemes, and tax-advantaged schemes. *Encouraging positive public perceptions on accessibility and safety would help.*

Access to SME Lending

Creating a complete and well-functioning secured transactions regime: Security interests over movable assets should be easy and allowed on most assets and by every entity (both physical and juridical persons). Priority rankings should also be clearly defined among those who might have claims on property offered as collateral. The new secured transactions regime should also include a place (such as a registry) for making priority interests publicly known and enforcement of security interests for all assets should be fast and cheap.

Continued promotion of initiatives aimed at proving a demonstration effect of bank downscaling. These include attraction to the market of an institutional investor that has a track record in SME lending. This should ideally be achieved by selling SME Bank or giving controlling rights on its board to an institutional investor. To stimulate competition in the market from the very beginning, the GOP could also support long-term technical assistance programs for selected banks. As illustrated by the China SME lending program, for this program to be successful, the government needs to ensure correct market incentives are in place.

Access to Remittances

Bringing informal remittances into the formal system, particularly on the domestic front: The high share of banks in the international remittance market in Pakistan indicates that increasing bank accounts should help increase remittances through formal channels. Currently, the minimum account balance of Rs 10,000 (with the exception of basic banking accounts) is prohibitive for a large segment of the society. To encourage people to open bank accounts, uncomplicated paperwork and less stringent balance requirements are needed. Banks currently handling remittances can credit accounts within 24 hours; however, delivering money or sending money orders by Pakistan Post creates unnecessary delays, and the banking sector loses customers to money transfer organizations and informal means of transfer. An enabling environment for the private sector, encouragement for opening of bank accounts, as well as improved postal office efficiency will continue attracting remittance flows to the formal sector. Advances in technical and financial literacy will matter, as well, with appropriate education to alert people to the benefits of formal systems and how to use them.

Supporting remittance services of Pakistani banks abroad: Further encouragement for Pakistani banks might be required to continue to boost international remittances and forge alliances with international banks. One strategy would be to set the reimbursement rate through partner banks higher than remittances coming solely through Pakistani bank networks.

Pakistani missions abroad could do a survey of options available in their respective markets and disseminate the information to immigrants on the cheapest and best sources of money transfer. For example, the Mexican mission to the United States publishes such information. A further successful policy carried out by the Mexican embassy in the USA is that it has issued a type of identification card (*Matricula Consular*) for their immigrants, and with this card Mexican immigrants in the USA can open bank accounts. Perhaps the GOP can discuss something similar with the U.S. and other authorities.

Promoting the structuring of international flows into investments: Channeling remittance flows directly into investment in the tradable sectors of the economy has been pursued successfully in the international experience, to counteract loss of international competitiveness associated with elevated remittance flows. International good practices include packaging remittances with payment services (such as Bansefi in Mexico). Successful policies to structure international flows into investments have also focused on organizing and targeting diaspora networks rather than actual remittances flows. At the macrolevel, diaspora bonds issues (for example, in Israel, India, and Ghana) or securitization of future remittances flows (in Brazil, Salvador) have been used, although securitization has proven costly. At the micro level, governments have facilitated targeted diaspora funds.

The Role of Public-Private Partnerships

A concrete way to make progress in expanding access to the underserved is to form public-private working groups on microfinance, small enterprise finance, and remittances. This would enable a dialogue between the government and private companies (banks, MFIs, exchange companies, money transfer organizations, as well as telecoms and other market participants where relevant) to tackle key challenges in the sector. Priority themes should include, among others, legal and regulatory issues, market transparency, competition and cost, and research and data issues. On branchless banking, the private sector has yet to fully respond to recent SBP regulations, and public-private discussions could focus on barriers to recent SBP regulatory incentives, as well as review the Payment and Electronic Fund Transfer Act, a possible data privacy or security law to facilitate e- or m-payments, and the branchless banking regulations providing for bank-nonbank partnerships and use of agents in money transfer services. The United Kingdom has had a successful experience in this regard with a Public-Private Working Group on Remittances, which led to the creation of a private sector–led UK Remittances Task Force. The World Bank has also convened a similar group at the international level, bringing together key actors from the public and private sectors. Pakistan can draw on this considerable experience.

Data Methodology and Calibration

Access to Finance Survey: Sampling Methodology and Calibration

The Pakistan Access to Finance (A2F) survey is a comprehensive national household survey of all the main financial services (transaction banking, savings, credit, and insurance), needs, and usage among consumers, in both the formal and informal sectors. The survey was conducted between October 2007 and March 2008.

The Survey Instrument

The A2F survey followed a joint methodology developed by FinMark Trust (South Africa) and the World Bank. The survey covered 10,305 households in all regions of Pakistan except the federally and provincially administered tribal and northern areas (FATA, FANA, and PATA). At an initial stage, the standardized questionnaire was customized to Pakistani conditions to ensure high-quality data. Focus interviews were held in urban and rural areas of Sindh, Punjab, North West Frontier Province (NWFP), Balochistan, and Azad Jammu and Kashmir (AJK), for purposes of calibration and gathering of supplementary qualitative information. At a second stage, households were surveyed on the following topics in detail:

- Basic household demographics, financial literacy
- Socioeconomic characteristics, psychographics/attitudinal
- Household income
- Access to financial services, banks, provider differentiations
- Savings
- Loans/credit
- Insurance

- Money transfer/remittances
- Payment and receipts
- Attitudes to risk and coping mechanisms.

Each of the above sections explores in detail individuals' habits on banking, saving, loans and credit, money transfers, and insurance.

To route the respondents to these sections, there is a backbone section within the questionnaire that first establishes the ratio of people involved in the five areas mentioned above. This section is based on an exhaustive list of products and services pertaining to the five themes and asks the respondents whether they have never used, used in the past, or are currently using these products. Only those respondents who mention that they are currently using these products are further routed to the respective section of the questionnaire.

Summarized versions of the questionnaire and the database of survey responses are on the report's CD-Rom.

Choice of Household Versus Individual Level of Analysis

Given the highly individual nature of financial data, as opposed to most standard data that are available at the household level, the questionnaire attempts to measure both aspects. As such, some questions are initially asked of the household head, and permission is subsequently sought from that person to interview a houschold member, selected at random, from among the adult household members (defined as above 18 years of age). This approach, worked out as a compromise, permits the identification of financial attitudes, literacy, and preferences, as well as needs, at the individual level, as those are highly specific to age, employment status, and gender, among other characteristics (within the household, income levels can differ significantly, especially along gender lines). At the same time, such variables as income would be more precisely defined at the household level, given resource sharing. Yet, we have observed that household members are not always aware of one another's financial transactions, even between husband and wife.

Sample Design

The survey design was carried out by the Pakistan Federal Bureau of Statistics (FBS). The survey was designed to cover all four provinces in Pakistan (Baluchistan, Singh, Punjab, and AJK), except the tribal and northern areas (FATA and FANA), the latter for security reasons. The survey used the population frame of the FBS, which divides the entire country into rural and urban enumeration blocks. The latest census on which these enumeration blocks were based was the Population Census 1998, where the enumeration blocks in rural areas were fixed in 1998, those in urban areas in 2003. Following the identification of the randomly selected (stratified) list of enumeration blocks (see first stage of sampling process, below), A.C. Nielsen, the survey firm contracted to carry out the survey, visited each selected enumeration block and conducted a detailed listing of the households in the block and their exact location. Given the lists, a random selection procedure was used to select 15 households from each enumeration block. The following sections provide details on the sampling procedure.

A two-stage stratified sample design has been adopted for this survey.

Selection of primary sampling units (PSUs): Enumeration blocks in the urban domain and *mouzas/dehs* (villages) in rural domain were used as primary sampling units (PSUs). Sample PSUs from each ultimate stratum/substratum were selected by probability proportional to size (PPS) method of the sampling scheme. In this survey, population of rural areas and households for urban areas were adopted as a measure of size for selecting PSUs from the strata/substrata formed in urban and rural subuniverses of the survey.

Selection of secondary sampling units (SSUs): Households within each sample PSU were considered as secondary sampling units (SSUs). Fifteen households were selected from each sample village and enumeration block by random systematic sampling scheme with a random start.

Sample Frame

FBS uses different sampling frames for urban and rural areas. The definition of areas as urban and rural is based on the classification provided by the Population Census Organization and by the local government and rural development department of each province. With regard to the rural areas, the lists of *mouzas/dehs* (villages) according to the Population Census 1998 are used as sampling frames.

For urban areas, the FBS has developed its own urban areas frame, adopting the quick-count record survey technique. All urban areas comprising cities/towns have been divided into small compact areas known as enumeration blocks identifiable through maps. On average, each enumeration block comprises 250-350 households. Each enumeration block has been further divided into low-, middle-, and high-income groups based on a subjective comparison with other households in the area. As per latest survey publications conducted by FBS, the urban area sampling frame has been updated in 2003.

Sample Size

The total sample size for this survey was 10,500 interviews to be conducted throughout Pakistan. To conduct these interviews in total 700 enumeration blocks were selected by FBS and demarcation and listing activity was conducted by the survey firm.

The breakdown of these 700 enumeration blocks is as shown in tables A1 and A2.

Stratification

The stratification scheme is based on geographical and (in the case of urban areas) also income considerations. The details of the stratification procedure are below.

Table A1 Initial Distribution of Enumeration Blocks/Villages (PSU)

Province/Area	Urban	Rural	Total
Punjab	130	200	330
Sindh	80	80	160
NWFP	38	66	104
Baluchistan	30	46	76
AJK	12	18	30
Total	**290**	**410**	**700**

Table A2 Initial Distribution of Households (SSU)

Province/Area	Urban	Rural	Total
Punjab	1,950	3,000	4,950
Sindh	1,200	1,200	2,400
NWFP	570	990	1,560
Baluchistan	450	690	1,140
AJK	180	270	450
Total	**4,350**	**6,150**	**10,500**

Urban areas: The urban areas—Bahawalpur, Faisalabad, Gujranwala, Hyderabad, Islamabad, Karachi, Lahore, Multan, Peshawar, Quetta, Rawalpindi, Sargodha, Sialkot, and Sukkur—have been treated as independent strata. Each of these cities has further been substratified according to low-, middle-, high-income groups based on the information collected in respect to each enumeration block.

After excluding the population of large cities, the remaining urban population in each administrative division in all provinces has been grouped and treated as an independent stratum. The entire area of AJK was considered a separate independent stratum.

Rural areas: In the rural areas, the population of each district in Punjab, Sindh, and NWFP provinces were grouped together to constitute a stratum. For Baluchistan, each distinct administrative division was taken as a stratum. Again, the AJK province has been considered as an independent stratum in rural areas.

Demarcation of Enumerator Blocks

Provision of sample areas: The FBS head office provided a list of the enumerator blocks for the urban areas and a list of the villages for rural areas with all possible identifiers (for example, *patwar* circle, *qanoongo* circle, *tehsil,* and district) where the fieldwork for the study will be conducted.

Demarcation of sample areas: FBS regional offices assisted the regional offices of the survey firm in physically demarking urban enumerator areas. The firm's regional offices provided sufficient notice to the FSB regional offices so they could arrange for their staff to accompany the firm's regional staff to physically identify the boundaries of the enumerator areas. Each of the firm's nine regional offices were responsible for coordinating this with all FSB regional offices (about 35) that fall within its coverage area.

Facilitating demarcation: To facilitate timely demarcation, the FBS head office provided a list of all its regional offices that included their addresses, phone numbers, and main contact person and deputy in charge in the focal person's absence.

The FBS head office also communicated to all of its regional offices about the assistance in demarcation that would be required from them by the survey firm. The regional staff of the survey firm was thus put in touch with the FBS regional offices and cooperated on the demarcation and listing exercise.

Similarly, the survey firm briefed its regional offices about the study and the protocol for coordinating and working with the FBS regional staff: call in advance of visiting the office, set up a timetable for demarcation agreeable for both parties, honor the commitments made, and so forth.

Training of survey firm staff by FBS: FBS staff trained the survey firm staff on listing protocols that were to be undertaken in each of the selected enumeration blocks. These trainings were conducted in three main cities of the country to keep the group size per session manageable and the trainings effective. The main areas of training were:

- How to select a starting point to demark the entire area
- What to be included in listing with a block
- How to fill in the listing form
- Difference in listing methods between urban and rural areas.

Listing of Households

In each selected PSU, listing of households was carried out to estimate the updated population statistics and develop the systematic scheme of selection of household within the PSU. This was undertaken as a simple census activity in which, once the FBS identified the PSU, the survey firm counted each house and noted its household number and name.

Selection Procedure

The households within each PSU were selected by a systematic sampling technique with a random start. In each PSU, 15 households were selected and interviewed. This was done from a list of households, which was produced by listing carried out in each selected PSU as described above.

Selection of a respondent: If a household had more than one potential valid respondent, the Kish Grid was used to select the actual respondent. This enabled selection of respondent in a randomized manner. If the selected respondent was not available, three callbacks were made to locate that respondent. If after three callbacks the respondent still was not available or refused to participate, a substitute from the same vicinity was selected and contacted.

Substitution: Substitution of a selected respondent within a household was done only if the original respondent was found to be of unsound mind. In other cases, the entire household was substituted.

Substitution Methodology and Listing in the Substitute Areas

FBS elected to avoid oversampling and therefore gave out substitution enumeration blocks in very limited cases, when a security risk or natural disaster (floods) was involved or when there was an insufficient number of households for valid selection because the government had razed houses for land development. If the survey firm found that a substitution was needed, it had to obtain a letter from the relevant authority (for example, the local *tehsil* administration) verifying that the area is not suitable for work because of law and order or any other reason. FBS first did its own confirmation of the situation and then provided a substitute enumeration area for the listing exercise. In the end, there were 12 substituted blocks; their distribution is provided in table A3.

Blocks dropped: In addition to the substitutions, 13 areas had to be dropped altogether for security reasons and no substitutions were possible. The breakdown of these blocks is provided in table A4.

Table A3 Distribution of Substituted Blocks/Villages (PSU)

Province/Area	Urban	Rural	Total
Punjab	4	—	4
Sindh	—	2	2
NWFP	1	—	1
Baluchistan	—	4	4
AJK	—	1	1
Total	**5**	**7**	**12**

Table A4 Distribution of Blocks/Villages Dropped

Province/Area	Urban	Rural	Total
Punjab	—	—	—
Sindh	2	2	4
NWFP	2	6	8
Baluchistan	—	1	1
AJK	—	—	—
Total	**4**	**9**	**13**

Table A5 Final Distribution of Blocks/Villages

Enumeration Blocks/Villages (PSU)				Households (SSU)			
Province/Area	Urban	Rural	Total	Province/Area	Urban	Rural	Total
Punjab	130	200	330	Punjab	1,950	3,000	4950
Sindh	78	78	156	Sindh	1,170	1,170	2340
NWFP	36	60	96	NWFP	540	900	1440
Baluchistan	30	45	75	Baluchistan	450	675	1125
AJK	12	18	30	AJK	180	270	450
Total	**286**	**401**	**687**	**Total**	**4290**	**6015**	**10305**

The final distribution of enumeration blocks and households is provided in table A5.

Weights

Using the initial and final sample distribution, as well as taking into account the stratification by geography and income, FBS computed and provided to the World Bank a set of household weights for each of the 10,305 interviewed households. The survey firm then used the household weights to compute the weight of each respondent's function in their household composition (the number of household members). Household weights are used for variables that are defined at the household level, such as household income. Individual weights are used for metrics focused on personal aspects, such as banking relationships, preferences, and attitudes to risk.

Calibration of Survey Results

The A2F Household Survey was calibrated to publicly available results from FBS, State Bank of Pakistan (SBP), and other supply-side sources, to determine possible latent biases and gauge the credibility of the data collected. This was particularly important for the A2F data set since it was the first of its kind in Pakistan and used a methodology that had not before been used in Pakistan. Calibration was done according to:

✓ Population data
✓ Income data
✓ Basic financial access data.

Population Calibration

Based on the household survey data, estimates of total population are derived using the following methodology. The total population is estimated as follows:

$$P = \sum (P_i)$$

$$= \frac{\sum (A_{iu} * S_{iu}^w)}{AS_{iu}^w} + \frac{\sum (A_{ir} * S_{ir}^w)}{AS_{ir}^w}$$

$$= \frac{\sum \{SH_{iu} * \sum (IW_{iu})\} * S_{iu}^w)}{AS_{iu}^w} + \frac{\sum \{SH_{ir} * \sum (IW_{ir})\} * S_{ir}^w)}{AS_{ir}^w}$$

where   P is total population,

$P_{i(u, r)}$ is the urban (resp. rural) province population;

$A_{i(u, r)}$ is the total urban (resp. rural) number of adults per province;

$S^w_{i(u, r)}$ is the urban (resp. rural) weighted average household size per province;

$AS^w_{i(u, r)}$ is the urban (resp. rural) weighted average adult household size per province; and

$SH_{i(u, r)}$ are the urban (resp. rural) sampled households per province;

$IW_{i(u, r)}$ are the urban (resp. rural) individual weights per province; and

i € (Punjab, Sindh, Baluchistan, NWFP, AJK).

The total households per province are estimated as:

$$H_i = SH_{iu} * \sum(HW_{iu}) + SH_{ir} * (HW_{ir}),$$

where H_i are total the urban (resp. rural) households per province,

$SH_{i(u, r)}$ are the urban (resp. rural) sampled households per province;

$HW_{i(u, r)}$ are the urban (resp. rural) household weights per province; and

i   (Punjab, Sindh, Baluchistan, NWFP, AJK).

Given the above calculations, the resulting population figures are presented below (table A6).

For the household survey, enumeration blocks in urban areas are based on 2003 estimates and in villages in the rural domain on 1998 estimates, per the latest population census. During each census, FSB fixes enumeration blocks at the size of about 250 people. The survey used the old enumeration blocks (1998/2003), but was based on a fresh listing done in 2007. Given this constraint, the calibration exercise begs the question of relevant population figures for comparison. The natural option is to compare the implicit total population from the household survey to the mix of rural population of 1998 and urban population of 2003. Another possible comparator is the 2007 population figure, as the survey was conducted in October 2007–March 2008. The choice would depend on the pattern of population growth we believe we have observed during the past decade. If we believe growth mostly occurred in the number of enumeration blocks, but not within blocks, the relevant comparator is the 1998/2003 mix. If, however, we believe that growth mostly

Table A6 Population Counts per A2FS Survey Results

Province	Total Households (HHs)			Total 18 Years Population			Total Population		
	Urban	Rural	Total	Urban	Rural	Total	Urban	Rural	Total
Punjab	3,970,977	7,587,990	**11,558,967**	15,047,579	27,949,635	**42,997,214**	26,275,084	52,187,201	**78,462,284**
Sindh	2,514,365	1,991,098	**4,505,463**	10,710,184	9,625,282	**20,335,466**	17,913,027	17,581,638	**35,494,665**
NWFP	449,841	1,763,546	**2,213,387**	1,939,424	7,385,777	**9,325,201**	3,577,497	14,667,675	**18,245,172**
Baluchistan	214,964	812,793	**1,027,757**	909,233	3,685,858	**4,595,091**	1,601,401	6,557,489	**8,158,890**
Total	**7,150,147**	**12,155,427**	**19,305,574**	**28,606,420**	**48,646,552**	**77,252,972**	**49,367,009**	**90,994,003**	**140,361,011**

occurred within blocks (through birth rate), the 2007 population is the more accurate comparator figure. Naturally, there will be some of both effects at work, so we would expect the A2F population to fall somewhere in between (as is the case, see below). We believe the first option is a more reasonable assumption, but we present both comparisons.

The change in population over the past 10 years can be attributed to migration (growth in the number of enumeration blocks) and birth rates (growth within enumeration blocks). The number of urban households in all four provinces has shown a positive increase from 1998 to 2008, while the total rural households have declined over the same period, which clearly suggests migration. The strong urbanization trend echoes this conclusion. On the other hand, the population increase attributable to birth rates for a 10-year period would affect total population strongly, but adult population figures less so (much of the increase will be in the population under 18 years of age). There are no factual population (or household count) figures since the latest census—to arrive at more recent population figures, public sources use extrapolated growth rates. Therefore, the comparator tables below present only total population comparisons. For those reasons, we believe calibration should be done in comparison with a mix of 1998/2003 figures as described above, instead of comparing with the extrapolated 2007 population figure.

Taking this limitation into account, one would expect that the household survey, which was based on "old" enumeration blocks devised during the latest census in 1998/2003, would affect the data in the following way: while some growth has occurred within the 1998/2003 enumeration blocks up to 2007/2008, most growth would be expected in the form of new enumeration blocks in peri-urban areas, which the household survey perforce does not capture. As such, the relevant comparisons would be with the population of 1998 (rural) and 2003 (urban), as below (see table 2). The biases stemming from this limitation of FBS data are discussed throughout the text; however, one obvious example is that new clusters of rural migrants to cities, the people who are most likely to engage in some microentrepreneurial activity, are poorly captured by the household survey, biasing downwards the microfinance access estimates. In the report, we caution the reader in each instance where the above bias is relevant.

This compares closely to FBS figures for population (table A7).

Thus, the relevant total population for comparison is the addition of urban population in 2003 and rural population in 1998, which is 139.5 million. Based on table A1, the total population from the household survey is estimated at 142.2 million, or within 1.9 percent of the relevant comparator figure for total population.

For completeness, we also present the comparison with 2007 population estimates. Estimated population from the household survey (142.2 million) is an underestimation if we consider the current population estimates from various sources: 159 million (World Resources Institute) for 2006, 164 million (World Resources Institute) for 2007, and 164 million (Population Census Organization) for 2008. Population estimates based on the household survey have to be interpreted with a caveat that FATA, FANA, and PATA were not included in the sampling frame

Table A7 **Population Counts per Census, Using Urban/Rural Mix per Enumeration Block Dates**

Province	Urban 1998	Growth rate*	Urban 2003	Rural 1998	Total
Punjab	23,548,205	**19%**	28,082,663	50,878,320	**78,960,983**
Sindh	14,839,862	**14%**	16,977,598	15,600,031	**32,577,629**
NWFP	2,994,084	**13%**	3,369,045	14,749,561	**18,118,606**
Baluchistan	1,568,780	**22%**	1,910,626	4,997,105	**6,907,731**
AJK	80,271	**17%**	93,912	2,892,729	**2,986,641**
Total Pakistan	**43,031,202**	**17%**	50,339,933	**89,117,746**	**139,457,679**

Source: AJK total population data from http://www.ajk.gov.pk/site/index.php?option=com_content&task=view&id=2256&Itemid=144.

*The AJK urban growth rate estimate is not available; average urban growth rate for the country was used instead. Given the tiny urban population in AJK, the impact of this approximation is negligible.

(estimated population for these two areas is approximately 3–4 million, not counting some 2 million registered Afghani refugees). That still leaves a population difference of more than 15 million. Some of that will be explained by children born since 1998, and will not affect the adult population figure. However, some of this increase is a genuine bias in the data due to the usage of dated enumeration blocks per FSB records. The above comparison shows the extent of possible downward bias in coverage, because of growth within enumeration blocks (as opposed to growth in the number of blocks). This bias is less worrisome as compared with bias caused by not covering new migration clusters created post 2003, for the following reason. Although the estimated population figures from the household survey are understated, and some of the increase in population may be attributed to migration, most of the increase in population is accounted for in an increase in the number of underage children, which are not considered by the survey for purposes of access/usage of financial services. Thus, the results based on the survey still remain valid and representative of the overall population of Pakistan, with the provision that coverage of newly created enumeration blocks since 1998/2003 has not been ensured.

Income Calibration

As a further robustness check, we have calibrated the A2F survey results to the National Household Survey of FBS, in terms of household income/consumption. This calibration is based on potential concerns that respondents understate their incomes relative to the Pakistan Social and Living Standards Measurement Survey (PSLM) 2005/06 consumption figures (perhaps because of underreporting or/and not counting some income as such because of lack of knowledge of all household members' income sources, or lack of literacy to estimate income correctly). Misstatement of income considerations (income is a particularly hazardous variable in self-reported surveys) led us to estimate income based on objective characteristics (type of house, type of basic amenities, and so forth), as explained below.

The benchmark data used are the monthly household consumption data of the total expenditure figures from PSLM 2005/06, based on monthly consumer price index data from FBS. Consumption data are used as a proxy for income data, as monthly household income data is not available in Pakistan national household surveys. The PSLM consumption data was adjusted for a 22.9 percent inflation rate between the collection periods of PSLM (January 2006) and the A2F survey (January 2008).

The tables below present the calibration of the A2F and PSLM models at two levels:

- Frequencies of households within monthly household expenditures/income thresholds in figure A1 (and associated cumulative frequencies in figure A2)

- Monthly household expenditures/income thresholds corresponding to frequency distribution of households in figure A3.

Calibration results show that the distribution of the A2F survey income results is wider than the PSLM 2005/06 expenditure data. The lowest income quintile of the A2F survey reported higher incomes relative to consumption expenditure, while the richest quintile reported lower income than consumption. Such deviation of income from consumption is typical in the data, the difference being accounted for by savings. While the savings of low-income groups are negligible, upper-income groups

Figure A1 Percentage Population within Monthly Household Expenditures/ Income Thresholds

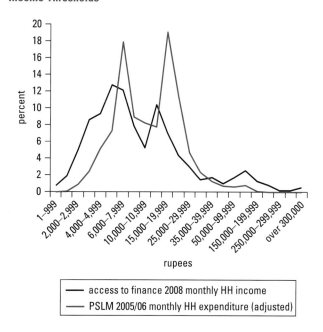

Figure A2 Cumulative Percentage Population within Monthly Household Expenditures/Income Thresholds

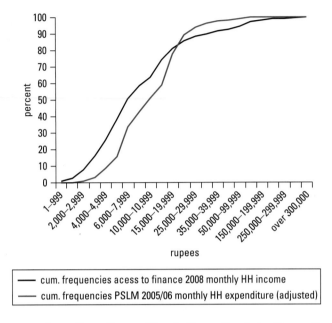

— cum. frequencies acess to finance 2008 monthly HH income
— cum. frequencies PSLM 2005/06 monthly HH expenditure (adjusted)

Figure A3 Upper Expenditures/Income Thresholds per Population Percentile

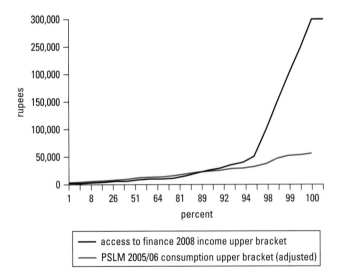

— access to finance 2008 income upper bracket
— PSLM 2005/06 consumption upper bracket (adjusted)

tend to save a considerable part of their incomes. Except for these differences at the upper and lower margins of the income data, the A2F income curve can be considered to overall fit the national expenditure curve.

While the overall income results are deemed calibrated to PSLM expenditure data, the range of factors that could explain the observed differences at the margins are discussed below.

Household Survey Measurement Bias

1. *Respondent bias:* As frequently observed in household surveys, because of lack of knowledge of all household members' income sources or lack of literacy to estimate income correctly, poor respondents of the A2F survey may have understated their incomes relative to consumption expenditure, while rich respondents may have overstated their income.

2. *Questionnaire bias* introducing differences linked to consumption from home production factors: A2F income survey responses on monthly household income may not have captured home consumption from the poor in agriculture, while this additional income flow would be reported in the consumption survey. This anticipated bias was, however, mitigated by an additional question in the A2F survey to capture "consumption from things the family grew" as income.

Consumption and Current Income Bias

3. *Differences between income and consumption levels among poor and rich households:* The differences in fit[[w/c]] at the lower- and upper-income/consumption ends could be explained by the observation that consumption may be higher than income among poor households and lower among rich households, more likely to save or invest excess income over consumption.

4. *Current versus permanent income bias:* While the standard hypothesis is that consumption captures permanent income, the calibration is conducted between consumption and the current income levels measured by the A2F household survey. The standard deviation of current income data would be larger than of the permanent income, hence higher percentages of households within bottom/top income thresholds than consumption threshold equivalents.

Corrective Techniques for Biases Identified Above

To correct for potential measurement bias, we use an alternative methodology to measure current income, pioneered for Pakistan by Dr. Mark Schreiner. The index developed by Dr. Schreiner calibrates income by the amenities used by households, such as type of house and other household assets. This methodology has been proven to be an adequate proxy to measure income levels of the Pakistani population. We use both variables in tests, for robustness, and obtain very similar results.

Calibration of Demand-side Financial Access Variables to SBP Supply-side Measures

Number of Bank Accounts

The total number of bank accounts, as quoted by SBP (most recent figures are for December 2006), is that in Pakistan there are 26.6 million bank accounts. These include both business and individual accounts. We do not have figures for the breakdown between those two categories, but we have that breakdown in the case of bank loans specifically. In that case, out of 4.9 million total loan accounts outstanding, 1.8 are private business loans, and 3.2 million are individual loans. If one assumes that a similar proportion holds for all bank accounts (admittedly, a leap-of-faith assumption), we end up with an estimate of 17.4 million bank accounts.

The A2F survey does not measure the number of accounts, but what we can observe is the number of adults who have at least one (and possibly more) bank accounts. We observe 12.2 million people who report to currently have bank accounts, and 18.9 million people who have now or have had in the past a bank account (weighted population figures, adults only). These figures are quite compatible if one takes into account that people, especially household heads, would make use of more than one account, for the use of spouse and grown children, and noting that those with bank accounts are mostly the urban high-income groups.

On *Islamic loans,* we have 11,500 people who hold such loans, and 61,000 have now or have had them in the past. The SBP quotes 22,200 loans, which gives about two loans per person. Note, again, that Islamic loans are mostly held by richer urban males. We find 127,000 clients for Islamic products, and 349,000 have now or have had such a product in the past.

Microfinance

On *microfinance* we have not been able to reconcile the data. The A2F survey points to 231,000 people who have at least one microfinance product, and 601,000 who have it or have had it in the past. The respective SBP figure is much higher, at 1.7 million microfinance products as reported by MFIs to SBP. There are several reasons to explain the divergence in estimates. First, microfinance clients may have multiple accounts or work with more than one MFI. Second, the A2F survey microfinance figures do not isolate microfinance insurance products (all insurance products are collected in a single measure, which precludes any distinction of microfinance insurance from traditional products). Third, and perhaps most significant, microfinance clients tend to cluster in urban areas and may be underrepresented in the A2F survey. This bias is pointed out in relevant sections of the report, and SBP figures are used.

To understand in detail the clustering bias, consider the following thoughts on population growth patterns. If the calibration above correctly identifies the bias of undercoverage of newer (urbanized) enumeration blocks, which appeared after the latest census and are therefore systematically not covered by the survey, that will result in severe undercoverage of younger village migrants. There is considerable evidence that microfinance products are predominantly used in clusters in urbanized areas, which lends even further credence to this conjecture. Figure A4, presenting a map of active microfinance borrowers, exhibits significant clustering of borrowers around urban areas and further confirms the above bias.

Figure A4 Distribution of Active Microfinance Borrowers

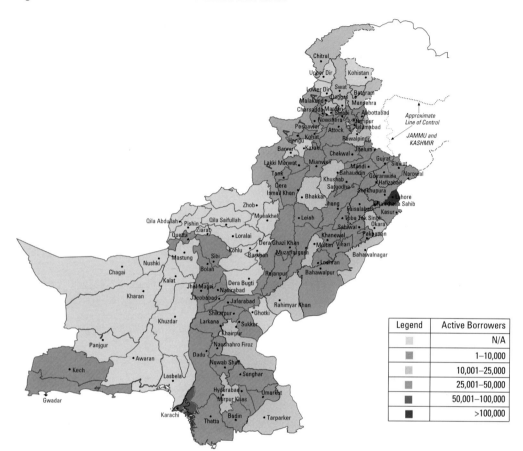

Legend	Active Borrowers
	N/A
	1–10,000
	10,001–25,000
	25,001–50,000
	50,001–100,000
	>100,000

Source: Microwatch, Issue 7 Quarter 1, 2008.

Pakistan Post Office

Finally, respondents report 1.7 million people with a Pakistan Post savings account, and 5.7 million have ever had such an account. The SBP-reported figure is 3.6 million post office savings accounts. Whereas it is unreasonable to assume multiple accounts in most of the cases (these are low-income savings, for the most part), some of the reasons for this difference lie most likely in the number of inactive accounts—that is, accounts that have not been closed but are not used and therefore are not considered as existing by the owner—whereas Pakistan Post maintains the account in its records, according to its reporting requirements or because of faults with automation or computerization of reporting.

Variable Description

Variable	Description
Financially served	= 1 if availing any financial service/s from any formal or informal provider; 0 if otherwise
Financially excluded	= 1 if not availing any financial service/s from any formal or informal provider; 0 if otherwise
Formally served	= 1 if availing saving/loans/insurance/payment facilities of any formal financial institution, including post office and microfinance institutions; 0 if otherwise
Informally served (organized sector)	= 1 if availing saving/loan/payment facilities of informal financial providers from the organized sector, such as moneylenders, shopkeepers, hawala/hundi money transfers, and committees; 0 if otherwise
Informally served (unorganized sector)	= 1 if availing saving/loan/payment facilities of informal financial providers not belonging to the organized sector, such as family and friends; 0 if otherwise
Interested in financial matters	= 1 if interested or strongly interested in financial matters; 0 if otherwise
Want a bank account	= 1 if would like to have a bank account; 0 if otherwise
Banked	= 1 if availing saving/loans/insurance/payment facilities of any bank; 0 if otherwise
Formal borrowers	= 1 if borrowing from any formal financial institution including microfinance institutions, Islamic loans, and leasing companies; 0 if otherwise
Informal borrowers	= 1 if borrowing from any informal lenders, such as moneylenders, shopkeepers, hawala/hundi money transfers, committees and family friends; 0 if otherwise
Borrowers	= 1 if borrowing from any formal or informal lenders; 0 if otherwise
Formal savers	= 1 if saving with formal financial institutions, including post office, Islamic savings scheme, and savings in financial form, including provident fund, prize bonds, shares, and government saving certificate; 0 if otherwise
Informal savers	= 1 if saving with informal sources, such as committees, friends and family and in gold, livestock, and land; 0 if otherwise

(continued)

Variable	Description
Savers	= 1 if saving with formal or informal sources; 0 if otherwise
Credit/debit card users	= 1 if have credit/debit/ATM card; 0 if otherwise
Female	= 1 if female; 0 if male
Age	Age in years
Education	= 1 if none; 2 = if completed up to class 4; 3 = if completed primary; 4 = if completed class 6–9; = 5 if completed grade 10; 6 = if completed intermediate/technical training; 7 = if graduate; 8 = if postgraduate
Rural	= 1 if from rural area (that is, from population clusters that are not metropolitan/municipal corporations or municipal/town committees); 0 if otherwise
Urban	= 1 if cluster with the status of metropolitan/municipal corporations or municipal/town committees; 0 if otherwise
Employed	= 1 if work full-time/part-time/self-employed in formal/informal sector or is a farmer or work for salary/wage from a company/government/individual/irregular or offer labor or receive goods in return for goods/services/things made/things grown/for livestock; 0 if otherwise
Household head	= 1 if household head; 0 if otherwise
Collateral	= 1 if has investment in land or owns a house or has investment in another house/flat/property that is rented out or has investment in a plot/vacant land or has investment in farm land; 0 if otherwise
Corporate	= 1 if work for a salary/wage from a company; 0 if otherwise
Government	= 1 if work for a salary/wage from government; 0 if otherwise
Farmer	= 1 if farmer or self-employed formal sector (own agriculture) or received goods in return for things grown/for livestock raised; 0 if otherwise
Laborer	= 1 if work for salary/wage—irregular or work for wage/salary from an individual (for example, domestic worker) but is not a farmer or for offering labor or received goods in return for services/goods/things made; 0 if otherwise
Type of house	= 1 if roof and walls of the house both concrete and both kitchen and toilet present; 0 if otherwise
Household income	Household income quintiles. Household income is self-reported by selecting 1 of 23 income brackets, and it also includes noncash income.
Personal income	Personal income quintiles. The calculation of personal income follows methodology of Schreiner (2007) explained in the note below this table.
Formal sector	= 1 if work full-time/part-time/self-employed in the formal sector or work for salary/wage from a company/government or self-employed formal sector (own enterprise/own agriculture); 0 if otherwise
Cell phone use	= 1 if use cell phone regularly; 0 if otherwise
Cell phone access	= 1 if has access to a cell phone; 0 if otherwise
Anti-Islamic	= 1 if the respondent considers paying interest on loans is unacceptable from a religious point of view; 0 if otherwise
Punjab	= 1 if from Punjab; 0 if otherwise
Sind	= 1 if from Sind; 0 if otherwise

(continued)

Variable Description

Variable	Description
NWFP	= 1 if from NWFP; 0 if otherwise
Baluchistan	= 1 if from Baluchistan; 0 if otherwise
Azad Jammu and Kashmir (AJK)	= 1 if from AJK; 0 if otherwise
Food and household needs	= 1 if using or needing funds for food or household goods; 0 if otherwise
Medical needs	= 1 if using or needing funds for medical expenses; 0 if otherwise
Education needs	= 1 if using or needing funds for school fees; 0 if otherwise
Investment needs	= 1 if using or needing funds for investment needs (to start a business or to invest in existing business [agriculture or others]); 0 if otherwise
Provision for accident and death	= 1 if using or needing funds to provide for the family in case something happens to the respondent; 0 if otherwise
Social and religious needs	= 1 if using or needing funds to meet marriage, Hajj/Umrah costs; 0 if otherwise
Old age needs	= 1 if using or needing funds for retirement/old age; 0 if otherwise
Medical, accident, and funeral needs	= 1 if using or needing funds to pay for unforeseen emergency costs (hospital/medical bills/funeral/childbirth expenses); 0 if otherwise
Agricultural investment needs	= 1 if using or needing funds to purchase goods for agriculture (livestock, farming) business/productive activity; 0 if otherwise
Nonfarming investment needs	= 1 if using or needing funds to meet expenses of a new or existing business, purchase productive assets (nonfarming); 0 if otherwise
Home investment and home improvement	= 1 if using or needing funds to purchase/build/renovate a residence, such as a house or apartment; 0 if otherwise
Check users	= 1 if have cashed a check in the past month; 0 if otherwise
Savings account users	= 1 if have savings with formal financial institutions, including post office or have savings in financial form including provident fund, prize bonds, and government saving certificate; 0 if otherwise
Current account users	= 1 if have debit/ATM card or basic banking account or current/check account; 0 if otherwise
Islamic clients	= 1 if have Islamic savings/loans/insurance (*Takaful*) or have Hajj/Umrah scheme with banks
Post office clients	= 1 if availing postal savings/insurance/payment facilities; 0 if otherwise
Insurance users	= 1 if availing insurance facilities offered by formal financial institutions, including post office and Islamic insurance; 0 if otherwise
Committee users	= 1 if saving with committees; 0 if otherwise
Self-employed in the formal sector	= 1 if self-employed in the formal sector (own nonfarm enterprise or own agriculture); 0 if otherwise
Self-employed in the informal sector	= 1 if self-employed in the informal sector, such as street vending, hawking; 0 if otherwise

(continued)

Note: The personal income variable (derived from Schreiner [2007]) is based on an easy-to-use, objective poverty scorecard. All scorecard weights are positive integers, and scores range from 0 (most likely "poor") to 100 (least likely "poor"). Personal income variable has quintiles based on this score. The scorecard is based on 10 indicators. Each indicator gets a point based on the value it takes. Addition of these points gives a score. The indicators include (points in parenthesis):

- Do all children ages 6 to 17 attend school? No, or 5 children (0); or Yes, 3 or 4 children (10); Yes, 2 children (15); Yes, 1 child (20); No children (23)
- What is the household's main source of drinking water? Hand pump (0); Other (10)
- Does the household own a refrigerator or freezer? No (0); Yes (15)
- What type of toilet is used by the household? All others (0); Flush connected to a pit (7); Flush connected to public sewage (10)
- Does the household own a cooking stove? No (0); Yes (9)
- How many household members have salaried employment? None (0); One (3); Two or more (9)
- Does the household own any type of land? No (0); Yes (7)
- Does the household own any livestock? Rural, no (0); Urban (1); Rural, Yes (4)
- Does the household own a scooter or motorcycle/car? No (0); Yes (11)
- Does the household own a radio or cassette player or stereo deck or CD player or TV? No (0); Yes (5)

Bibliography

Adams, R. 2006. "Remittances and Poverty in Ghana." World Bank Policy Research Working Paper No. 3838.

Adams, R., and J. Page. 2005. "Do International Migration and Remittances Reduce Poverty in Developing Countries?" *World Development* 33(10), pages 1645–69.

Aggarwal, Demirguc-Kunt, and Martinez-Peria (2006). "Do Workers' Remittances Promote Financial Development?" World Bank Policy Research Working Paper 3957.

Ahmed, Syed Mohsin, and Mehr Shah. October 2007. "Amendments to the Microfinance Institutions Ordinance 2001: Implications for the Sector, Essays on Regulation and Supervision." College Park, Maryland: IRIS Center, University of Maryland.

Akhtar, Shamshad. 2006. "Development of Microfinance." Keynote Address at the Seminar on Commercial Opportunities in Micro and Small Business Lending, Islamabad, June 6, 2006. http://sbp.org.pk/about/speech/governors/dr.shamshad/2006/Development-Microfinance-13-Jun-06.pdf.

———. 2007a. "Building Inclusive Financial System in Pakistan." DFID and HM Treasury, Financial Inclusion Conference, London, June 2007. http://www.sbp.org.pk/about/speech/governors/dr.shamshad/2007/Draft-Agriculture-PRs-18-04-05.pdf.

———. 2007b. "Expanding Microfinance Outreach in Pakistan." Presentation made to the Prime Minister of Pakistan, February, 2007. http://www.sbp.org.pk/about/speech/governors/dr.shamshad/2007/MF-PM-17-Apr-07.pdf.

———. 2008. "Financial Sector—Ten Year Vision and Strategy." Presentation, July 1, 2008.

Al-Hussainy, Edward, Thorsten Beck, Asli Demirguc-Kunt, and Bilal Zia. 2008. "Household Use of Financial Services." World Bank Working Paper, draft.

Ananth, Bindu, Bastavee Barooah, Rupalee Ruchismita, and Aparna Bhatnagar. 2004. "A Blueprint for the Delivery of Comprehensive Financial Services to the Poor in India." Working paper. Chennai, India: Center for Microfinance. http://ifmr.ac.in/pdf/workingpapers/9/blueprint.pdf.

Ara, I. 2003. "Urban Migration in Pakistan: Evidence from 1998 Population Census." Mimeo. Karachi: Arshad Zaman and Associates.

Azam, F. 2005. "Public Policies to Support International Migration in Pakistan and the Philippines." Paper presented at New Frontiers of Social Policy, World Bank, Washington, DC.

Bagazonzya H., A. K. M. Abdullah, Safdar Z., Riley T., Niang C., Rahman A. 2009a. "Linking Up And Reaching Out "ICT As An Enabler And Catalyst For Microfinance." World Bank Report No. 47068-Bd.

Bagazonzya H., Safdar Z., Riley T., Niang C. 2009a. "Maximizing the Outreach of Microfinance in Nepal: The Case for a Technology Platform." World Bank Report No. 46985-Np.

BancoSol Bank. Bolivia. http://www.bancosol.com.bo/en/intro.html.

BRAC Bank. Bangladesh. http://www.bracbank.com/.

Basu, Priya. 2006. "Improving Access to Finance for India's Rural Poor." Washington, DC: World Bank.

Beck, T., and R. Levine. 2004. "Stock Markets, Banks and Growth: Panel Evidence." *Journal of Banking and Finance* 28 (3):423–42.

Beck, T, A. Demirguc-Kunt, and S. Martinez Peria. 2004. "Finance, Inequality and Poverty: Cross-country Evidence." Policy Research Working Paper 3338. Washington, DC: World Bank.

———. 2005. "Reaching Out: Access to and Use of Banking Services across Countries." Policy Research Working Paper 3754. Washington, DC: World Bank.

———. 2006. "Banking Services for Everyone? Barriers to Bank Access around the World." Policy Research Working Paper 4079. Washington, DC: World Bank.

Beck, T, A. Demirguc-Kunt, and R. Levine. 2004. "Law and firms' access to finance." Policy Research Working Paper 3194. Washington, DC: World Bank.

Beck, Thorsten, and Augusto de la Torre, 2006. "The Basic Analytics of Access to Financial Services."

Beegle, K., R. H Dehejia, and R. Gatti. 2003. "Child Labor, Income Shocks, and Access to Credit." World Bank Policy Research Working Paper 3075. Washington, DC: World Bank.

Bossoutrot, Sylvie. 2005. "Microfinance in Russia: Broadening access to finance for micro and small entrepreneurs." Washington, DC: World Bank.

Buchenau, Juan. 1997. "Financing Small Farmers in Latin America." Paper presented at the First Annual Seminar on New Development Finance, Frankfurt University, Germany.

Buchenau, Juan, and Richard L Meyer. 2007. "Introducing Rural Finance into an Urban Micro-finance Institution: The Example of Banco ProCredit El Salvador." Paper presented at the International Conference on Rural Finance Research: Moving Results into Policies and Practice, Food and Agriculture Organization, Rome, March 19–21.

Bureau of Immigration and Overseas Employment. 2006. http://www.beoe.gov.pk/download.htm.

Burki, Hussan-Bano, and Mehr Shah. June 2007. "The Dynamics of Microfinance Expansion in Lahore." Pakistan Microfinance Network and ShoreBank International.

Burki, Hussan-Bano, and Shama Mohammed. January 2008. Mobilizing Savings from the Urban Poor in Pakistan. Research Paper 01, ShoreBank International.

Business and Finance Consulting. 2005, Demand Survey.

Carpenter, Seth B., and Robert T. Jensen. 2002. "Household Participation in Formal and Informal Savings Mechanisms: Evidence from Pakistan." Review of Development Economics 6(3, October 2002): 314.

CGAP (Consultative Group to Assist the Poor). March 2005. Occasional Paper No. 10.

———. June 2007. Notes on Regulation of Branchless Banking in Pakistan.

Chidzero, Anne-Marie, Karen Ellis, and Anjali Kumar. 2006. "Indicators of Access to Finance through Household Level Surveys: Comparisons of Data from Six Countries."

Christen, Robert Peck. 2000. "Commercialization and Mission Drift: The Transformation of Microfinance in Latin America." CGAP Occasional Paper 5. Washington, DC: Consultative Group to Assist the Poor.

Cirasino, M., and O. Andreassen. 2007. "Reducing Costs for Remittances: A New People's IDA." Presentation at Global Conference "Exploring Frontiers in Payment System Development." World Bank, Washington, DC.

Claessens, Stijn, and Konstantinos Tzioumis. May 2006. "Measuring firms' access to finance." World Bank manuscript.

Cole, Shawn, Bilal Zia, and Thomas Sampson. 2008. Evaluation the Impact of Bank Accounts on Households Welfare Outcomes in Indonesia. Unpublished manuscript.

Competitiveness Support Fund. 2008. "Expanding Women's Access to Financial Services: Commitment and Scale." Report prepared for United States Agency for International Development (USAID) and Ministry of Finance, Pakistan. Islamabad.

Courcelle-Labrousse, Antonie. 2005. "IFC SME Banking Advisory Services." Presented at the Conference on SME Financing—Issues and Strategies, May 2005, Lahore, Pakistan. http://www.sbp.org.pk/bpd/conference.htm.

Cull, Robert J., Asli Demirguc-Kunt, and Jonathan Morduch. Forthcoming. "Microfinance and the Market." *Journal of Economic Perspectives*.

De la Torre, Augusto, Juan Carlos Gozzi, Sergio L. Schmukler. 2007. "Innovative experiences in access to finance: market friendly roles for the visible hand?" Policy Research Working Paper No. 4326. Washington, DC: World Bank.

Dellien, Hans, and Olivia Leland. 2006. "Introducing Individual Lending." New York: Women's World Banking.

Dellien, Hans, Jill Burnett, Anna Ginchermann, and Elizabeth Lynch. 2005. "Product Diversification in Microfinance: Introducing Individual Lending." New York: Women's World Banking.

Department for International Development (DFID) and USAID (2005) "FMFB Pakistan—Serving the Domestic Money Transfer Market." *Migrant Remittances Newsletter*.

Duflos, Eric, Alexia Latortue, Rochus Mommartz, Graham Perrett, and Stefan Staschen. April 2007. Pakistan Country-Level Effectiveness and Accountability Review with a Policy Diagnostic. Washington, DC: CGAP.

Esser, Ekkehard. 2005. "Upgrading and Incentivising Staff." Presentation at the Conference on SME Financing—Issues and Strategies, May 2005, Lahore. http://www.sbp.org.pk/bpd/conference.htm.

Finmark Trust. 2003. "Access to Financial Services in Lesotho." Finmark Trust Research Paper 2. Johannesburg.

Firpo, Janine. 2005. "HP's Remote Transaction System: A Technology Solution to Scale Microfinance." New York: United Nations Capital Development Fund. http://www.uncdf.org/english/microfinance/pubs/newsletter/pages/2005_05/news_hp.php.

Fleisig, Heywood, Mehnaz Safavian, and Nuria de la Pena. 2006. "Reforming Collateral Laws to Increase Access to Finance." Washington, DC: World Bank.

Gazdar, H. 2003. "A Review of Migration Issues in Pakistan." Paper presented at Regional Conference on Migration, Development Pro Poor Policy Choices, Dhaka.

GC University. "SME Development in Pakistan: Issues and Strategies." Lahore. http://www.gcu.edu.pk/Publications/VC-SME.pdf.

Government of Pakistan. "Developing SME Policy in Pakistan: SME Issues Paper for Deliberation." SME Task Force Prepared by the Small and Medium Enterprise Development Authority, Lahore.

———. 2006. "Small and Medium Enterprise Policy: 2006." Prepared by the Small and Medium Enterprise Development Authority, Lahore.

———. 2007. "Small and Medium Enterprise Policy: 2007." Prepared by the Small and Medium Enterprise Development Authority, Lahore.

———. 2007. "SME Policy 2007: SME Led Economic Growth: Creating Jobs and Reducing Poverty." Islamabad: Ministries of Industries, Production, and Special Initiatives.

———. "SMEDA Report of Working Committee on the Business Environment." Prepared by the Small and Medium Enterprise Development Authority, Lahore.

———. Federal Bureau of Statistics. 2006. "Household Income Integrated Survey (HIES) 2005–06."

———. Federal Bureau of Statistics. PSLM CWIK 2004-05. Islamabad.

Hewlett-Packard. 2005. "Remote Transaction System." Solution Brief. Palo Alto, California. http://www.hp.com/e-inclusion/en/project/microfin_brief.pdf.

Holden, Paul, and Vassili Prokopenko. 2001. "Financial Development and Poverty Alleviation: Issues and Policy Implications for Developing Countries." IMF Working Paper 01/160. Washington, DC: International Monetary Fund.

Honohan, P. 2004. "Financial Development, Growth, and Poverty: How Close are the Links?" In C. Goodhard, ed. Financial Development and Economic Growth: Explaining the Links. London: Palgrave Macmillan.

Honohan, P. 2005. "Measuring Microfinance Access: Building on Existing Cross-country Data." Policy Research Working Paper 3606. Washington, DC: World Bank.

Husain, Ishrat. 2003. "SME Financing—Issues and Prospects." Keynote address at the SMEDA-IBP seminar on Issue of SME financing held at Lahore on October 24, 2003. http://www.sbp.org.pk/about/speech/2003/SME-financing(24102003).pdf.

———. 2005. "SME Financing: Issues and Strategies." Welcome Address at the Conference on SME Financing—Issues and Strategies. May 2005. Lahore. http://www.sbp.org.pk/about/speech/financial_sector/2005/SME_Financing_10_May_05.pdf.

———. 2005. "Conference on SME Financing—Issues and Strategies." Closing remarks at the Conference on SME Financing—Issues and Strategies. May 2005. Lahore. http://www.sbp.org.pk/bpd/Conference/Day_Two/Governor_Closing_Remarks.pdf.

IFAD. 2006. "Sending Money Home: Worldwide Remittance Flows to Sending Countries."

International Finance Corporation (IFC). 2006. "Access to finance for women entrepreneurs in South Africa: challenges and opportunities." Washington, DC.

INAFI (International Network of Alternative Financial Institutions). 2007. "Reducing Vulnerability of the Poor through Social Security Products: A Market Survey on Microinsurance in Bangladesh." Research paper. Dhaka.

IPC (Internationale Projekt Consult). 2006. "Building Up Capacities for Successful Lending to Micro, Small and Medium-sized Businesses." Presented at the Up-scaling SME Lending: New Tools seminar, organized by Small Industries Development Bank of India (SIDBI), September, New Delhi, India.

Ivatury, Gautam. 2006. "Using Technology to Build Inclusive Financial Systems." CGAP Focus Note 32. Washington, DC: Consultative Group to Assist the Poor.

Ivatury, G., and Mas, I. 2008. "The Early Experience with Branchless Banking." CGAP (Consultative Group to Assist the Poor) Focus Note No. 46.

Kashf Foundation. 2006. "Market for Microfinance: Analysis of the Punjab."

Kazi, S. 1989. "Domestic Impact of Overseas Migration: Pakistan." In Amjad (ed.):167–96.

Khandker, S., and R. Faruqee. "The Impact of Farm Credit in Pakistan." http://unpan1.un.org/ intradoc/groups/public/documents/APCITY/UNPAN026319.pdf.

Khawaja, Shahab. 2005. "Small and Medium Enterprises in Pakistan." Presented at the Conference on SME Financing—Issues and Strategies, May 2005, Lahore. http://www.sbp.org.pk/ bpd/conference.htm.

Khwaja, Asim I., Atif Mian, and Bilal H. Zia. April 2006. "Dollars Dollars Everywhere and Not a Dime to Lend?" World Bank Working Paper. Washington, DC.

King, R.G., and R. Levine. 1993. "Finance and Growth: Schumpeter Might Be Right." *Quarterly Journal of Economics* 108(3):717–38.

Kumar, Anjali. 2004. "Access to financial services in Brazil." Washington, DC: World Bank.

Kumar, Anjali, Thorsten Beck, Christine Campos, and Soumva Chattopadhvay. 2005. "Assessing financial access in Brazil." World Bank Working Paper Series No. 50. Washington, DC.

Kumar, Anjali, Mukta Joshi, Ergys Islamaj, and Vidhi Chhaochharia. 2007. "Access to Firm Finance in MENA Countries: Country-level, Institutional, and Firm-level Factors."

Levine, R., N. Loayza, and T. Beck. 2000. "Financial Intermediation and Growth: Causality and Causes." *Journal of Monetary Economics* 46 (1):31–77.

Lindh de Montoya, Monica, and Aban Haq. June 2008. "Pakistan—Country Level Savings Assessment." Pakistan Microfinance Network.

Lyman, Timothy, Gautam Ivatury, and Stefan Staschen. 2006. "Use of Agents in Bankless Banking for the Poor: Rewards, Risks and Regulation." CGAP Focus Note 38. Washington, DC: Consultative Group to Assist the Poor.

Malik, Sohail J. October 2003. "Rural Credit Markets in Pakistan: Institutions and Constraints." Background paper prepared for the World Bank-sponsored study of Rural Factor Markets in Pakistan.

Manuamorn, Ornsaran Pomme. 2005. "Scaling Up Micro-Insurance: The Case of Weather Insurance for Smallholders in India." Washington, DC: World Bank, Commodity Risk Management Group.

Mehkari, M. R. 2002. "Hawala." Presented at the International Conference on Hawala.

Mellyn, K. 2003. "Worker Remittances as a Development Tool: Opportunities for Philippines." Asian Development Bank.

Microfinance Information Exchange, Consultative Group to Assist the Poor, and the World Bank. January 2006. "Performance and Transparency: A Survey of Microfinance in South Asia."

Nabi, I. 1989a. "Entrepreneurs and Markets in Early Industrialization." San Francisco, California: ICS Press.

———. 1989b. "Investment in Segmented Capital Markets." *Quarterly Journal of Economics*. August 1989.

Nawaz Kasim. 2006. "Microfinancing by Commercial Banks: The Regulatory Initiatives." Presented at the Roundtable Discussion on Opportunities for Commercial Banks in Microfinance jointly organized by the State Bank of Pakistan and Pakistan Microfinance Network, Karachi, November 2006. http://sbp.org.pk/about/micro/comm&mic.htm.

Oda, H. 2007. "Dynamics of Internal and International Migration in Rural Pakistan." *Asian Population Studies* 3(2):169–179.

Omar, Marzunisham. 2005. "Focused and Coordinated Development of Small and Medium Enterprises (SMEs): The Malaysian Experience." Presented at the Conference on SME

Financing—Issues and Strategies, May 2005, Lahore. http://www.sbp.org.pk/bpd/conference.htm.

Orozco, M. 2003. "Workers' Remittances: An International Comparison." Working Paper commissioned by the Multilateral Investment Fund of the Inter-American Development Bank. http://www.iadb.org/exr/prensa/images/RemittancesInternational.pdf.

Pakistan Enterprise Development Facility and National Productivity Organization. 2006. "Why are Pakistan's SMEs Bank Shy?" Unpublished report for the European Commission.

Pakistan Microfinance Network. 2003. "Performance Indicators Report." Islamabad, Pakistan. http://www.pmn.org.pk/link.php?goto=pir.

———. 2005. "Performance Indicators Report." Islamabad. http://www.pmn.org.pk/link.php?goto=pir.

———. 2006. *Microfinance Spotlight* 01.

———. 2006. "Performance Indicators Report." Islamabad. http://www.pmn.org.pk/link.php?goto=pir.

———. 2006. *Microwatch*, Issue 6.

Pakistan Post. 2005. "Annual Report." Islamabad.

Pakistan Telecommunication Authority. 2007. *Annual Report* 2007.

———. 2008. *Quarterly Report March 2008*.

Passas, N. 2004. "Informal value transfer system (IVTS) and their mechanics." Presented at APEC Initiative on Remittance Systems, Tokyo.

Pelzer, I. 2006. "The Access Frontier for Housing Finance in South Africa: How Low Can You Go?" Presentation prepared for the FinMark Trust.

Porteous, D. 2005. "The Access Frontier as an Approach and Tool in Making Markets Work for the Poor." Prepared for the Department For International Department (DFID).

Procredit Bank. 2007. Annual Report. Ukraine. http://www.procreditbank.com.ua/data/AnnualReports/AR%202007_ENG.pdf.

Qadir, Adnan. December 2005. "A Study of Informal Finance Markets." Pakistan Microfinance Network.

Qureshi, U., and S. Zaka. 2007. "Survival or Take-off: A Study of MSEs in the Lahore Small Business Market." Prepared for the United States Agency for International Development (USAID) and ShoreBank International.

Ritchie, Anne. 2007. "Community-Based Financial Organizations: a solution to access in remote rural areas." Washington, DC: World Bank.

Sa-Dhan. 2006. "Slide by Slide: A Slice of Microfinance Sector in India 2006." India. http://www.sa-dhan.net/ResMaterials/SidebySideASliceofMicrofinanceOperationsinIndia2006.pdf.

Safavian, Mehnaz, Heywoood Fleisig, and Jevgenijs Steinbuks. 2006. "Unlocking Dead Capital: How Reforming Collateral Laws Improves Access to Finance." *Viewpoint 307*. Washington, DC: World Bank.

Schreiner, Mark. February 2006. "A Poverty Scorecard for Pakistan." Saint Louis, Missouri: Microfinance Risk Management, LLC.

Securities and Exchange Commission and State Bank of Pakistan. 2003. "Anti Money Laundering Initiative." *Newsletter* 1:1.

Shah, T. 2005. "Informal Finance Markets in Pakistan: A Rural Finance Perspective." Presentation at the Seminar on Informal Finance Markets in Pakistan, Islamabad. http://www.pmn.org.pk/link.php?goto=seminar.

Shah, V, H. Sharif, and S. Khan. "Scoping study of migrant remittance flows in to Pakistan and earthquake affected areas." Unpublished. Department for International Development.

Shehzad, Muhammad Kamran. 2005. "SBP's Initiative for SMEs Financing." Presented at the Conference on SME Financing—Issues and Strategies. May 2005. Lahore. http://www .sbp.org.pk/bpd/conference.htm.

ShoreBank International and Pakistan Microfinance Network, 2006. Microfinance Performance in Pakistan.

Siddiqui, R., and A. Kemal. 2002. "Remittances, Trade Liberalization, and Poverty in Pakistan: The Role of Excluded Variables in Poverty Change Analysis." Islamabad: Pakistan Institute for Development Economics, Working Paper, 2006:1. http://www.gapresearch.org/production/ RizwanaRemittR2.pdf.

SME (Small and Medium Enterprise) Bank, Pakistan. 2007. Financial Statement. http://www.smebank.org/pdf/Finance%202007.pdf.

State Bank of Pakistan (SBP). 2002a. "Calculation of Microfinance Market Size." In the Report of the Committee on Rural Finance. Karachi, Pakistan. http://www.sbp.org.pk/report/ Annex-VI.pdf.

———. 2002b. "Microfinance Institutions, Branch Licensing Policy." http://www.sbp.org. pk/bsd/2002/C13.htm.

———. 2002c. Prudential Regulations for agriculture financing, corporate/commercial banking, SME financing, consumer financing, Microfinance banks. Karachi. http://www.sbp .org.pk/publications/prudential/index.htm.

———. 2002d. Prudential Regulations for Microfinance Banks/Institutions. Karachi. http://www.sbp.org.pk/bsd/2002/Anex-C18.pdf.

———. 2002e. Prudential Regulations for Small and Medium Enterprises. SBP Banking Policy and Regulation Department. http://www.sbp.org.pk/publications/prudential/ PRs-SMEs.pdf.

———. 2002f. Report of the Committee on Rural Finance. Karachi. http://www.sbp.org .pk/report/Annex-I.pdf.

———. 2003. Credit Rating of Microfinance Banks. Prudential Regulation 29 for Microfinance Banks. Karachi. http://www.sbp.org.pk/bsd/2003/C10.htm.

———. 2003. Guidelines for the Mobile Banking Operations of Microfinance Banks/ Institutions. Karachi. http://www.sbp.org.pk/bsd/2003/C2.htm.

———. 2005a. "Annual Report 2004–2005." Karachi.

———. 2005b. "Pakistan: Financial Sector Assessment." State Bank of Pakistan-Research Department. Karachi. http://www.sbp.org.pk/publications/FSA/2005/.

———. 2005c. Prudential Regulations for Small and Medium Enterprise Financing. Karachi.

———. 2006a. "Annual Report 2005–2006." Karachi.

———.2006b. "Banking Statistics of Pakistan." Karachi. http://www.sbp.org.pk/publications/ anu_stats/2006.htm.

———. 2006c. "Scaling Up Microfinance in Pakistan." Note prepared by the Pakistan Microfinance Network.

———. 2006d. "Financial Stability Review 2006."

———. 2007a, "Annual Performance Review." Karachi.

———. 2007b. "Annual Report 2006–07." Volume I. Karachi. http://www.sbp.org.pk/ reports/annual/arfy07/.

———. 2007c. "Annual Report 2006–07." Volume II. Karachi. http://www.sbp.org.pk/ reports/annual/arfy07/vol2/index.htm.

———. 2007d. "Building Inclusive Financial Systems in Pakistan." Speech by Governor at Financial Inclusion Conference, London.

————. 2007e. "Guidelines for Branchless Banking." Karachi.

————. 2007f. "Islamic Banking Bulletin." SBP Islamic Banking Department. July–September 2007, November 2007. http://www.sbp.org.pk/ibd/Bulletin/2007/Mar-Jun-Bulletin.pdf.

————. 2007g. "Payment Systems and Electronic Fund Transfer Act 2007." http://sbp.org.pk/psd/2007/EFT_ACT_2007.pdf.

————. 2007h. "Quarterly Performance Review of the Banking System." June 2007. SBP Banking Surveillance Department. Karachi. http://www.sbp.org.pk/publications/q_reviews/q_review_june_07.pdf.

————. 2007i. "Third Quarterly Report of the Payment Systems Department 2007." Karachi, Pakistan.

————. 2008a. "Country-wise Workers' Remittances." Available on economic data. http://www.sbp.org.pk/Ecodata/Homeremit.pdf.

————. 2008b. Credit/Loans Classified by Borrowers. Available on economic data. http://www.sbp.org.pk/ecodata/CreditLoans.pdf.

————. 2008c. "Understanding Credit Information Bureau: Consumer Awareness Program." http://www.sbp.org.pk/bsd/CIB_Awareness.pdf.

————. 2008d. "SME finance quarterly review—First quarter 2008." Issue 02. SBP SME Department. http://www.sbp.org.pk/publications/index2.asp Accessed Sept 5, 2008.

————. 2008e. "Quarterly Housing Finance Review." SBP Infrastructure and Housing Department. October-December 2007. Page 5. www.sbp.gov.pk Accessed Sept 5, 2008.

————. 2008f. "Banking System Review 2008."

————. 2008g. "Scheduled Banks Position Based on Weekly Returns, Liabilities and Assets." Money and Credit, Chapter 5. Economic Survey of Pakistan 2007–2008.

————. 2008i. "Industry Progress and Market Share." *Islamic Banking Bulletin* Jul–Sept 2007:2. SBC Islamic Banking Department. http://www.sbp.org.pk/publications/index2.asp 2008.

————. 2008j. Statistical Bulletin, June 2008. http://www.sbp.org.pk/reports/stat_reviews/Bulletin/2008/Dec_08/index.htm.

Suleri, A. Q., and K. Savage. 2006. "Remittances in Crises: A case study on Pakistan." Humanitarian Policy Group, Overseas Development Institute.

Swamy, G. 1981. "International Migrant Workers' Remittances: Issues and Prospects." World Bank Staff Working Paper No. 481. Washington, DC.

Swiss Re. 2006. "World Insurance in 2005: Moderate Premium Growth, Attractive Profitability." SIGMA Report 5/2006. Zurich: Swiss Re Economic Research and Consulting.

Tamagaki, Kenichi. 2006. "Effectiveness of ITCs on the Dual Objectives of Microfinance." Presented at the International Conference on ICT and Higher Education–E-governance, Japan. http://www.iac-japan.org/06spring/tamagakip.pdf.

Tarin, Shaukat. 2005. "SME Financing—Is it Really a …?" Presented at the Conference on SME Financing—Issues and Strategies. May 2005. Lahore. http://www.sbp.org.pk/bpd/conference.htm.

USAID (United States Agency for International Development). 2005. "Microfinance Performance in Pakistan." Prepared for USAID by Pakistan Microfinance Network and ShoreBank International Limited. http://www.pmn.org.pk/link.php?goto=trends.

Vincelette, Gallina A. June 2006. "Pakistan's Saving Determinants." Washington, DC: World Bank Discussion Paper.

Wisniwski, S. 2005. "The Art of SME Loan Appraisal." Presented at the Conference on SME Financing—Issues and Strategies, May 2005, Lahore. http://www.sbp.org.pk/bpd/conference.htm.

Women's World Banking. 2004. "Remittances: ICICI Builds Technology Based Financial Literacy and Remittance Products for Rural Markets." Innovation Brief. New York: Global Network for Banking Innovation in Microfinance.

World Bank. 1996. Bangladesh Rural Finance. Agriculture and Natural Resources Division, South Asia Region. Washington, DC.

———. 2002. "Household participation in formal and informal institutions in rural credit markets in developing countries: evidence from Nepal?" Background paper prepared for *World Development Report 2001/2002: Institutions for Markets*. Washington, DC.

———. 2003d. "Improving Investment Climate in Pakistan," South Asia Finance and Private Sector Development Unit.

———. 2004. "Credit Bureau Development in South Asia." Washington, DC. http://siteresources.worldbank.org/INTSOUTHASIA/Resources/Credit_Bureau_Development_in_South_Asia.pdf.

———. 2005a. "Crediting Small Enterprises: Bank Lending to Small Businesses in Pakistan." Prepared for the World Bank by Business and Finance Consulting, Germany.

———. 2005b. "Sri Lanka - Improving access to financial services: selected issues." South Asia Region, Finance and Private Sector Development Unit. Washington, DC.

———. 2006a. "Getting Finance in South Asia: An Analysis of the Commercial Banking Sector." South Asia Region, Finance and Private Sector Development Unit. Washington, DC.

———. 2006b. "Meeting Development Challenges: Renewed Approaches to Rural Finance." South Asia Region, Finance and Private Sector Development Unit. Washington, DC.

———. 2006c. "Microfinance in South Asia: Toward Financial Inclusion for the Poor." Washington, DC.

———. 2006c. "Performance and transparency : a survey of microfinance in South Asia," by Stephens, Blaine; Tazi, Hind [editors]; Ahmed, Syed Mohsin; Sa-Dhan; Mali, Prahlad; Wijesiriwardana, Indrajith; Athapattu, Anura; Washington, DC.

———. 2006d. "The Role of Postal Networks in Expanding Access to Financial Services." World Bank Discussion Paper. Washington, DC.

———. 2006e. "Enterprise Survey Database: India." Washington, DC.

———. 2006f. "The Role of Postal Networks in Expanding Access to Financial Services." Volume 1. Discussion paper, Global ICT Department, Washington, DC.

———. 2007a. "Access to Financial Services in Nepal," by Aurora Ferrari, Guillemette Jaffrin, and Sabin Raj Shreshtha. South Asia Region, Finance and Private Sector Development Unit, Washington, DC.

———. 2007b, Colombia: Bank Financing to Small and Medium-Sized Enterprises, Washington, DC.

———. 2007c. "Crediting Small Enterprises Bank Lending to Small Businesses in Pakistan." Business & Finance Consulting (BFC).

———. 2007d. "Investment Climate Survey." Washington DC.

———. 2007e. "South Asian Domestic Debt Markets Study, Main Report." Draft. South Asia Region, Finance and Private Sector Development Unit. Washington, DC.

———. 2008a. "Banking the Poor," Financial Access Unit, Finance and Private Sector Development. Washington, DC.

———. 2008b. *Doing Business Indicators*. Washington, DC.

———. 2008c. "Finance for All?: Policies and Pitfalls in Expanding Access," A World Bank Policy Research Report. Washington, DC.

————. 2008d. "Increasing Access to Rural Finance in Bangladesh: The Forgotten 'Missing Middle,' by Aurora Ferrari. South Asia Region, Finance and Private Sector Development Unit, Washington, DC.

————. 2009. "Investment Climate Assessment of Pakistan." South Asia Finance and Private Sector Development Unit.

————. Forthcoming. "Microfinance Strategy for South Asia." by Priya Basu and Mehnaz Safavian, South Asia Region, Finance and Private Sector Development Unit. Washington, DC.

————. Financial sector development indicators. Washington, DC. http://www.fsdi.org/.

————. *World Development Indicators* database. http://devdata.worldbank.org/dataonline.

Yang, Dean, and Claudia Martinez. 2005. "Remittances and Poverty in Migrants' Home Areas: Evidence from the Philippines." In Caglar Ozden and Maurice Schiff (eds.), International Migration, Remittances and the Brain Drain, Chapter 3, pp. 81–122. Washington, DC: World Bank.

Yaron, Jacob. 2002. "What Makes Rural Financial Markets Successful?" In the *Report of the Committee on Rural Finance by the State Bank of Pakistan, Karachi, Pakistan.* http://www.sbp.org.pk/report/Annex%20%96%20XI.pdf

Yusuf, M Abdullah. 2007. "Management of Tax Debt Collection." Presented at the ITD Global Conference on Taxation of SMEs. Buenos Aires, Argentina.

Zia, Bilal H. July 2006. "Access to Finance and Industrial Composition in Emerging Markets." World Bank Working Paper. Washington, DC.

Zia, Bilal H., and Robert T. Jensen. 2002. "Household Participation in Formal and Informal Savings Mechanisms: Evidence from Pakistan." *Review of Development Economics* 6(October 2002): 314–28.

Index